S0-BAJ-885

Black Men, White Cities

The Institute of Race Relations was founded as an independent body in 1958. The main aims are to promote the study of the relations between groups racially defined, to make available information on race to different groups, and to give advice on proposals for improving relations. In its work, the subject of 'race relations' is regarded as primarily referring to the social relationships between groups that are influenced by prejudice and beliefs about race, but 'race' is inevitably related to the many factors affecting group relations, including the major problems of political and economic relationships. The Institute has responded to a changing situation by extending its work and services to members of minority groups. The Institute cannot itself hold a corporate opinion: the opinions expressed in this work are those of the author.

IRA KATZNELSON

Black Men, White Cities

Race, Politics, and Migration in the
United States, 1900–30, and Britain, 1948–68

The University of Chicago Press
Chicago and London

This Phoenix edition
is published with the permission of
Oxford University Press.

The University of Chicago Press, Chicago 60637
The University of Chicago Press, Ltd., London
© Institute of Race Relations 1973. © 1976 by
The University of Chicago. All rights reserved
Published 1973 by Oxford University Press for the
Institute of Race Relations. Phoenix edition 1976
Printed in the United States of America
80 79 78 77 76   987654321
International Standard Book Number: 0-226-42671-8
Library of Congress Catalog Card Number: 76-8376

Jessica, my love,
Seize your time

'Rabbi Ishmael said: "He who learns in order to teach will be afforded the opportunity both to learn and to teach. But he who learns in order to practise will be afforded the opportunity to learn and to teach, to observe and to practise."'

THE TALMUD (Pirke Abot IV, 6)

'To educate man to be *actional*, preserving in all his relations his respect for the basic values that constitute a human world, is the prime task of him who, having taken thought, prepares to act.'

FRANTZ FANON, *Black Skin White Masks*

Contents

List of tables

Preface

So much social science demonstrates what is abundantly clear from everyday experience that the archetypal social scientist in the United States has been likened to a man who spends $50,000 to find his way to a whorehouse. Much work on race has this flavour. The relative condition of blacks in the United States and Britain, as compared to the white population, is no longer, if indeed it ever was, a secret. The primary need is not for more data, but for more action. Yet one need not be a Leninist to recognize that action without prior information, careful thought, and theoretical direction is likely to be diffuse and ineffective at best. Hence the aim of this study is not simply the generation of more information. Rather it is hoped to contribute to a re-orientation of the way in which we perceive what appears to be familiar reality, recognizing, as Robert Lynd put it, that 'the controlling factor in any science is the way it views and states its problems'.

This book examines the political responses to black migration and the political relationships formed in the early, and fluid, periods of inter-racial contact in the Northern cities of the United States, 1900–30, and in the United Kingdom, 1948–68. The focus is on the development of racial–political linkages that have shaped and limited available choices and the space of racial justice. The thrust of the work is two-pronged: it is a study in comparative race politics and, too, an examination of the capabilities of the two leading liberal democracies to incorporate and deal with the politics of race.

The systematic study of race politics is in its infancy. Accordingly, the first section of the book deals with developments and directions in this field, with the study's choice of subject and locale, and proposes a research orientation to the subject. Part II explores the genesis of struc-tured racial relationships in the United States, and Part III examines much the same issues in the United Kingdom. The final section attempts cross-national comparisons, examines the consequences of the patterns of political linkage, and reflects on the amalgam of liberal politics and institutional racism.

In preparing this study for publication, I have accumulated many debts, more than I can adequately repay. I was introduced to the study of race relations, and to the joy and demands of disciplined research, by the late Richard Hofstadter, a kind, brilliant mentor, who supervised my B.A. thesis, on racial violence in America in 1919.

As a graduate student, I was more than fortunate to have Henry Pelling as my dissertation supervisor. His probing, demanding, supportive comments and sympathetic assistance were invaluable to me. For their interest and suggestions, I wish to thank the following people, some of whom read portions of earlier drafts of the manuscript: Benjamin Barber, Nicholas Deakin, Daniel Lawrence, Robert Reinders, John Rex, William Taylor, and my students at Columbia. Thanks to the editorial work of Simon Abbott and Dale Gunthorp the readability of the manuscript has been improved. I owe a very special debt to A. Sivanandan, the Librarian at the Institute of Race Relations, London, whose intellectual and personal sensibilities have challenged and shaped my concerns.

The staff of his unique library, and the librarians at the Library of Congress, the Schomburg Collection of the New York Public Library, the New York Historical Society, the New York City Municipal Archives, the Columbia University Library, the Cambridge University Library, the Howard University Library, and the British Museum graciously assisted my work. The study has received generous financial assistance from the Danforth Foundation, the Euretta Kellett Fund, the Columbia College Council for Research in the Social Sciences, and the European Institute, Columbia University.

The usual disclaimer is not meant to be perfunctory. The manuscript's stylistic lapses and errors of fact or judgement are my own. But it should be said that without my wife's critical, persistent encouragement this work would not have been possible.

IRA KATZNELSON
Columbia University

Introduction to the Phoenix Edition

"To BEGIN to apprehend a text," Edward Said has written, "is to begin to find intention and method in it . . . to construct the field of its play, its dispersion, its distortion."[1] Paradoxically, the distortions of a text, be it a novel or a work of social science, are essential to its function of knowing society.[2] But the distortions inherent in writing about society are distortions nevertheless, and a writer had better self-consciously grasp the consequences of the analytical fictions he or she embraces. It is probably the essense of the revolution in late nineteenth-century art to have been able to concretize this homily about the uncertainty of vantage points. Thus Cezanne, for example, never just painted a tree, but several possible trees. He captured on canvass what every child knows: what you see depends on where you are and on the available constructed tools of vision.

Most books never approach this achievement, in part because of the limits of linear prose. But since they depend on distortion for their pursuit of truth, it is important at least that authors create a calculus of distortion for their own work, assessing the benefits and costs of their choices. The early chapters of *Black Men, White Cities* represent such an attempt. But while books have an unchanging textual life and coherence (the product of a distinctive conjuncture of biography, history, and analytical perspectives), new self-critical assessments are possible with the passage of time. In this Introduction, I should like to assay the distinctive play and distortions of *Black Men, White Cities,* and to clarify, and in some cases modify, a number of the book's positions.

I

Black Men, White Cities explores and reflects the concerns and intel-

[1] Edward W. Said, *Beginnings: Intention and Method* (New York: Basic Books, 1975), p. 59.

[2] Said stresses that "writing is not coterminous with nature," that it "deforms its subjects . . . more than it forms them," and that truth "can only be approached indirectly, by means of a mediation that, paradoxically, because of its falseness makes the truth truer." Ibid, pp. 59, 90.

lectual currents of the late 1960s and early 1970s. It focuses on the *political* and *participatory* causes of *racial* conflict in the United States and Britain. Like much radical scholarship of the period, it rightly recoiled from reductionist approaches to race. Following Weber, the dominant approach of Western social science has subsumed racial groups under the rubric of "status," and thus distinguishes them from classes. To this profound simplification, the archetypal Marxist response of the period was the flawed attempt to reduce issues of race to issues of class. Black and white workers are identically exploited by the capitalist class. Racism is only the artifact of a divide-and-conquer strategy. To this view, *Black Men, White Cities* stridently (the tone was deliberate) asserted that the racial order must be understood in its own terms, and that for many facets of social action the racial contradiction takes precedence over the class divide. This feature of social experience in Anglo-American societies is especially pronounced in the domain of politics and the state.

From this starting point, the book counterposed a modified Weberian perspective to the "class" versus "status" debate. For Weber, status has a dual, and partially contradictory, set of meanings. It denotes groups with noneconomic *origins,* and it denotes groups which share a *style* of culture and consumption. As I argued in chapter 1, the attempt to distinguish between classes and racial groups seen as status groups in either or both of these senses is flawed, since racial groups function as economic, status, and political units of the social structure concurrently. Indeed, the dominant feature of a racial order is that the characteristics of race come to identify systemic dividing points in all three of Weber's stratification arenas.

Having made these points, the book treats racial groups in the United States and Britain in the early formative periods of interracial contact by isolating for analysis their possibilities and behavior as political conflict groups in the process of fashioning a structure of linkages to liberal democratic regimes. Though this mode of proceeding still makes analytical and expositional sense to me, it was more distorting than it need have been because it was framed by an inadequate understanding of the possible utility of a Marxist agenda and methods (I confused the flaws of Marxists with the possibilities of Marxism), and of the potential for a meaningful, even urgent, set of conceptual connections between Marx and Weber.

Put more concretely, not only was the choice between Marxist and Weberian approaches misperceived as a choice at the same plane or level of analysis, but the act of choosing as I did missed the opportunity to locate the book's modified Weberian perspective within the frame of an essentially Marxist analysis of race and racism in their international and domestic settings. Both the "class" and "status" approaches to race miss the point that from the very outset of the creation of the post-feudal modern order race and racism have been integral components of capitalist development. From this starting point the integrity of the racial contradiction can be assessed and the political-citizenship dimensions of racial conflict understood.

The capitalist world economy which emerged in the sixteenth century has been both a class *and* a racial order from its birth to the present. As Immanuel Wallerstein has recently stressed, the meaning of Marx's assertion that "the capitalist era dates from the sixteenth century" can be comprehended only in terms of a unique global disjuncture. The new world economy whose defining characteristics were those of merchant capitalism linked a large number of political units together not, as heretofore, in the framework of an empire, but by regular, unequal market patterns of trade. The connecting solvent was money, not direct political control from a single center. Nation-states became the crucial units of a global stratification system. The dominant core states of western Europe (principally Britain and the Netherlands) pioneered in the development of commercialized agriculture and new forms of industrial production. An intermediate, or semiperipheral, group of states were somewhat less diversified in their economies, and, as in the case of Polish wheat production, became increasingly dependent on core state markets. At the bottom of this international order were the peripheral regions which specialized in the export of primary products, largely to western Europe.

Most importantly for this discussion, the new order was also distinguished by corresponding modes and sources of labor supply. Core states increasingly organized labor on the basis of contractual freedom (workers sold their time, not the total disposition of their lives). Sharecropping was the principal form of labor supply in the semiperiphery; and the peripheral areas were the repositories of unfree modes of labor, slavery being the paradigm case. This division of labor was also a racial and cultural division. In Wallerstein's words,[3]

A moment's thought will reveal that these occupational categories were not randomly distributed either geographically or ethnically within the burgeoning world economy. After some false starts, the picture rapidly evolved of a slave class of African origins located in the Western Hemisphere, a "serf" class divided into two segments: a major one in Eastern Europe and a smaller one of American Indians in the Western Hemisphere. . . . The wage workers were almost all west Europeans.

Though racial and status distinctions clearly predate this seminal era,

---

[3] Immanuel Wallerstein, *The Modern World-System: Capitalist Agriculture and the Origins of the European World-Economy in the Sixteenth Century* (New York: Academic Press, 1974), p. 87.

race has never simply denoted communitarian differences in the modern world. Thus the traditional Marxist view has been correct in rejecting "status" categories as adequate to capture the place and meaning of race and racism. Modern racial groups do not have unambiguously extra-economic origins; nor have they been distinguished only, or even principally, along cultural lines. Rather, from at least the sixteenth century, race has been a *material* category rooted in relations of production and a cultural division of labor.[4]

Quite clearly this feature of the modern world is not limited to global stratification, but is also crucially germane to an understanding of the dynamics of national social structures. An important example of recent scholarship concerned with the racial experience in the United States that takes this point of departure is the work of Robert Blauner. He undertakes a major revision of traditional Marxist scholarship on race by stressing that racial realities "are part of the base as well as the superstructure of . . . those capitalist nations which developed out of colonial conquest and imported African slaves to meet labor needs."[5] In the essay "Colonized and Immigrant Minorities," a comparative study of black and white workers in the United States in the nineteenth century, he persuasively argues that the essential distinguishing feature resided in the near exact correlation between color and the mode of labor: "The key equation was the association of free labor with people of white European stock and the association of unfree labor with non-Western people of color."[6] The global distinctions analyzed by Wallerstein were reproduced within the embrace of a core nation-state.

With the commercialization of Southern agriculture and the massive migration of blacks to the cities of the North in this century, this distinction has been eroded. Yet race continues to function as an important material marker in the base of advanced capitalist societies. Happily, since *Black Men, White Cities* was written, a number of social theorists have attempted to come to grips with this dimension of the racial experience.

Much of the most important work has focused on "segmented" or "dual" labor markets. Edna Bonacich has fashioned a theory of ethnic antagonism based on the differential capacities of workers grouped by ascriptive characteristics to command a high price for their labor power. In her view, antagonism between groups of workers "is specifically produced by the competition that arises from a price differential"; business

---

[4] An important elaboration and concrete application of these perspectives to the Celtic fringe in British development may be found in Michael Hechter, *Internal Colonialism* (Berkeley: University of California Press, 1975).

[5] Robert Blauner, "Marxian Theory and Race Relations," unpublished ms.

[6] Robert Blauner, *Racial Oppression in America* (New York: Harper and Row, 1972), p. 57.

tries to pay as little as it can for labor, regardless of ethnicity, but is held in check by the class capacities of some workers (for example, whites collectively in the United States) as opposed to the lack of class resources of others (for example, blacks). Though this approach, as William Wilson notes, understates the extent to which capitalist classes have manipulated such antagonisms, it does have significant historical explanatory power, as Bonacich's recent empirical work demonstrates. Moreover, it importantly stresses the extent to which racial markers have come to be inextricably bound to uneven capitalist development in this century.[7]

Focusing on western Europe in the recent past, Manuel Castells has compellingly located the place of immigrant workers as a culturally and racially distinctive part of the proletariat. Following Marx, Castells stresses that the central mechanism of capitalist societies is the extraction of surplus value from the working class, and that over time the capitalist system faces an increasingly severe crisis of profitability which can be counteracted only by intensifying the rate of exploitation. Immigrant workers play a critical role in this respect, because they have allowed capital "to pay a proportionately smaller value for the reproduction of the labor force," and to increase "the duration and intensity of work." The newcomers from western Europe, including Britain, have been recruited primarily from the young and productive. As a result, both government and capital have been able to avoid paying for the costs of rearing and socializing the immigrant work force. Moreover, since a disproportionate number of migrants have been males (without families or with families left behind to be called for later) who live in substandard housing, there are significant savings on schools, health costs, welfare benefits, and other social expenditures; and immigrants underwrite the profits of discrimination in housing that would be unacceptable for the mass of the working population.[8]

Castells further stresses that in the post-Keynesian world, minority immigrant workers perform the function of moderating the impact of what now seems to be an endemic problem of the combination of recession and inflation. The newcomers, he argues, are constrained to act as

[7] Edna Bonacich, "A Theory of Ethnic Antagonism: The Split Labor Market," *American Sociological Review,* vol. 37 (October 1972); William J. Wilson, "Ethnic and Class Stratification: Their Interrelation and Political Consequences—North America," paper delivered to the Research Committee on Social Stratification of the Eighth World Congress of Sociology, Toronto, Canada, August 1974; Edna Bonacich, "Abolition, the Extension of Slavery, and the Position of Free Blacks: A Study of Split Labor Markets in the United States, 1830–1863," *American Journal of Sociology,* vol. 81 (November 1975).

[8] Manuel Castells, "Immigrant Workers and Class Struggles in Advanced Capitalism: The Western European Experience," *Politics and Society* 5 (winter 1975): 33–66.

workers and consumers in ways that mitigate this dilemma. They are productive in the expansionary phase of the business cycle, yet consume little, thus reducing inflationary pressures. In the recessionary phase of the cycle, they can be excluded from productive employment with much less difficulty than is entailed in laying off other workers; thus the minority work force acts as an economic buffer against the dangers of overproduction.

While the empirical work of Blauner and Bonacich is not directly applicable to an analysis of the place of blacks within the northern political economy of the United States between 1900 and 1930, and while the work of Castells is not directly applicable to the position of blacks in Britain since 1948, their scholarship nevertheless presents a compelling agenda of questions, generated from within a Marxist problematic, that must be addressed to the periods of migration if they are to be understood in their fullness. The most promising line of analysis in this respect for the United States and Britain in the periods under study in this book is suggested by work on uneven development and the dual economy by such scholars as James O'Connor, Robert Averitt, and John Kenneth Galbraith.[9]

They suggest that the major feature of private sector capitalist development in this century lies in the developing boundaries between small and large capital. Each sector has distinctive characteristics with respect to levels of technology, size and market power of firms, the extent of unionization, and levels of wage rates. Over time the differences between the sectors have grown wider, as those who control the investment of capital have reinvested in products, machinery, workers, and geographic areas that yield the highest returns. In the United States and in the Commonwealth, blacks were largely lodged in the periphery of traditional unfree occupations before they moved in large numbers to the North and to Britain. Since their arrival, they have been largely concentrated in employment in the sector of small capital, which is not only economically but spatially distinctive. Blacks, in both countries, have been confined on the whole to the declining urban cores of developing dual economies. This observation suggests a very large research agenda, focusing on causes and consequences, a task too large to be attempted here (with much of it beyond my competence). But what can be said is that *Black Men, White Cities* provides some of the elements of this kind of analysis. In particular, it points to the significance of political linkages and therefore pinpoints those aspects of the groups' relationships to the state which have made blacks vulnerable to the processes of uneven develop-

---

[9] James O'Connor, *The Fiscal Crisis of the State* (New York: St. Martin's Press, 1973); Robert T. Averitt, *The Dual Economy* (New York: Norton, 1968); John Kenneth Galbraith, *Economics and the Public Purpose* (Boston: Houghton Mifflin Company, 1973).

ment. For as a consequence of the tales told in this book, blacks in both countries became, in Castells' phrase, a nineteenth-century proletariat in twentieth-century capitalism, lacking in substantive political and economic rights and protections.

II

Similarly situated ethnic or racial segments of the working class are today a part of the social structure of virtually every advanced capitalist country, from South Africa to Switzerland. To be sure, the quantitative economic importance of these groups varies considerably from place to place, but their qualitative role is strikingly close in function. Against this backdrop of rather consistent material roles are a set of *political* differences in the ways racial and ethnic subordinates are linked to their national political systems.

Simplifying the universe of possibilities somewhat, there are three dominant ways in which racially and ethnically distinct proletarians have been politically connected to modern capitalist states. At one end of the continuum is the definition of citizenship rights by race. In the American South until the passage of the Voting Rights Act of 1965, and even more nakedly in South Africa, citizenship criteria have been racial. As a result, the racial-labor system and the realm of citizenship are in isomorphic relation. By law, black South Africans who come to work in the cities are attached to white-defined "homelands." Urban workers are assigned "rights" to citizenship in Bantustans where their families are obliged to live, and to where they must return from time to time. As a result, the urban black worker lacks all of the protections of citizenship at the points of production and almost full-time residence. "Although he is not permitted to bring his family to the city, the black migrant laborer is in reality an urban proletarian—except that he may never have the right of settlement and security which would make him one effectively."[10] Such a system within the embrace of one nation-state in which a demographic minority is a sociological majority must be undergirded, of course, by visible and pervasive repression. Over 10 million South Africans have been arrested and prosecuted under the Pass Laws since 1948. Thus questions of citizenship and political linkages for the majority are kept off the political agenda; and potential contradictions between material inequality and citizenship equality do not directly arise.

The less repressive but functionally equivalent "contract" status of Continental migrant labor also allows most European countries to avoid dealing with this potential contradiction between economic and political

---

[10] Neal Ascherson, "Room at the Bottom," *The New York Review of Books,* February 15, 1976, p. 23.

structures.[11] The North Africans, Portuguese, Spaniards, Turks, and Italians who are recruited in periods of boom are exported, as they are today, in periods of stagnation. Most disadvantageously placed in the uneven capitalism of north and west Europe, these migrants are the first to be let go from their jobs and the least able to utilize the state to enlarge or defend their class position. As Neal Ascherson has recently argued, the separateness of national political boundaries and responsibilities has been a vital factor in maintaining the cohesion of advanced European capitalism: "It enables the industrialized country to export to another government the responsibility for the social and political consequences of exploitation and of trade cycles as they affect employment." The burden of unemployment is visited on the country of origin. "When they lose their jobs, they do not stay around to form embarrassing mobs waiting for relief, or gather dangerously behind banners in the town hall square. Instead, they vanish."[12]

In the third possibility, they have not. Blacks moving north in the United States between 1900 and 1930 (and later in even larger numbers during and after the Second World War) and to Britain from the Commonwealth after 1948 came in search of jobs in expanding economies. But, crucially, *they came as citizens*. They posed, from the outset, the issues of political incorporation. The analysis of the processes of incorporation in the United States and Britain, of course, forms the centerpiece of *Black Men, White Cities*. In the book, these matters are conceptualized and treated almost exclusively on the political plane. But perhaps even more usefully, the book may be read as a comparative treatment of two cases in which contradictions between economic imperatives and the political structures of the liberal state could not be avoided by immigration laws and exclusionary citizenship patterns. Rather they had to be dealt with directly by the state and the relevant party institutions.[13] Put plainly, *Black Men, White Cities* is an analysis of how formal democratic rights and possibilities were made substantially compatible with a materially subordinate economic place for the migrants through the elaboration of distinctive mechanisms of linkage to the state. In this sense the book's preoccupation with issues of representation may be best understood.

In both cases, political linkages institutionalized racism and established quasi-colonial patterns of interaction which simultaneously reflected

---

[11] The most comprehensive treatment is Stephen Castles and Godula Kosack, *Immigrant Workers and Class Structure in Western Europe* (London: Oxford University Press, 1973).

[12] Ascherson, "Room at the Bottom."

[13] Albeit reluctantly in the British case, and, after 1961, by shifts in immigration legislation which come closer to replicating the Continental contract labor status of the migrants.

economic imperatives and were autonomous bases of conflict with their own logic of development. Viewed in these terms, the political incorporation of blacks in the United States and Britain are condensed cases of the central problem of cohesion of the liberal capitalist state: that of developing a modus vivendi between a politics of mass participation and the dynamics of capitalist inequality and exploitaton.

The recrudescence of interest in Gramsci, and the powerful analytical currents of recent Marxist work on the state by such scholars as Poulantzas, Miliband, O'Connor, Offe, and Habermas has placed issues of cohesion, legitimation, and the political integration of the working class on the analytical agenda.[14] The issues raised most extensively by liberal theorists of democratic stability are now being grappled with intensively by Marxist analysts as well, whose work is differentiated from the liberal tradition by defining the activities of the state with regard to the reproduction of the forces and social relations of capitalist production. Though not intentionally written to contribute to this literature, *Black Men, White Cities* may retrospectively be located as part of this enterprise in that it suggests tools for the analysis of the *functioning* of the state's functions of control, and applies those tools to show concretely how, in Alford and Friedland's terms, "a principal consequence of the democratization of the electoral process may have been the development of mechanisms by political and economic elites to neutralize or cancel out the potential consequences of that democratization."[15] And, too, the book at least implicitly raises questions not only about how economic imperatives may shape the construction of political structures, but also about how the relative independence of the political may in turn provide opportunities for subordinates of major consequence.

III

In retrospect, there are a number of assertions in the book which might have been developed differently. The argument in chapter 7, a restatement of the conventional wisdom that the political linkages of white ethnics to the state through political machines produced significant mass mobility opportunities, needs at least to be reexamined, and possibly rejected. For the machine more usefully may be seen as a solution for white workers equivalent to black political arrangements for incorpora-

[14] See O'Connor, *The Fiscal Crisis;* Nicos Poulantzas, *Political Power and Social Classes* (London: New Left Books, 1973); Ralph Miliband, *The State in Capitalist Society* (London: Weidenfeld and Nicolson, 1969); Claus Offe, "The Abolition of Market Control and the Problem of Legitimacy," *Kapitalistate* 1 (1973); Jürgen Habermas, *Legitimation Crisis* (Boston, Beacon Press, 1975).

[15] Robert R. Alford and Roger Friedland, "Nations, Parties, and Participation: A Critique of Political Sociology," *Theory and Society* 1 (1974): 324.

tion on terms that did not disturb capitalist development. In any event, my position on these matters is now more agnostic. Better answers must await more systematic research.

Also, the labelling of pre-1958 race politics in Britain as "pre-political," while correct at the level of purposive elite action, seems misperceived in more systemic terms. The attempt to keep race off the political agenda was in fact an eminently political attempt to manage the contradiction of citizenship and material subordination by suppressing its expression. The term "pre-political" obscures this dynamic. There are still other matters, large and small, which are incompletely developed. But instead of launching into a detailed textual exercise, permit me to conclude by raising some questions about the volume's treatment of social control.

In a recent article, Morris Janowitz has sought to reassert the distinctive meaning "social control" had in the emerging discipline of American sociology at the turn of the century. In the work of E. A. Ross, Charles Horton Cooley, Robert Park, and other members of the Chicago School, social control referred not to the array of mechanisms of imposed compliance, but to the ability of social groups to regulate themselves; and at the macro-level, "to the capacity of a society to regulate itself according to desired principles and values."[16] This tradition portrays matters of social control in terms of the clash between the thoughts and actions of free individuals and the imperative of social order at the level of society. As Georges Gurvich has noted, it sees order and social reality itself in accord with the classical liberal view "in a nominalistic way, as rather an assemblage of isolated individuals, whose connection and emergence in a whole stems from social control."[17]

Though this tradition has permitted rich research at the "interface between micro- and macro-analysis," its assertion that "the *opposite* of social control can be thought of as coercive control"[18] clearly reveals its limitations as well; for such an assertion indicates the failure of this tradition to specify the place of individuals (and clusters of individuals) in society. Lacking a convincing theory of the sharply inegalitarian and exploitative social structure of capitalist societies (or even of industrial societies more generally), and of the material bases of social and political behavior, the liberal tradition of social control has tended, normatively, to assert the paramount importance of order, and, scientifically, to reify society and leave unexamined the sources of threat to social cohesion. "Social control" is reduced to one kind of technique of co-

[16] Morris Janowitz, "Sociological Theory and Social Control," *American Journal of Sociology* 81 (July 1975): 82.

[17] Georges Gurvich, "Social Control," in Georges Gurvich and Wilbert Moore, eds., *Twentieth Century Sociology* (New York: Philosophical Library, 1945), p. 272.

[18] Janowitz, "Sociological Theory," pp. 87, 84.

hesion (perhaps the most important technique, though this is a matter that clearly varies in time and place), rather than being an analytical tool for assessing the entire scope of means (including self-regulation) for the fashioning of order in societies faced with the disjunction between the formal legal equality of citizenship and the franchise, and the structural inequities produced by the routine operation of the economic system.

For these reasons, the discussion of social control in *Black Men, White Cities* commenced with Joseph Roucek's definition: "Social control occurs when one group determines the behavior of another group, when the group controls the conduct of its own members, or when individuals influence the responses of others." This approach is more inclusive than Janowitz's by incorporating both coercive and behaviorally voluntaristic means of compliance. "Social control takes place when a person is induced or forced to act according to the wishes of others, whether or not in accordance with his own individual interests."[19]

The book sought further to move beyond the liberal sociological tradition by firmly linking social control to an analysis of social structure. A society's apparatus of social control was thus conceptualized as an interlocking set of coercive, symbolic, and institutional buffers which soften the impact of basic social contradictions, and which produce behavior in which people act against their interests (often by not acting at all). In a capitalist political economy, as I have written subsequently, stability does not imply the absence of structurally rooted conflicts, but reflects the operation of the buffering mechanisms that shape and limit behavior. The state's function of social control consists in managing the consequences of making capitalism work, and can best be understood as an attempt to manage but not overcome the contradictions of the capitalist system.[20]

But while this formulation focuses on the need to trace the links between the interests and intentions of political elites and political outcomes, it does not sufficiently focus on the more dynamic or conflictual aspects of social control. The dimensions of social control are not givens or outcomes, but parts of an ongoing process. The state is not simply or exclusively the instrument of a dominant class or the carrier of the structural imperatives of capital. Because of the degree of autonomy the state has from the economy, and because the members of the liberal state are citizens, political arrangements themselves may act as constraints on the capacity of a dominant class to realize its interests. Thus class and race conflicts occur in distinctive ways within the state in the form of competing political capacities.

¹⁹ See below, chapter seven, p. 105.

²⁰ Ira Katznelson, "The Crisis of the Capitalist City: Urban Politics and Social Control," in Willis Hawley and Michael Lipsky, eds., *Theoretical Perspectives on Urban Politics* (Englewood Cliffs, N.J.: Prentice-Hall, 1976).

At any given moment, the political capacity of a class or group, dominant or subordinate, depends not only on its material resources but also on distinctively political factors: on the heritage of previous political decisions (the English gentry of 1832, for example, was ill-placed to resist reform precisely because its victories in the seventeenth century had produced a weak central state); on the strength of alternative ideologies; on available mechanisms of physical coercion; and on prevailing patterns of political institutionalization by which the dominant and the subordinate are linked to the state.

Black Men, White Cities may thus be read as an analysis of competing capacities of class and race, and of their political structuration. Subsequent racial turmoil in the United States and Britain has been conditioned by the political structures discussed in this volume and has in large measure been about their alteration.

Part One

Comparative Race Politics

Chapter One

Towards Comparison: Problems, Concepts, Possibilities

SICKENED by the vision of 'great, ugly whirlwinds of hatred, and blood and cruelty' of impending racial conflicts, W. E. B. DuBois, both deeply pessimistic and realistic, wondered in 1920: 'If I cry amid this roar of elemental forces, must my cry be in vain, because it is but a cry—a small and human cry amid Promethean gloom?'[1] A half century later, despite massive racial upheavals and the demise of most formal, overt colonial arrangements (including the end of legally sanctioned segregation practices in the United States), the realist must remain a pessimist. Paradoxically, today's 'realistic pessimism' follows a long period characterized by what Harry Hoetink has called 'sociologistic optimism'; most race relations scholars, especially American scholars, were convinced that by revealing the nature of racial myths and prejudice they could administer therapy to their racist societies.

This optimistic, hopeful vision has been mocked by recent events. In the United States the illusion of marked racial progress promoted by the passage of the omnibus Civil Rights Act in 1964 was shattered by widespread violent ghetto rebellions in the middle years of the decade. Likewise, in England, the Labour Government's White Paper limitations on Commonwealth immigration in 1965 and the exclusion of Kenyan Asians with British passports three years later brought the optimistic 'Liberal Hour'[2] to an abrupt end. As a consequence of these developments, race relations scholars, and white scholars in particular, have been compelled to re-examine their role and the nature and direction of their research.

This chapter addresses itself to these questions. Its purpose is to

[1] W. E. B. DuBois, *Darkwater* (New York, 1920), p. 52.
[2] See Harry Hoetink, *The Two Variants in Caribbean Race Relations* (London, 1967), pp. 86–90; E. J. B. Rose and associates, *Colour and Citizenship: A Report on British Race Relations* (London, 1969), pp. 10–26. An extended discussion of approaches to the study of race appears in Peter Rose, *The Subject is Race* (New York, 1968), especially Chapters 3 and 4.

delineate some of the problems of the white social scientist concerned with race, to review major trends in race research, and propose new links between race relations scholarship and the study of comparative politics. Each of these matters might be seen as peripheral to the book's central enterprise, the comparative study of American and British race politics during the critical early periods of migration. They are dealt with at some length here, however, because the book provides the occasion for an examination of what I take to be crucial themes that must be faced up to by those who write and act to help secure racial and political liberation; because these themes haunted me as I wrote the book; and because what follows in the remaining sections is meant to be taken as an example of the kind of work I hope may be emulated elsewhere.

Hence, the study is not meant to be a comparative study only (though that is its central focus), but also a book that addresses itself concretely to the concerns examined in this section. The general reader can, of course, read the case studies on their own terms. To do so, he need not dwell on the materials in this chapter. But I would urge that he work his way through the discussion in Chapters 2 and 3, since they provide the conceptual apparatus for making the most sense of what follows.

I

The relationships that link social scientists and their work to their social and political locale raise difficult, nettlesome issues. Given present patterns of racial dominance, these issues need to be raised with great urgency; the easy shibboleths about scholarly independence, appropriateness, objectivity, and value-neutrality cannot be uttered confidently except by the most facile and insensitive. The insistent struggles by Third World (non-European, non-Western, non-white) peoples for decolonization and liberation have overtaken these comforting formulations.

Hence the role of the white scholar, who recognizes that to be a man is to be responsible, is an anomalous role. One is reminded of Albert Memmi's vivid characterization of the colonizer who refuses, who resists the colonial arrangements from which he benefits, who can usually only observe the nationalistically oriented struggles from afar, and who remains, despite his good intentions, politically impotent.[3] The scholar resembles, as a result, the lonely adolescent, who, in Octavio Paz's words, 'is astonished at the fact of his being, and this astonishment leads to reflection: as he leans over the river of his consciousness, he asks himself if the face that appears there, disfigured by the water, is his own. The singularity of his being, which is pure sensation in children, becomes a problem and a question.'[4]

[3] Albert Memmi, *The Colonizer and the Colonized* (Boston, 1965), pp. 19ff.
[4] Octavio Paz, *The Labyrinth of Solitude* (New York, 1961), p. 9.

In the past decade, many white social scientists have been increasingly, and painfully, puzzled by the issues of race. Well-intentioned liberal scholars, who have subscribed to the view that colour should be irrelevant, that the political and academic worlds should be colour-blind, are troubled at the rejection by many blacks of racial integration. In sincere, but insensitive, response they accord equal weight to the positions of white racists and black separatists, not realizing, as a black Englishman has put it, that 'white racism is at one level a matter of choice, at another a matter of privilege, but at all levels an exercise in oppression. White racism incurs somewhere down the line the denial of human dignity; black "racism" envisages the destruction of that denial.'[5]

Their puzzlement reflects, in part, the limitations of focus and perspective of the most important traditional approaches to the study of race: the concern with racial contact, assimilation, and a race relations cycle; and the dominant concern with prejudicial attitudes and discriminatory behaviour.

The first of these two research foci is associated with the seminal work of Robert Park. Generalizing from the Hawaiian and West Coast Asian experiences, he argued, 'In the relations of the races there is a cycle of events which tends everywhere to repeat itself. . . . The race relations cycle which takes the form, to state it abstractly, of contacts, competition, accommodation, and eventual assimilation is apparently progressive and irreversible.'[6] This mechanistic, determinist approach has been aptly criticized by Michael Banton who notes that 'cyclical theories . . . make little allowance for the characteristics of the interacting groups or for the institutional context within which contact occurs. In so far as they posit assimilation as an inevitable conclusion, events of recent years have cast further doubt upon their validity.'[7]

Similarly, recent experience compels a re-examination of the assumptions of much research that has focused on prejudice and discrimination. The stress on prejudice, which dates academically from the 1930s,[8] achieved its most brilliant expression in Gunnar Myrdal's *An American Dilemma*. In the keynote paragraph of his massive, still invaluable, study, Myrdal summed up his organizing thesis:

The American Negro problem is a problem in the heart of the American. It is there that the interracial tension has its focus. It is there that the decisive struggle

[5] A. Sivanandan, 'The Revolt of the Natives', *Twentieth Century* (Vol. I, Third Quarter 1968), p. 13.

[6] Robert Ezra Park, *Race and Culture* (New York, 1950), p. 150.

[7] Michael Banton, *Race Relations* (London, 1967), p. 76: Emory Bogardus, Park's student, later postulated a more detailed, but equally irreversible cycle—curiosity, economic welcome, industrial and social antagonism, legislative antagonism, fair-play tendencies, quiescence, second-generation difficulties; Emory Bogardus, *Immigration and Race Attitudes* (Boston, 1928). For an extended discussion of race relations cycles, see Brewton Berry, *Race and Ethnic Relations* (Boston, 1965), pp. 129–35.

[8] See R. A. Schermerhorn, *Comparative Ethnic Relations* (New York, 1970), p. 6.

B

goes on. This is the central viewpoint of this treatise. Though our study includes economic, social and political race relations, at bottom our problem is the moral dilemma of the American.[9]

Besides being empirically suspect (events subsequent to the publication of *An American Dilemma* indicate that most Americans are *not* torn by contradictions of creed and behaviour), Myrdal's ethical–moral approach to prejudice begs the question: what are the social, economic, and political origins of relationships of racial inequality, and what social, economic, and political factors sustain such relationships? It is a distortion to posit the perceptual, subjective notion of prejudice as the central independent variable in analysing social and political reality. As R. A. Schermerhorn has put it,

If we begin with the matter of prejudice, any approach to the field from this viewpoint has a subtle tendency to psychologize group relations by seeing them as personality processes writ large. . . . If research has confirmed anything in this area it is that prejudice is the product of *situations*, historical situations, economic situations, political situations; it is not a little demon that emerges in people because they are depraved.[10]

The focus on attitudes as independent variables has comparative limitations as well, not only because prejudice is difficult to measure, but because prejudicial attitudes have no meaning apart from concrete contexts. The focus on discrimination also misleads to the extent that it diverts attention from the structured differential distribution of wealth, status, and political power, and from the examination of the linkages of racial groups in society to each other and to the polity.

Like the well-intentioned liberal scholar, many Marxist and quasi-Marxist scholars have had difficulty in dealing with race. They are disturbed by what they see as the deflection of class consciousness and conflict into racial consciousness and conflict, typically arguing that 'anyone who assumes race exists . . . is playing the racialist game'.[11] Much Marxist work on race reduces the issues of race to issues of class; thus Oliver Cox, in the classic American Marxist analysis of race relations, insists that, 'We can understand the Negro problem only in so far as we understand their position as workers . . . this fundamental fact identifies the Negro problem in the United States with the problem of all workers regardless of color.'[12]

These Marxist sentiments, like those of the archetypal liberal, are noble, but not rooted in reality. Colour has been a mark of oppression related to, yet quite independent of, class. Among other striking indica-

---

[9] Gunnar Myrdal, *An American Dilemma* (New York, 1944), p. xxi.

[10] Schermerhorn, op. cit., p. 6.

[11] Nigel Harris, 'Race and Nation', *International Socialism* (Vol. 9, Autumn 1968), p. 24.

[12] Oliver C. Cox, *Caste, Class, and Race* (New York, 1948), p. xxxii.

tions, the blue-collar vote for George Wallace in 1968 and the fierce resistance by members of construction unions to black membership in the United States, and the massive outpouring of support for the inflammatory speeches of Enoch Powell by dockworkers and other working-class white Englishmen indicate, at a minimum, that at least for the present class and colour do not share a common denominator.[13] An insistent Marxist might reply with appropriate arguments about false consciousness (with which I would concur), yet he can no longer argue intelligently that corrosive racial distinctions, whatever their origin, have not created categories of events and behaviour that must be dealt with on their own terms.

In his 1956 letter of resignation from the French Communist Party, the Martinique poet, Aimé Césaire, affirmed the duality of class and race. He wrote to Thorez:

One fact, crucial in so far as I am concerned, is this: that we coloured men, in this specific moment of historical evolution, have consciously grasped, and grasped in its full breadth the notion of our peculiar uniqueness, the notion of just who we are and what, and that we are ready, on every plane and in every department, to assume the responsibilities which proceed from this coming into consciousness.

The peculiarity of 'our place in the world' isn't to be confused with anybody else's. The peculiarity of our problems aren't to be reduced to subordinate forms of other problems. . . .

In these conditions, it will be understood that we cannot delegate anyone to think for us; to do our searching, to make our discoveries; that we cannot henceforth accept that anyone at all, be he our best friend, answer for us.[14]

If we take Césaire's last point seriously, as we should, then we must indicate with some precision what the role of white social scientists should be in this area. It is possible, of course, to resolve the question by counselling white withdrawal from the field, temporarily at least. But this categorical position, in my view, confuses on one hand the tasks of indigenous decision-making and community autonomy, with on the other contextual issues of black–white interaction, with those structural economic, social, and political linkages that define the limits of choice and racial justice, and which, therefore, must be of as much concern to whites as to blacks. To state explicitly what should be obvious: however benevolent the intention, white scholars have no role to play in resolving internal black community disputes, no role to play in directing black organizations, no role to play in defining black community goals or the direction of black political activity. Perhaps less obviously, but equally compellingly, more or less conscious nascent tendencies of cultural imperialism—the product of historical and contemporary patterns of dominance—must consciously be overcome.

[13] see Sivanandan, op. cit., p. 13.
[14] Aimé Césaire, *Letter to Maurice Thorez* (Paris, 1956), pp. 6, 11.

An appropriate role for white social scientists dealing with race has a great deal to do with the appropriate task of the social scientist whatever his subject matter, and to that I will return. But first, a discussion of two well-meaning approaches that are misdirected should help clarify the issue.

One approach to race studies now in vogue is that of urban ethnography, the attempt to apply the field techniques of the anthropologist to racial minority groups in complex industrialized societies. To date, many, though not all, urban ethnographers have focused on what the late Oscar Lewis called the culture of poverty, or the culture and personality problems of the poor.[15] Many ethnographers argue that these patterns, which are dysfunctional for mobility in American society, must be modified so that blacks can take advantage of the *existing* opportunity structure. The direct policy implications are clear, and were spelled out, to cite a leading example, in Daniel Moynihan's report on the black family:

What then is the problem? We feel the answer is clear enough. Three centuries of injustice have brought about deep-seated structural distortions in the life of the Negro American. At this point the tangle of pathology is capable of perpetuating itself without assistance from the white world. *The cycle can be broken only if these distortions are set right. In a word, a national effort towards the problems of Negro Americans must be directed towards the problems of family structure.*[16]

This approach to urban ethnography and the policy uses to which it has been put have been attacked vigorously, perhaps most convincingly by Charles Valentine in his excellent little volume, *Culture and Poverty*.[17] Valentine argues that many ethnographers misleadingly portray racial problems as black problems of personality and behaviour, ignoring the interdependence of systemic arrangements, cultural patterns, and debilitating effects on personalities. The life cycle of the American ghetto poor can more fruitfully be seen as a cluster of related adaptations to structural–situational factors that limit the chance to choose. Thus, if society is conceptualized in terms of a hierarchy of choice behaviour possibilities, the ghetto poor are at the bottom with the fewest choices. It is crucial, therefore, to analyse those structured economic, social, and political relationships that limit choice and destroy psyches.

On the face of it, this is what social scientists who have participated in the research and writing of many of the recent riot commission reports

---

[15] For a discussion of the culture of poverty, see Oscar Lewis, *La Vida* (New York, 1966), pp. xlii–lii. A good anthology of urban ethnography that at least partially transcends the limitations discussed is Norman E. Whitten, Jr. and John F. Szwed, *Afro-American Anthropology* (New York, 1970).

[16] United States Department of Labor, Office of Policy Planning and Research, *The Negro Family*, by Daniel Moynihan (Washington, 1965). Emphasis in original.

[17] Charles Valentine, *Culture and Poverty* (Chicago, 1968).

published by government agencies at the local, state, and national levels in the United States have been doing. But in this respect, Robert Lynd's classic question obtains, *Knowledge for What?*[18] Most of the reports—the McCone Commission report on Watts being the most glaring example[19]— have sought to discover the means to secure the greatest level of black docility at the lowest cost to the wider society. Put another way, many social scientists have become interested in race relations only since American blacks, using the most effective tactic available to the relatively powerless—disruption—have been able to make inputs into the political system. It is noteworthy that of the 2,611 articles published by the *American Political Science Review* between 1906 and 1963, only thirteen contained the words 'Negro', 'Race', or 'Civil Rights' in their titles.[20] Simmel noted an analogous phenomenon when he commented on welfare assistance programmes to the poor in Germany in the early years of the century:

It becomes clear that the fact of taking away from the rich to give to the poor does not aim at equalizing their individual positions and is not, even in its orientation, directed at suppressing the social differences between the rich and the poor. On the contrary, assistance is based on the structure of society, whatever it may be. . . . The goal of assistance is precisely to mitigate certain extreme manifestations of social differentiation, so that the social structure may continue to be based on this differentiation.[21]

Consider the best of the riot reports, the Kerner Commission's *Report of the National Advisory Commission on Civil Disorders,* which dramatically indicted 'white racism', concluding, 'Our nation is moving toward two societies, one black, one white—separate and unequal.'[22] Even this report, as two critical observers have noted, 'contained almost no criticism of established institutions or programs'.[23] The organizational ties of the Commission membership—which included legislators, a union leader, the chairman of a corporation board, a Mayor, and a Police Chief— made it difficult, perhaps impossible, to explore the institutional context and expression of the 'white racism' the Commission considered so central to its findings. Looked at this way, the report is no more than a placatory symbolic document that provided the Johnson Administration

---

[18] Robert Lynd, *Knowledge for What?* (Princeton, 1945).

[19] See Robert Blauner, 'Whitewash Over Watts', *Trans-Action* (Vol. 3, March–April 1966), pp. 3ff.; and Lewis Coser, *Continuities in the Study of Social Conflict* (New York, 1968), pp. 101ff.

[20] Donald Matthews, 'Political Science Research on Race Relations', in I. Katz and P. Gurin, *Race and the Social Sciences* (New York, 1969), p. 113.

[21] Georg Simmel, 'The Poor', in Chaim Waxman, ed., *Poverty: Power and Politics* (New York, 1968), pp. 8–9.

[22] *Report of the National Advisory Commission on Civil Disorders* (New York, 1968), p. 1.

[23] Michael Lipsky and David Olson, 'Riot Commission Politics', *Trans-Action* (Vol. 6, July–August 1969), p. 17.

with the opportunity to delay implementation of its minimal programmes. The report, Parenti has observed,

... treats the obviously abominable living conditions as 'causes' of disturbance but never really inquires into the causes of the 'causes,' viz., the ruthless enclosure of Southern sharecroppers by big corporate farming interests, the subsequent mistreatment of the black migrant by Northern rent-gouging landlords, price-gouging merchants, urban 'redevelopers,' discriminating employers, insufficient schools, hospitals and welfare, brutal police, hostile political machines and state legislators, and finally, the whole system of values, material interests and public power distributions from the state to the federal capitols which gives priority to 'haves' than to 'have-nots,' servicing and subsidizing the interests of private corporations while neglecting the often desperate needs of the municipalities.[24]

Thus, like some urban ethnographers, the riot commission policy-proposers focus on the poor, 'ignoring the system of power, privilege, and profit which makes them poor. It is a little like blaming the corpse for the murder.'[25]

By ignoring the structure of power, riot commission studies have usually missed the political side of the ghetto rebellions. Those who participated in the urban uprisings of the 1960s focused their attention on symbols of public authority and political legitimacy; thus the riots have been realistically compared to 'native' uprisings against oppressive, colonial-like relationships.[26] Those social scientists who have serviced the needs of the government-appointed commissions at best have unwittingly played a symbolic game, leaving themselves open to the charge of having helped to perpetuate the network of structured relationships that produced the conditions they claim to abhor.

II

Writing about race relations research, Melvin Tumin recently observed 'that never has social research been so substantial, in the first instance, and relevant in the second instance, to matters of pressing moment, and *so quickly followed up with social action and policy that run directly against the major grain of that research.*'[27] Whether intended or unintended, research in this field has social consequences. To avoid the question of consequences is to obscure a central and inescapable dilemma, one that is characteristic of the social sciences as a whole.

The problem of intention and consequences, of course, is not a new

---

[24] Michael Parenti, 'The Possibilities for Political Change', *Politics and Society* Vol. I, (November 1970), p. 81.

[25] Ibid., p. 82.

[26] Blauner, 'Whitewash over Watts', op. cit.

[27] Melvin Tumin, 'Some Social Consequences of Research on Racial Relations', in Hans Peter Dreitzel, *Recent Sociology* (New York, 1969), p. 254.

one for social scientists. Recently, Ralf Dahrendorf has made an interesting attempt to reformulate the issue by compartmentalizing the sociologist and his sociology. On the whole, he accepts the canons of scientific objectivity that seek to maintain a distance between the social scientist and his subject, but cautions, 'Our responsibility as sociologists does not end when we complete the process of scientific inquiry.' Thus,

. . . it is the sociologist's business to consider what a modern, open, civilized society might look like, and what roads might lead to it. This is the domain of theory. It is also the sociologist's business, once he is equipped with his theories, to take part in the process of changing reality, in making what is reasonable real. This is the domain of practice.[28]

Though this formulation has appeal, the neat dualism of theory and practice is unconvincing, for however detached or conventional the intent, 'no two arrangements of social knowledge have quite the same uses or political implications.'[29]

Moreover, as Dankwart Rustow has argued, the social scientist *qua* social scientist is heavily involved in the area of values whether he likes it or not as a result of his relationship, unique for the sciences, with his subject matter and his audience: 'As social scientists we are cast in the awkward role of men in society trying to explain to other men in society how men live in society.'[30] Seen in this light, objectivity cannot possibly be achieved in the physical science sense. The professed objectivity of the social scientist can more aptly be seen as a particular solution, fulfilling particular needs for social scientists seeking a particular kind of linkage with society. Thus, Gouldner perceptively sees objectivity as 'the way one comes to terms and makes peace with a world one does not like but will not oppose.'[31]

Counterpoised to the pose of objectivity is the more appealing approach of 'disciplined subjectivity' (the phrase is Erikson's),[32] involved with the subject of inquiry, yet disciplined by the canons of scholarship. This approach recognizes the essential links between scholar, subject, and audience; the social scientist is both in and of his world. This is a persuasive approach, for why study society unless you care about society? Moreover, since social science scholarship has political and moral consequences, social scientists must face up to their political and moral responsibilities.[33]

These considerations are magnified in the field of race relations. Given

[28] Ralf Dahrendorf, *Essays in the Theory of Society* (Stanford, 1968), p. 278.
[29] Hugh Stretton, *The Political Sciences* (London, 1969), p. 64.
[30] Dankwart Rustow, 'Change as the Theme of Political Science', unpublished paper, p. 9.
[31] Alvin Gouldner, *The Coming Crisis of Western Sociology* (New York, 1970), p. 103.
[32] Erik H. Erikson, 'On the Nature of Psycho-Historical Evidence: In Search of Gandhi', *Daedalus* (Summer 1968), p. 683.
[33] This is a paraphrase of Gouldner, op. cit., p. 410.

the social scientist's web of relationships, attempts at value-free race relations scholarship are not simply absurd, but dangerous. We do not write and work in a moral and political vacuum. Therefore, race relations scholarship is today, whatever our degree of regret, more than an exercise in understanding. Given the subject matter, to write is to be implicitly political. For that reason, it is crucial that we be as clear as possible as to the meaning and potential consequences of our work. And, given the burden of our racial history, white scholars must be doubly aware.

The parameters of the white social scientist's role in the area of race can be assessed by a consideration of the broader question of the social scientist's relationship to those with power. C. Wright Mills examined three alternative public roles social scientists may seek to assume. The scholar might seek political power, coveting the role of philosopher-king. Alternatively, he might counsel those with power in a subsidiary, advisory role, as in the case of those who serviced the riot commissions. Mills urged a third course, with which I concur: 'It is to remain independent, to do one's own work, to select one's own problems, but to direct this work *at* kings as well as *to* publics.'[34] In this role, the social scientist imputes responsibility to those with power for the consequences of their decisions, and educates those without power by examining the consequences of public decisions for their private lives. In this role, to both those with and without political power, the social scientist clarifies the range and consequences of choice.

At its best, an independent social science of 'disciplined subjectivity' adopts approaches similar to those of Gandhi's *satyagraha*. In her acute analysis of the Gandhian philosophy of conflict, Joan Bondurant asks, 'What does it mean to be a satyagrahi?'

Gandhi repeatedly addressed himself to this question. He not only thought, spoke, and wrote about the continuing exploration of truth, but he fashioned a method of conflict in the exercise of which a man could come to know what he is and what it means to evolve. In satyagraha, dogma gives way to an open exploration of context. *The objective is not to assert propositions, but to create possibilities.* In opening up new choices and in confronting an opponent with the demand that he make a choice, the satyagrahi involves himself in acts of 'ethical existence.' The process forces a continuing examination of one's own motives, an examination undertaken within the context of relationships as they are changed towards a new restructured, and reintegrated pattern.[35]

Thus, a social science of 'disciplined subjectivity' seeks to fuse moral commitment, rigorous research, and theoretical illumination to define and extend the range of choice. It is imperative, therefore, to focus on those structured relationships that limit behavioural possibilities. Stretton has put the point clearly:

[34] C. Wright Mills, *The Sociological Imagination* (New York, 1959), p. 181.
[35] Joan Bondurant, *The Gandhian Philosophy of Conflict* (Berkeley, 1969), pp. vi–vii.

We need a science of choice and possibilities. Such a science needs moral as well as technical originality. It must invent as well as discover. Inescapably, it must include political as well as technical debate. It cannot be a science only of durable laws and extrapolated trends. . . . For us, the purpose of knowledge is often to erode constants, escape from regularities, reduce the certainty of prediction; or if the regularities seem valuable, then to replace their causes, so that men may now choose what they once suffered from necessity.[36]

Given these sets of commitments, social scientists concerned with race have as a first-order task the identification and analysis of the relationships, linkages, and structures—social, economic, political, and normative —that define the limits of choice behaviour and racial justice. The discussion that follows in this chapter and the next proposes an approach to the study of race that might facilitate this task.

III

In the last decade and a half, under the impact of considerable methodological development, much of political science's most exciting work has been done by students of comparative politics who have moved away from the constraints of formalist, descriptive, institutional approaches. It is an unfortunate irony that despite the considerable gains in methodological sophistication, and despite a growing recognition that the issues of race are of global significance, to date, to their mutual impoverishment, race relations scholars have usually operated within the relatively closed world of the traditional literature on race, while students of comparative politics remain largely uninformed by that literature.

Comparative politics and race relations scholarship would be enriched by an exchange of ideas, research foci, and methodological orientations. In particular, many students of comparative politics, including pioneers of the post-institutional developments, have been uneasy about aspects of the present state of their discipline. The papers presented at a conference on the comparative method at the City University of New York in May 1968, later published in the inaugural issue of *Comparative Politics*,[37] are a representative expression of this unease. Treating this corpus of work in unitary fashion for the sake of economy, the following shared criticisms and points of departure seem most persuasive: Echoing Cobban's classic observation that most of what is called political science seems to be 'a device, invented by university teachers, for avoiding that dangerous subject politics, without achieving science',[38] the participants lamented

[36] Stretton, op. cit., pp. 261-2.

[37] I refer especially to the papers by Roy Macridis, 'Comparative Politics and the Study of Government: The Search for Focus', Dankwart Rustow, 'Modernization and Comparative Politics: Prospects in Theory and Research', and Joseph LaPalombara, 'Macrotheories and Microapplications in Comparative Politics: A Widening Chasm', in *Comparative Politics* (Vol. 1, October 1968).

[38] Alfred Cobban, 'The Decline of Political Theory', *Political Science Quarterly* (Vol. 68, September 1953), p. 335.

the depoliticization of political science (as a consequence of behaviouralism), and the unsatisfactory dual focus on 'grand theory' (defined by Wright Mills as 'thinking so general that its practitioners cannot logically get down to observation'),[39] and empirical trivia. As a corrective, LaPalombara called for studies 'involving partial segments of the polity' and Rustow for monographs that focus sharply on one theme within one or more political systems.[40] Other compelling themes included the exhortation that more emphasis be placed, than has been to date, on shedding a Western (and by implication, white) bias; that there has been undue attention to *status quo* oriented notions of consensus, and integration, at the expense of the centrality of change and conflict; and that there has been over-emphasis on process to the virtual exclusion of the study of political content.[41]

The avoidance of race studies by comparativists has aggravated the disciplinary shortcomings noted here, since a focus on race, almost self-evidently, addresses itself to these important concerns. By themselves, the physical facts of race are of little or no analytical interest. Racial–physical characteristics assume meaning only when they become criteria of stratification.[42] Thus studies of race inescapably put politics—which, fundamentally, is about organized inequality—at the core of their concern. Analyses of the politics of race that are informed by developments in comparative politics can avoid the often meaningless abstractions of grand theory jargon on one hand and methodological overkill that amasses refined data about trivia on the other. Too, a focus on race has the potential to liberate social scientists from culture-bound assumptions, and a near obsessive concern with systems maintenance, and with procedures as opposed to substance. The subject matter of race which deals with questions of subordination and superordination provides the opportunity to ask not only who gets what and how, but who gets left out and how,[43] thus aiding the development of political studies which recognize, in Phil Green's words, that 'a political science which does not know who the victims are is no political science at all.'[44]

In complementary fashion, race relations scholarship could be enriched and refined by attention to the systematic work and insights of comparative research. Pierre van den Berthe's recent critique of the

[39] Mills, op. cit., p. 33.

[40] LaPalombara, 'Macrotheories and Microapplications . . .', op. cit.; Rustow, 'Modernization . . .', op. cit.

[41] La Palombara, 'Macrotheories . . .', op. cit.

[42] For a discussion, see Pierre van den Berghe, *Race and Racism* (New York, 1967), pp. 21–5.

[43] Paraphrase of Peter Bachrach and Morton Baratz, *Power and Poverty* (New York, 1970), p. 105.

[44] Philip Green, 'Decentralization, Community Control, and Revolution; Reflections on Ocean-Hill Brownsville', in Philip Green and Sanford Levinson, *Power and Community: Dissenting Essays in Political Science* (New York, 1970), p. 273.

dominant trends in the study of race aptly summarize the major short-comings of the traditional literature:

Much of the literature on race relations during the last three decades has dealt with the United States and has been written by scholars who lacked comparative experience. . . . For every hundred published racial attitude studies done in the United States, we could perhaps find five to ten in all the rest of the world. This lack of comparative approach has led, among other things, to an implicit or explicit overgeneralization of American findings.[45]

He noted the relative lack of methodological rigour of most race studies, especially those with a comparative focus; their low degree of integration with the social sciences; their stress on *immediate* policy payoffs; their aversion to historical analysis. And, he stressed that at least in the case of American work, the field is dominated by an optimistic, reformist definition of the race problem as one of the successful assimilation of minorities.[46] R. A. Schermerhorn has also noted that much of what ails race relations research stems from a 'general ignorance of related cross-cultural studies made by social scientists in other disciplines.'[47]

Given the present state of the systematic study of comparative race politics, described accurately by van den Berghe as 'so incoherent and embryonic that almost any cross-cultural study, however poorly designed and executed, is destined to be regarded as "pioneering",'[48] how best to proceed? Needed now, I will argue below, are theoretical guidelines that can organize possibilities, not assert certainties; a conceptual approach that will yield the interesting and significant questions (interrogative theory, if you like, for, as Runciman has put it, 'even the most ingenious answers will prove inadequate when it is the wrong question which is being asked').[49] A conceptual approach productive of heuristic questions and analysis has analysis, not neo-scholastic classification, as its objective.

The raison d'être of the approach would not be a search for iron laws of race relations, but the development of propositions at the level of what Michael Scriven has called normic statements—not universal hypotheses or statements open to exact quantitative validation, but rather at the level of theory, 'which leaves open the question whether people are doing what people invariably do in these uniquely compli-cated circumstances or are doing one of the comparatively few things which people . . . choose to do in such circumstances.'[50]

The development of a heuristic framework for race research will be valuable to the extent that the questions asked 'extricate the essential

[45] Van den Berghe, op. cit., p. 4.
[46] Ibid., pp. 4–8.
[47] Schermerhorn, op. cit., p. 5.
[48] Van den Berghe, op. cit., p. 5.
[49] W. G. Runciman, *Social Science and Political Theory* (Cambridge, 1965), p. 165.
[50] Stretton, op. cit., p. 327.

factors in the constitution of reality under study',[51] and to the extent that they permit internal comprehension and external confirmation; that, in other words, they both have comparative utility and respect the uniqueness of national historical circumstance.

And, perhaps most importantly, the framework will be valuable to the extent that it facilitates research that is actional, in the sense of creating possibilities and widening the arenas of choice and racial justice. In his description of the colonizer who refuses, to whom the white race scholar was compared early in this chapter, Memmi concluded,

If he cannot stand this silence and make his life a perpetual compromise, he can end up by leaving the colony and its privileges. And if his political ethics will not permit him to 'run out' he will make a fuss. He will criticize the authorities until he is 'delivered to the disposal of the *metropole*,' as the chaste administrative jargon goes. By ceasing to be a colonizer, he will put an end to his contradiction and uneasiness.[52]

But the white American or British social scientist's reluctance to 'run out' is more than a question of political ethics or sensibilities. Just as the colonized in America or Britain (to extend the image) cannot physically separate from the mother country—the colony being in the mother country—so the colonizer who refuses cannot resolve his contradictions by flight to the mother country. Only domestic decolonization can resolve his contradictions; he and the colonized are inextricably bound. His research that identifies and analyses those racial structures that shape and limit choice and racial justice may create new possibilities of just, restructured relationships. In this direction lie his hopes, and those of the colonized, for their mutual liberation.

[51] Lucien Goldmann, *The Human Sciences and Philosophy* (London, 1969), p. 115.
[52] Memmi, op. cit., pp. 43-4.

Chapter Two

A Framework for Research: Priorities and Guidelines

THE systematic study of comparative race politics is in its infancy. The following research guide proposes a number of considerations and elements that, by informing the development of comparative race studies, might overcome some of the shortcomings of the literature and stimulate productive research. In any event, they have guided the writing of this book. They express a commitment to a *political* science that seeks to widen the space of political choice.[1]

Both for normative and methodological reasons, I will propose that the priority task of race studies be the identification and analysis of those structural periods, decisions, arrangements, and relationships that define the parameters of group and individual choice. Put another way, following Schermerhorn,[2] behavioural patterns, including rates of political participation, subjective feelings of satisfaction or dissatisfaction with existing arrangements, and patterns of protest, are seen as dependent variables, with structural factors seen as independent variables. The identification and analysis of structural factors, I will argue, can be facilitated by regarding race as a special case of stratification; by adhering to the Weberian tripartite approach to stratification to open up new, revealing areas of inquiry; by acknowledging that a conflict model orientation, in this field, is an advance on the emphasis of consensus and value integration; by evaluating structured racial group relationships along the dimensions of both formal and substantive representation coupled with an assessment of the direction or flow of decision-making capabilities made possible by those relationships; and by examining the institutional expressions of these linkages, with particular attention to the degree of access to the scarce resources of economic, social, and political power that they make possible.

---

[1] See Henry Kariel, 'Expanding the Political Present', *American Political Science Review* (Vol. LXIII, September 1969), pp. 768–76.

[2] R. A. Schermerhorn, *Comparative Ethnic Relations* (New York, 1970), pp. 14–16, 238–40.

I

Unless racial characteristics are given ascriptive social meaning, the physical facts of colour are of no real concern to the social scientist. Racial groups acquire social meaning when their physical features become features that divide men hierarchially. Racial groups, it must be noted, should not be confused with ethnic groups, though the categories often overlap: ethnic groups are groups that are socially defined on the basis of their cultural characteristics (religion, language, etc.), while racial groups are socially defined by their immutable physical characteristics.[3] Thus, a racial group is defined both by its relationship to other groups and by its potential as well as actual consciousness. In Etzioni's terms, racial groups, as collectivities, are meaningful stratification units whose members share positions, and, therefore, objective interests, similar vantage points, and a shared consciousness, actual or potential.[4] It follows that the analysis of objective interests and structure should precede the analysis of subjectively perceived interests and behaviour.

Since race, if socially significant, is a basis of stratification, race studies, like other stratification studies, would profit in conceptual clarity by adhering strictly to Max Weber's multi-dimensional approach to the forms and elements of stratification. In his uncompleted, posthumously published essay, 'Class, Status, Party', Weber implicitly took issue with Marx's view that property relations and economic class reference is the substructure and all else is superstructure. Weber retained stratification as a fundamental concept, but urged that society be seen conceptually as composed of discrete, separate, yet interacting spheres, each marked by the uneven distribution of available, and scarce, resources. The three major discrete spheres are the *economic*, divided into classes 'as a resultant from either (1) the given distribution of property, or (2) the structure of the concrete economic order'; the *social*, divided into 'status groups' marked by specific 'styles of life' based on the subjective distribution of honours and prestige; and the *political*, stratified by the unequal distribution of political power based on the possession or non-possession of political offices which have a monopoly of the legitimate means of coercion.[5]

In a recent essay, W. G. Runciman argues convincingly that, in spite

[3] See Pierre van den Berghe, *Race and Racism* (New York, 1967), pp. 9–11, 21–5.

[4] Etzioni defines a collectivity as 'a macroscopic unit that has the potential capacity to act by drawing on a set of macroscopic normative bonds which tie the members of a stratification category . . . the cohesion of a collectivity is not based on face to face contact. Unlike class position in the stratification structure, the position of a collectivity is not necessarily horizontal nor is its prime base necessarily economic.' Amitai Etzioni, *The Active Society* (New York, 1968), pp. 98, 439.

[5] Max Weber, 'Class, Status, Party', in H. Gerth and C. Wright Mills, eds., *From Max Weber* (New York, 1958), pp. 180ff.

of the operational difficulties in retaining these Weberian categories, stratification theories, for the sake of accuracy and clarity, should be expressed in their terms since they can be shown to be empirically as well as conceptually distinct.[6] The multi-dimensional approach, he has written, is particularly valuable in dealing with concrete situations of inequality (race relations being a salient example).

Any classification, of course, is legitimate if it answers to the purpose at hand. But if there are three, and only three basic dimensions in which societies are stratified—class, status, and power—then it necessarily follows that all social inequalities (in the sense opposed to individual inequalities such as height and weight) are inequalities of one or another of these three, and only three, kinds. It is perhaps self-evident that inequalities of class, status, and power need not always coincide. But surprising as it seems, there is as far as I know no major writer on social inequality who has explicitly formulated and consistently retained the tripartite distinction. Indeed, I would go so far as to say that every one of the best known discussions of inequality, from Aristotle to Rousseau, to Tocqueville to Tawney, has been confused by the neglect of it.[7]

Adherence to the three-dimensional approach to stratification is conceptually liberating because it permits the asking of new questions. It is precisely because 'inequalities of class, status, and power need not always coincide' that we can isolate one and seek to establish its relationship, often complex, to the others. Each of society's stratified spheres is autonomous, yet in constant interaction with the others. Thus, no single developmental tendency emerges out of Weber's comprehensive picture of structured inequality. Within his schematic framework, a multitude of types of displacement, interaction, and conflict is conceivable. It is therefore possible to deal, for example, with rates of mobility for a racial group discretely for each stratification dimension. In doing so, Lipset and Zetterberg's complaint that political 'power as a vehicle for other kinds of social mobility has so far been a neglected area of research'[8] may be remedied.

When utilized in race studies, the Weberian multi-dimensional approach is usually used to distinguish between classes and racial groups, seen as status groups.[9] Weber's model, I would suggest, might also, less conventionally, be used to compare the hierarchical positions of racial groups in the three dimensions and to study their interactions. Groups dominant in one sphere may be subordinate in another (for example, Malaysian Malay's who are superordinate politically but subordinate

[6] W. G. Runciman, 'Class, Status, and Power', in J. A. Jackson, ed., *Social Stratification* (Cambridge, 1968), pp. 25–61.

[7] W. G. Runciman, *Relative Deprivation and Social Justice* (London, 1966), p. 37.

[8] S. M. Lipset and H. L. Zetterberg, 'A Theory of Social Mobility', in Lewis Coser and Bernard Rosenberg, eds., *Sociological Theory* (New York, 1966), p. 442.

[9] See, for example, Immanuel Wallerstein, 'Racial Tensions and National Identity in Independent Africa: The Concept of Status Group Reconsidered', in Ernest Q. Campbell, ed., *Racial Tensions and National Identity* (Nashville, 1972).

economically).[10] In this view, it is possible to assess racial groups as material groups,[11] status groups, and as political conflict groups. The central focus in this study is on the latter, but implicit is the more comprehensive picture.

Complementing Weber's schema is the assumption that 'typically speaking, nobody is satisfied with the position he occupies in regard to his fellow creatures; everybody wishes to attain one which is, in some sense, more favorable',[12] that 'the basic motive of politics is a striving motive to expand mobility opportunities, either for some special group or for large segments of the society.'[13] Central to this view is a concern with conflict and power; politics is seen as a process in which individuals and groups interact in competition for the scarce resource of political power.

Adherence to the Weberian framework might provide a corrective to the disinclination, which Joseph Roucek noted, in the 1950s, 'to view majority–minority relationships as another aspect of human power relations'; an orientation which reflects integrative theory's concern with stability and value consensus.[14] This kind of approach, M. G. Smith has argued, is particularly inappropriate in analysing societies that are divided by racial cleavages:

It is obvious that when societies are conceived as structural systems in equilibrium, their homogeneity is assumed, and heterogeneity is difficult to define, classify, or analyze. In consequence, one general model, namely that of homogeneous structural systems, is applied to quite different types of society, thereby obscuring their differences, misleading their analyses, and blocking the development of social theory. . . . From such presumptions, absurdities often follow.[15]

Thus, as eminent an analyst as Robert Dahl could write in 1956 that 'the full assimilation of Negroes into the normal system has already occurred in many northern states and now seems to be slowly taking place even in the South.'[16] The difficulty with this construction of reality, of course, was that it bore little relation to fact.

Opposed to the severely distorting position of the integrative theorists

[10] My knowledge of the Malaysian situation relies heavily on conversations with my colleague James Guyot.

[11] On the question of the material basis of racial groups, I have learned much from reading an early, yet unpublished, draft of Robert Blauner's 'Marxian Theory and Race Relations'.

[12] Kurt Wolff, ed., *The Sociology of Georg Simmel* (New York, 1950), p. 275.

[13] David Apter, 'A Comparative Method for the Study of Politics', in David Apter and Harry Eckstein, eds., *Comparative Politics* (New York, 1963), pp. 82–5.

[14] Joseph Roucek, 'Minority–Majority Relations in their Power Aspects', *Phylon* (Vol. 17, 1st quarter, 1956), p. 25. See Ralf Dahrendorf, *Class and Class Conflict in Industrial Society* (Stanford, 1959), pp. 171ff.

[15] M. G. Smith, *The Plural Society in the British West Indies* (Berkeley, 1965), pp. 77, xiii.

[16] Robert Dahl, *A Preface to Democratic Theory* (Chicago, 1956), pp. 138–9.

in the area of race is the Weberian (modified Marxist) conceptualization of society as a structure of organized inequality in the distribution of wealth, status, and political power; this differential distribution being the central dynamic for conflict and change.[17] Conflict, in this view, is an omnipresent characteristic of social relationships, the product of competition for scarce resources; 'no one is oppressed in the absolute, but always in relation to someone else, in a given context.'[18] Or as Simmel put it, 'if liberation from subordination is examined more closely . . . it almost always reveals itself as, at the same time, a gain in domination.'[19] Though conflict and consensus models of society represent two sides of the same coin and though each are abstractions of reality, in the area of race studies the conflict model is the more compelling, useful analytical approach.[20]

II

Power has already been referred to without elaboration. Some clarification is in order. Power involves the capacity to make and carry out decisions. John Champlin has defined having power as 'being in a position to get others to do what one wants them to do without having to make unacceptable sacrifices'.[21] Power, then, is relational. It is positional also, in that it depends on an individual or group's structural position in relation to others. Thus, for Gerth and Mills, the political order 'consists of those institutions with which men acquire, wield, or influence distributions of power.'[22]

The key methodological objection to the concept of power (that it can only be assessed after the event, after A gets B to do what A wants without unacceptable sacrifices to A) can be overcome by following Etzioni's suggestion that we should use power,

. . . not for a single exercise of it on a single issue over a single subject at one point in time, but rather to refer to a generalized capacity of an actor, in his relations with others, to reduce resistance in the course of action he prefers in a given field . . . about a set of matters over a period of time. This capacity can be anticipated with a certain degree of accuracy.[23]

To assess a group's power capacity, it is necessary to assess its assets which may be converted into power (like consciousness, power may be

---

[17] For an extended discussion, see Dahrendorf, *Class and Class Conflict* . . . .

[18] Albert Memmi, *Dominated Man* (Boston, 1968), p. 74.

[19] Wolff, ed., op. cit., p. 273.

[20] For a development of this argument, see Donald Henderson, 'Minority Response and the Conflict Model', *Phylon* (Spring 1964), pp. 18–26.

[21] John Champlin, 'On the Study of Power', *Politics and Society* (November 1970), p. 94.

[22] Hans Gerth and C. Wright Mills, *Character and Social Structure* (New York, 1954), pp. 192–3.

[23] Etzioni, op. cit., pp. 314–15.

C

actual or potential). These assets or resources include money and status but the most important political assets are positional. Thus, inevitably, there will be conflict between individuals and groups attempting to obtain the institutional positions which confer the legitimate right to make and carry out decisions (the number of such positions being limited, and as such being a scarce resource). But, the possession of these positions does not, by itself, fix immutably the individual's or group's power.[24] One President of the United States, for example, can be said to have been more powerful than another, even though the legal–institutional powers of the office were identical for both. Nevertheless, it is clear that to obtain the generalized capacity called political power, a person or group must have access to the resource of positions of political control. The prerequisite to that, of course, is participation in the political system.

This view of power contrasts sharply with the use of the term by consensus-oriented systems theorists. Consider, as a leading example, Talcott Parsons's essay, 'On the Concept of Political Power'. He conceives of power 'as a circulating medium, analogous to money'; thus Parsons views power not as the generalized capacity of an individual or group but as the generalized capacity of the *system* to secure outputs useful to its continuity and stability. As he states it, power

is the generalized capacity to secure performance of binding obligations by units in a system of collective organization when the obligations are legitimized with reference to their bearing on collective goals and where in the case of recalcitrance there is a presumption of enforcement by negative situational sanctions.[25]

Parsons does not focus on who has power or on the consequences of the distribution of power. Not only is the implicit moral valuation repugnant—that what is legitimate is collectively good—but empirically, this formulation begs the most important questions about power: who can attain the capacity to make and carry out decisions, on behalf of whom and to what ends. As Gouldner has noted, Parsons looks at power from the standpoint of those on top; viewed from the perspective of the subordinate, power cannot be seen as a morally neutral generalized systemic currency. It is imperative to ask '*whose* legitimate claims are being met and whose are being ignored?' As the generalized capacity of individuals and groups, power often exists quietly:

It exists as a factor in the lives of subordinates, shaping their behavior and beliefs, at every moment of their relations with those above them. Attitudes towards their superiors are continually influenced by the *awareness*—sometimes focal and sometimes only subsidiary—that superiors can give or withhold at

---

[24] An informative selection of approaches to the study of power can be found in Reinhard Bendix and Seymour Martin Lipset, eds., *Class, Status, and Power* (New York, 1966), Section 3.

[25] Talcott Parsons, 'On the Concept of Political Power', in Bendix and Lipset, op. cit., pp. 243–4.

will things that men greatly want, quite apart from their own agreement or dissent, and that crucial gratifications depend upon allocations and decisions by their superiors.[26]

Moreover, power often takes the form of keeping certain issues *off* the political agenda, what Bachrach and Baratz call nondecision-making, which they defined as,

. . . a decision that results in suppression or thwarting of a latent or manifest challenge to the values or interests of the decision-maker . . . nondecision-making is a means by which demands for change in the existing community can be suffocated before they are even voiced; or kept covert; or killed before they gain access to the relevant decision-making arena; or, failing all these things, maimed or destroyed in the decision-implementing stage of the policy process.[27]

Nondecision-making, we should note, is as much of a form of action as decision-making; it is not a non-event.[28] In short, as C. Wright Mills put it, 'the problem of who is involved in making [decisions] (or not making them) is the basic problem of power.'[29]

The relative power of racial groups to make and carry out decisions and nondecisions—institutionally expressed and organized—is the most significant independent variable for the student of race politics. Accordingly, the remainder of the chapter suggests questions and issues to be explored in the analysis of structural–institutional relationships of racial groups and the political system.

III

In 1948, Charles Beard compellingly argued that 'many of our neglects, overstresses, and simplifications are due to the divorce of political science from history.' This unnatural separation that characterizes much of the work of the social sciences has had negative consequences, he argued, for the uses of political knowledge, producing, in John Burgess's words, a 'theoretical, superficial, and speculative' social science, or, worse, studies that are 'merely "practical," that is, subservient to vested interests and politicians temporarily in power.'[30] To remedy the separation of history from the social sciences, recognizing that 'every social fact is a historical fact and vice versa',[31] Nisbet has urged that time be envisaged in the manner now largely reserved for space. Similarly, Levi-Strauss sees time not merely in mechanical or cumulative or statistical terms, but in

[26] See Alvin Gouldner, *The Coming Crisis of Western Sociology* (New York, 1970), p. 103.

[27] Peter Bachrach and Morton Baratz, *Power and Poverty* (New York, 1970), p. 44.

[28] Ibid., p. 46.

[29] Mills, *The Sociological Imagination*, p. 40.

[30] Charles Beard, 'Neglected Aspects of Political Science', *American Political Science Review* (Vol. XLII, April 1948), pp. 220, 222.

[31] Lucien Goldmann, *The Human Sciences and Philosophy* (London, 1969), p. 23.

social terms as well ('social time') deriving its properties from concrete social phenomena.[32]

In social terms, the student of race politics can distinguish between critical and routine historical periods, the former being the periods when critical structural political decisions were made institutionalizing power differentials between racial groups. Much as Barrington Moore has examined the periods of the social origins of democracy and dictatorship (combining comparison with detailed investigations of individual national cases), so it is important to explore the genesis of structured racial linkages that limit behavioural choices. Hypothesizing that the linkages fashioned between racial groups and the polity in the early, and fluid, periods of interracial contact have a determinative impact on the subsequent patterns of racial group behaviour, the examination of the formation of structured relationships is a priority research task.

Since 'organization is the mobilization of bias',[33] structure not only limits but also shapes the direction of choice. Thus, critical decisions, as opposed to routine decisions, are those that define the structural context that limits and shapes choice. With Apter 'the structure may be defined as the relationships in a social situation which limit the choice process to a particular range of alternatives', while 'the behavioral may be defined as the selection process in choice, i.e., deciding between alternatives.'[34] Utilizing this distinction, critical decisions are structural, routine decisions behavioural.[35]

Logically, then, as was noted above, structural factors should be the starting point of analysis. To begin with behaviour, stressing perceptions, socialization, voting behaviour, protest activity, and the like, would assume a knowledge of structure and the boundaries of choice possibilities. Without an analysis of context, an analysis of choice behaviour has little meaning. Hence, complementing Weber's stratification model and the focus on conflict and power, is a research focus on critical structure periods and decisions. We must ask who has the power to make the critical decisions affecting structure and 'who gets what and how, and who gets left out and how'[36] as a consequence of those structural arrangements.[37]

The structured political linkages that shape and limit the choices of racial groups may be assessed on the basis of the related criteria of (i) the

---

[32] Robert A. Nisbet, *Tradition and Revolt* (New York, 1970), p. 99; Claude Levi-Strauss, *Structural Anthropology* (New York, 1967), pp. 281–3.

[33] E. E. Schattschneider, *The Semi-Sovereign People* (New York, 1960), p. 71.

[34] Apter and Eckstein, op. cit., p. 732.

[35] For an elaboration of this distinction, see Andrew McFarland, *Power and Leadership in Pluralist Systems* (Stanford, 1969), especially Chapter 5.

[36] Bachrach and Baratz, op. cit., p. 105.

[37] See Lewis Lipsitz, 'On Political Belief: The Grievances of the Poor', in Philip Green and Sanford Levinson, eds., *Power and Community: Dissenting Essays in Political Science* (New York, 1970), pp. 141–72.

relative distribution of power they embody, and (ii) the degree and types of racial group representation they facilitate.

Manfred Halpern's work on political modernization usefully addresses itself to the first of these criteria. He enumerates six basic types of two-way relationships: emanation, subjection, direct bargaining, boundary management, buffering, and isolation, as well as two other special types of linkage which he calls incoherence, and transformation, and which need not detain us here.[38] Classifying his six basic types of relationship, according to their relative distribution of power, yields three classes of linkages: uni-directional power, linking actors and objects; bi-directional power, linking participant-equals; and non-directional or mediated power, either linking actors through buffers or the groups exist in isolation, paradoxically, a form of linkage.

In the uni-directional power class of relationships, the capacity to make and carry out decisions is the exclusive, or near exclusive, property of one of the linked groups. Thus, for Halpern, emanation 'is an encounter in which (1) one treats the other solely as an extension of one's personality, one's will and power—as an embodiment of one's self—and (2) the other accepts his denial of a separate identity as legitimate because of the mysterious source or nature of the overwhelming power of the other.'[39] In subjection, the second polarity in this class of relationships, the source of the power by which the actions of the other are controlled is not, as in emanation, mysterious or charismatic. Rather, the other complies simply because of the skewed distribution of power. In both emanation and subjection, the relationship links superior and subordinate, not participant-equals. Almost inevitably, decisions 'reached among actors who differ significantly in their power . . . reflect more of the needs of the mighty than those of the weak.'[40]

In the class of bi-directional power relationships, the capacity to make and carry out decisions is shared by the linked participants. In the linkage form Halpern calls boundary management, each of the participant groups claims zones of autonomous jurisdiction which can, for example, take the form of pressure group organization or direct control of geographical political units. Direct bargaining, a related form of relationship, refers to the linkage in which 'individuals and groups make demands on each other and negotiate directly with each other.'[41]

In the non-directional or mediated power class of relationships, the groups do not interact directly. Thus buffering, the fifth of Halpern's polarities, denotes an indirect encounter through a mediator, and isolation,

[38] Manfred Halpern, 'Conflict, Violence and the Dialectics of Modernization', unpublished paper, 1968; Manfred Halpern, 'A Redefinition of the Revolutionary Situation', *Journal of International Affairs* (Vol. 22, Winter 1968), pp. 65–75.

[39] Ibid., p. 61.

[40] Amitai Etzioni, 'Social Guidance: A Key to Macro-Sociology', *Acta Sociologica* (Vol. 4, fasc. 4, 1968), p. 204.

[41] Halpern, 'A Redefinition . . .', op. cit., pp. 63–4.

the absence of a functioning relationship. It should be stressed, of course, that relationships between racial (and other) groups in the 'real world' are most often quite complex and do not often yield to the neat classificatory schemes of social scientists. More often than not racial group linkages will approximate amalgams of Halpern's ideal-types.

The degree and types of racial group representation they facilitate is the second criterion for evaluating the structured relationships that shape and limit the choices of racial groups. An assessment of racial–structural linkages (utilizing Hanna Pitkin's distinctions)[42] should distinguish between the following modes of representation: formal, socially descriptive, symbolic, substantive, and actual.

Formal representation refers to the procedural, institutional mechanisms of representation, including the selection process of a racial (and other) group's leadership. Under this heading, we may inquire about the nature of the institutional mechanisms set up to link racial groups to the political system, the degree to which these institutions are enclosed or separated from the society's broader network of institutions, and the question of who selects and recruits a recognized, legitimated racial group leadership, and how it is chosen.

Socially descriptive representation, a measure of personnel,

. . . refers to the extent to which the representatives reflect accurately the characteristics of those whom they formally represent. . . . The representatives' social class, ethnic or racial background, age, and place of residence have all been considered by analysts and political actors as politically relevant social characteristics which affect descriptive representation.[43]

We may inquire if a racial group has access to decision-making positions in the polity proportional to its numbers, and we may ask if the group's representatives are descriptively representative of the group as a whole.

Substantive representation refers to the orientation, in action, of the representative. It is, in short, a behavioural measure of responsiveness, of the extent to which decision-making elites, whether descriptively representative or not, are oriented towards meeting the racial group's needs and demands. Rustow concluded his review of the literature on elites by stressing the distinction between descriptive representativeness and responsiveness: 'The study of the rulers' social background is only a supplement, not a substitute for the study of their performance in office —and (we may add) of the effect of that performance on the recruitment of future rulers.'[44] Utilizing this distinction, conflicts about power may

---

[42] Hanna Pitkin, *The Concept of Representation* (Berkeley, 1967); Paul Peterson, 'Forms of Representation: Participation of the Poor in the Community Action Program', *American Political Science Review* (Vol. LXIV, June 1970), pp. 491–4.

[43] Peterson, 'Forms of Representation . . .', op. cit., p. 492.

[44] Dankwart Rustow, 'The Study of Elites', *World Politics* (Vol. 18, July 1966), pp. 716–7.

be conflicts about the possession of positions that confer the ability to make and carry out decisions and/or about the use others make of their power capacity.[45]

Actual representation refers to influence or efficacy, a measure of the ability of representatives to produce desired effects or results. Representation that is inefficacious is at best symbolic. Given the extent of formal and descriptive representativeness and the degree of the representatives' responsiveness, we may inquire if the racial group's representatives are efficacious in carrying out their programmes and in achieving their aims. A major aim of comparative race research should be the assessment of concrete, structured, racial relationships along these dimensions of representation and an attempt to analyse the links between these dimensions.

A typology of group–polity, group–leadership relationships can be constructed using the three dimensions, descriptive representativeness, responsiveness (substantive representation), and efficacy (actual representation), yielding eight possible ideal-types (see Table 2.1):

TABLE 2.1 : A TYPOLOGY OF GROUP–POLITY RELATIONSHIPS AND INTERNAL GROUP STRUCTURE

| | *Representative* | | *Not Representative* | |
	Responsive	*Not Responsive*	*Responsive*	*Not Responsive*
Efficacious	1 Clear democracy	2 Detached oligarchy	5 Paternalism	6 Efficacious autocracy
Not efficacious	3 Ineffectual democracy	4 Apparent democracy	7 Ineffectual paternalism	8 Clear tyranny

1. The polity or the group's leadership is descriptively representative, responsive, and efficacious. We may call this case *clear democracy*.
2. The polity or the group's leadership is descriptively representative and efficacious, but is unresponsive to group needs. Here the forms of democracy are intact and are seen to be operating, but the group's participating leadership elite has been co-opted or bought off so that while it participates in the larger political system, it no longer speaks for those it claims to represent. We may call this case *detached oligarchy*.
3. The polity or the group's leadership is descriptively representative, responsive, but ineffectual. We may call this case *ineffectual democracy*.
4. In this fairly unlikely case, the polity or the group's leadership though descriptively representative is both unresponsive and ineffectual. The polity or group leadership's unresponsiveness is masked by its lack of effectiveness. We may, therefore, call this case *apparent democracy*.

[45] See Hugh Stretton, *The Political Sciences* (London, 1969), p. 329.

5. The polity or the group's leadership is responsive though not descriptively representative, but is efficacious in promoting its goals. We may call this case *paternalism*.

6. The polity or the group's leadership is neither descriptively representative nor responsive, but promotes its goals effectively. We may call this case *efficacious autocracy*.

7. The polity or the group's leadership, though ineffectual and not descriptively representative does try to be responsive. We may call this case *ineffectual paternalism*.

8. The polity or the group's leadership is not descriptively responsive, nor is it responsive or effectual. We may call this case *clear tyranny*.

Utilizing this typology, we can ask, cross-nationally, if racial group relationships are characterized by high or low descriptive representation, responsiveness, and efficacy; in what combination; and with what consequences.

IV

To sum up: convinced, both for normative and methodological reasons that the study of structure should precede the study of behaviour in the developing field of comparative race relations, this chapter has suggested a number of emphases and research directions for the analysis and evaluation of racial–group relationships and their institutional expression. Within the overarching framework of Weber's stratification model, the study of race politics that analyses critical structural periods, decisions, and relationships, focusing on power differentials and on types and degrees of representation can contribute not only in a systematic, comparative way to a developing research field, but most importantly can widen the space of political choice.

The guidelines proposed should be seen as research criteria and as tools to be used in the formulation of research questions that permit comparative analysis while respecting the uniqueness of national historical circumstance. For comparative race politics to move out of the infant stage, I would propose that similar heuristic questions, fashioned from the tools suggested in this chapter, be asked cross-nationally and cross-culturally. It is premature to assert certainties; let us explore the possibilities.

Chapter Three

The Immigrant–Colonial Amalgam

IN the early stage of systematic race politics scholarship, a conscious choice has to be made between possible research strategies: the inclusion of as many racial contact situations as possible, intensive single country case studies, or a middle course of limited comparisons. As Rustow has noted in his work on democracy, though comprehensiveness in a field in a preliminary stage of theorizing is desirable, very broad empirical coverage, given the enormity of possible variables, has a tendency to produce shallow, simplifying, superficial work.[1] Single country case studies, on the other hand, while avoiding these pitfalls, entail sacrificing the advantages of comparative work, comprising the very essence of the social sciences. To avoid the 'twin dangers of inconclusive scholasticism and of fact-grubbing',[2] I have decided to focus on racial contact situations in two countries—the United States and the United Kingdom—that share the features of what I shall call the immigrant–colonial amalgam. The time periods selected were chosen for their comparability in 'social time' terms; they are the periods of early, and fluid, interracial contact as a result of large scale migration; critical structural periods when critical structural decisions were made that fundamentally affected the future character of race relations.

A comparative study of British and American race relations must begin with an acknowledgment of formidable difficulties. Two leading British scholars in this field have recently cautioned would-be comparative students, 'It cannot be easy for an American observer to realize how different race relations in Britain are from those in the United States; the resemblances hit him in the eye; the differences he can easily ignore—but they are extremely important.'[3] They are correct in that there are significant features unique to each country. The United States, they note, has traditionally been a country of immigrant absorption, Britain

[1] Dankwart A. Rustow, 'Transitions to Democracy: Toward a Dynamic Model', *Comparative Politics* (Vol. 2, April 1970), pp. 349–50.
[2] Ibid., p. 350.
[3] Nicholas Deakin and Philip Mason, 'Racial Adjustments in Britain', *African Forum* (Vol. 2, Winter 1967), p. 98.

of emigration. The United States is an ethnically heterogeneous society, Britain relatively ethnically homogeneous. Americans have long practised the politics of ethnicity, the British the politics of class. Slavery and a legalized caste system based on segregation enforced by law existed on American soil. The British colonial experience, though similar in many ways, from the perspective of British society, was more remote. This list of dissimilarities could easily be extended.

In a preliminary way, I should stress that, with the leader writer of the *Guardian*, I am asserting that the correct parallel 'is with the northern cities of the United States at the turn of the century, not with the urban ghettoes of today.'[4] The British and American experiences of the 1960s were not comparable. The mass movement of Commonwealth blacks to Britain began only just over two decades ago; American blacks have moved to the North in substantial numbers for the past seventy-five years. And, secondly, we should note that the British–American comparison has already been made by some in facile, misleading fashion, without explanation or careful examination. In this manner, for example, Enoch Powell warned his countrymen in 1968: 'Time is running out against us and them. With the lapse of a generation or so we shall at last have succeeded— to the benefit of nobody—in reproducing "in England's green and pleasant land" the haunting tragedy of the United States.'[5]

But more significantly, by stressing the similarities here between important aspects of the American and British racial situations in the early periods of migration, I do not reject the differences that exist between them; indeed, one of the major tasks of the chapters to follow will be, by asking similar analytical questions of each situation, the explication of differences. Nevertheless, I would argue, with van den Berghe, that variations 'specific to a given place and time, far from preventing cross-cultural uniformities and making generalizations impossible, leave a large residual of similarities unaccounted for except in terms of the broad economic and political infrastructure.'[6] In a very real sense, it is the social scientist's perspective that creates comparability; by bringing objects together for comparison intelligently, he makes the comparison intelligible. 'All science is the search for unity in hidden likenesses. . . . The scientist looks for order in the appearances of nature by exploring such likenesses. For order does not display itself of itself: if it can be said to be there at all it is not there for the mere looking. . . . Order must be discovered and, in a deep sense, it must be created.'[7]

There are, in short, levels of comparability, and they depend on the perspective of the observer. As Simmel put it, 'We obtain different pictures of

---

[4] *Guardian* (13 November 1967).

[5] *Sunday Times* (17 November 1968), p. 8; the speech was delivered to the Rotary Club of London at Eastbourne the day before.

[6] Pierre van den Berghe, *Race and Racism* (New York, 1967), p. 26.

[7] J. Bronowski, *Science and Human Values* (New York, 1965), pp. 13ff.

an object when we see it at a distance to two, or of five, or of ten yards. At each distance, however, the picture is "correct" in its particular way. . . . All we can say is that a view gained at any distance has its own justification.'[8] The comparisons in this study are made at the level of inquiry and dimensions suggested by the research criteria proposed in Chapter 2, which focused on structured relationships, and their representational implications.

Yet, with Schermerhorn, we note that 'intergroup encounters and the relationships that develop from them are not self-subsistent phenomena but take their shape and form to a marked degree from the social organization and directional processes of the societies in which the encounters take place.'[9] No society of course is precisely like any other society. The shared features of the immigrant-colonial amalgam, however, discussed below, provided a strikingly similar context for interracial contacts, making possible comparative research that holds constant both the types of society under examination and the temporal sequences of interaction. Before proceeding to discuss the analytical parallels of the research locales, however, a bit of 'fact grubbing' on the migrations is in order.

I

In the history of American blacks, the period 1900-30 stands out as a key structural period. In 1900, American racial contacts were limited largely to the South.

By Federal Government count, 7,922,969 blacks lived in the South; only 902,025 blacks resided in all the other regions of the country combined. Though the percentage of American blacks who lived in the South had declined slightly from 90·6 in 1870 to 89·7 in 1900, most Americans, at the turn of the century, were convinced that the black population would remain a fixed element in Southern society.[10]

By the outbreak of the First World War, this assumption had to be reassessed. Approximately 150,000 blacks left the South for the metropolitan areas of the North in the first fifteen years of the century. The movement, which came to be known as the Great Migration,[11] rapidly

[8] Kurt Wolff, ed., *The Sociology of Georg Simmel* (New York, 1950), p. 7.

[9] R. A. Schermerhorn, *Comparative Ethnic Relations* (New York, 1970), p. 164.

[10] United States Chamber of Commerce, Bureau of the Census, *Negroes in the United States, 1920-1932* (Washington, 1935), pp. 9, 7. I use the term 'fixed' in social as well as demographic terms. The *New York Times* for instance wrote in 1900: 'Northern men . . . no longer denounce the suppression of the Negro vote in the South as it used to be denounced in the Reconstruction days. The necessity of it under the supreme law of self-preservation is candidly recognized.' Cited in Thomas Gossett, *Race: The History of an Idea in America* (New York, 1965), p. 285.

[11] The term 'Great Migration' has most often been used to denote the movement of blacks to the North during the First World War. It is both more correct and useful to accept John Roche's and Gilbert Osofsky's revisionist use of the term; namely, to use it to describe the black migration to the North which began at the turn of the century and which is continuing today. Roughly speaking, there have been two periods of 'Great Migration'—1900-30 and 1940 to the present.

accelerated during the war; by conservative estimate, 500,000 blacks migrated to the North in wartime.[12] In the 1920s, well over 550,000 left the South. The black population of the Middle Atlantic states alone in this decade increased (as a result of natural increase and migration) by 868,000. By 1930, the percentage of America's blacks in the South had declined dramatically to $78 \cdot 7$[13] (see Tables 3.1 and 3.2).

It is difficult to overstate the impact of this migration on the North and on the course of black history in America. Ray Stannard Baker aptly described the migration as 'probably next to emancipation the most noteworthy event which has happened to the Negro in America.'[14] In similar terms, August Meier has argued that the population movement was 'after Emancipation . . . the great watershed in American Negro history.'[15] In the second decade of the century alone, New York's black population increased by 66 per cent, Chicago's by 148, Cleveland's by 307, and Detroit's by 611. 'Recalling that the Negro population of the whole North Central region in 1900 was roughly half a million,' writes John Roche, 'we find that between 1900 and 1930 Illinois (largely Chicago) had a net immigration of 213,000 Negroes; Michigan (mainly Detroit)

TABLE 3.1: NUMBER AND PERCENTAGE DISTRIBUTION OF BLACK POPULATION BY SECTIONS, 1880–1930

Year	South	(%)	North	(%)	West	(%)	Total U.S.	(%)
1880	5,953,903	(90·5)	615,038	(9·3)	11,852	(0·2)	6,580,793	(100)
1890	6,760,577	(90·3)	701,018	(9·4)	27,081	(0·4)	7,488,676	(100)
1900	7,922,969	(89·7)	880,771	(10·0)	30,254	(0·3)	8,833,994	(100)
1910	8,749,427	(89·0)	1,027,674	(10·5)	50,662	(0·5)	9,827,763	(100)
1920	8,912,231	(85·2)	1,472,509	(14·1)	78,591	(0·8)	10,463,131	(100)
1930	9,361,577	(78·7)	2,409,219	(20·3)	120,347	(1·0)	11,891,143	(100)

SOURCE: U.S. Department of Commerce, Bureau of the Census, *Negroes in the United States*, p. 5.

added 127,000. The Northeastern increase was equally notable: with a 1900 base figure of 385,000 *for the whole region*, New York in these three decades gained 272,000 and Pennsylvania 217,000.'[16]

The numerical similarities, in relative, not absolute, terms between the 'Great Migration' in the United States and the movement of Third World immigrants to Great Britain since 1948 are striking. In 1910, 2 per cent

[12] See John Hope Franklin, *From Slavery to Freedom* (New York, 1964), p. 465; U.S. Department of Labor, *The Negro at Work During the World War and During Reconstruction* (Washington, 1921), p. 10; Ray Stannard Baker, 'The Negro Goes North', *The World's Work* (Vol. 34, July 1917), p. 315; and John P. Roche, *The Quest for the Dream* (New York, 1963), p. 80.
[13] U.S. Chamber of Commerce, op. cit., p. 7.
[14] R. S. Baker, 'The Negro Goes North', op. cit., p. 317.
[15] August Meier, *Negro Thought in America, 1880–1915* (Ann Arbor, 1966), p. 170.
[16] Roche, op. cit., p. 81.

TABLE 3.2: NUMBER AND PERCENTAGE DISTRIBUTION OF TOTAL
POPULATION BY SECTIONS, 1880–1930

Year	South	(%)	North	(%)	West	(%)	Total U.S.	(%)
1880	16,516,568	(32·9)	31,871,518	(63·5)	1,767,697	(3·5)	40,155,783	(100)
1890	20,028,059	(31·8)	39,817,386	(63·3)	3,102,269	(4·9)	62,947,714	(100)
1900	24,523,527	(32·3)	47,379,699	(62·3)	4,091,349	(5·4)	75,994,575	(100)
1910	29,389,330	(32·0)	55,757,115	(60·6)	6,825,821	(7·4)	91,972,266	(100)
1920	33,125,803	(31·3)	63,691,845	(60·2)	8,902,972	(8·4)	105,710,620	(100)
1930	37,857,633	(30·8)	73,021,191	(59·5)	11,896,222	(9·7)	122,775,046	(100)

SOURCE: U.S. Department of Commerce, Bureau of the Census, *Negroes in the United States*, pp. 5, 9.

of Chicago's and 2·6 per cent of New York's population was black; the respective figures for 1920 were 4·1 and 4·8. In Britain, the 1966 Sample Census revealed that the percentage of immigrants from the Caribbean, India, and Pakistan was 3·2 in Greater London and 3·3 in the West Midlands.[17]

The Third World immigrants to Britain, of course, are not a homogeneous group; they are West Indians, Pakistanis, Indians, African blacks, and African Asians whose social, cultural, and religious differences from each other are often greater than the intrinsic differences that distinguish them from white Englishmen. Nevertheless, they should be considered analytically as a single group because, as a collectivity, they form a meaningful stratification unit whose members share objective interests, similar vantage points, and a shared consciousness, actual or potential.[18] Most concretely, the immigrants share the dual bond of a colonial past and a skin colour darker than white, as well as similar residential and occupational positions in England where they have acted as a replacement population in declining urban cores of industrial regions unable to attract a sufficient number of domestic workers.[19] Moreover, most British politicians, in their rhetoric, legislation, and deeds, have dealt with the country's Third World population as a single group.

There were few Third World people in Britain before the Second World War. During the war, 8,000 West Indians came to work in British munitions factories and to serve in the armed forces, mainly in the R.A.F. By 1951, two-thirds of this group had returned to the Caribbean. In 1948, a new movement of West Indian workers to Britain commenced;

[17] Seth Scheiner, *Negro Mecca* (New York, 1965), p. 222; Allan Spear, *Black Chicago* (Chicago, 1967), p. 12; Institute of Race Relations, *Facts Paper on Colour and Immigration in the United Kingdom* (London, 1968), p. 2; see also, Joe Doherty, 'The Distribution and Concentration of Immigrants in London', *Race Today* (Vol. 1, December 1969), pp. 227ff.
[18] For a discussion, see footnote 4 of Chapter 2.
[19] For an extended discussion, see Ceri Peach, *West Indian Migration to Britain* (London, 1968), p. 82.

by September 600 skilled and semi-skilled Jamaican workers had arrived. All found work without difficulty. The number of West Indian immigrants in the early 1950s was very small—roughly 1,000 in 1951, 2,200 in 1952, 2,300 in 1953, and 9,200 in 1954.[20] However, in 1955, there was a sharp increase to 27,550, and from 1 January 1956 to 30 June 1962, the Home Office estimated the net immigration of West Indians to be 231,950.[21] In this period, up to July 1962, like the situation of the migrant blacks in the United States, the rate of migration was limited only by the will to come, the financial means to make the journey, and economic conditions in the United Kingdom.

Though most of the Third World immigrants in these years came from the Caribbean, there was a parallel migration from the Indian sub-continent. Between 1955 and mid-1962 there was a net movement into Britain of 75,850 Indians and 67,430 Pakistanis.[22]

From 1 July 1962, Commonwealth immigration has been controlled by statutory legislation through the device of labour vouchers. During the first six months of 1962, almost 32,000 West Indians, 19,000 Indians, and 25,000 Pakistanis came to Britain; the respective figures for the second half of the year were 3,241, 2,211, and 896. This drastic cut in the number of migrants was not indicative, however, of the size of the migration to come. Between 1 July 1962 and 30 June 1968, the net inward movement of West Indians numbered 75,849 (of whom 10,797 were voucher holders, most of the rest being dependants). The Indian in-migration numbered 95,506 (22,172 voucher holders), and the Pakistani 74,935 (21,582 voucher holders), (see Tables 3.3, 4, 5, and 6).

TABLE 3.3: ESTIMATED NET INWARD MOVEMENT FROM CERTAIN COMMONWEALTH COUNTRIES, 1955 to 30 JUNE 1962

	1955	1956	1957	1958	1959	1960	1961	1962	Total
West Indies	27,550	29,800	23,000	15,000	16,400	49,650	66,300	31,800	259,500
India	5,800	5,600	6,600	6,200	2,950	5,900	23,750	15,050	75,850
Pakistan	1,850	2,050	5,200	4,700	850	2,500	25,100	25,680	67,330
Cyprus	3,450	2,750	1,450	2,700	400	3,200	6,850	5,150	23,950
West Africa	1,500	2,000	2,200	950	750	-500	5,450	6,630	18,980
East Africa	700	700	650	400	150	250	2,650	1,930	7,480
Hong Kong	300	550	900	200	450	500	2,150	2,160	7,210
Others*	1,550	3,400	2,400	-300	-350	-3,800	4,150	5,050	12,100
Total	42,700	46,850	42,400	29,850	21,600	57,700	36,400	94,900	472,400

* Excluding Australia, New Zealand, Canada, Southern Rhodesia, and South Africa.
SOURCE: Home Office Figures cited in Labour Party Research Department *Immigration and Race Relations*, Information Paper No. 22 (November, 1968).

[20] Sheila Patterson, *Dark Strangers* (London, 1965), p. 359. These figures were originally provided in an answer given in the House of Lords on 15 February 1956.
[21] Home Office figures: cited in Labour Party Research Department, *Immigration and Race Relations*, Information Paper No. 22 (November 1968), p. 6.
[22] Ibid. The figures below also appear in the same source.

TABLE 3.4: COMMONWEALTH IMMIGRANTS ACT 1962: HOLDERS OF MINISTRY OF LABOUR VOUCHERS ADMITTED 1 JULY 1962 TO 30 JUNE 1968

	1962	1963	1964	1965	1966	1967	1968	Total
West Indies	1,600	2,077	2,635	2,987	628	630	240	10,797
India	646	8,366	3,828	3,794	2,433	2,175	930	22,171
Pakistan	391	13,526	3,296	2,520	721	754	374	21,582
Cyprus	162	610	539	274	80	96	46	1,807
Malta	154	679	793	716	651	537	331	3,861
West Africa	635	1,391	824	280	62	34	15	3,241
East Africa	33	108	92	44	16	18	7	318
Hong Kong	207	834	664	441	106	153	81	2,466
Australia	358	693	328	356	165	159	87	2,146
Canada	425	558	381	310	76	58	31	1,839
New Zealand	121	196	108	89	79	45	43	681
All other territories	389	1,087	1,217	1,069	444	339	293	4,838
Total	5,121	30,125	14,705	12,880	5,461	4,978	2,478	75,748

SOURCE: Commonwealth Immigrants Act, *Statistics*. (1 July 1962–31 December 1963, 1964, 1965, 1966, 1967, 1968, monthly), Cmnds. 2397, 2658, 2979, 3258, 3594.

TABLE 3.5: COMMONWEALTH IMMIGRANTS ACT 1962: DEPENDANTS ADMITTED 1 JULY 1962 TO 30 JUNE 1968

	1962	1963	1964	1965	1966	1967	1968	Total
West Indies	3,730	7,896	11,461	11,147	9,878	11,211	3,346	58,669
India	1,565	6,616	8,770	12,798	13,357	15,822	9,411	68,339
Pakistan	505	3,304	7,046	6,763	9,319	17,506	7,393	51,836
Cyprus	438	1,063	1,750	1,128	587	505	127	5,598
Malta	187	424	490	501	302	282	63	2,249
West Africa	886	2,292	2,492	2,452	1,882	1,103	305	11,412
East Africa	259	856	871	674	666	501	354	4,181
Hong Kong	97	288	675	933	951	1,236	346	4,526
Australia	285	731	677	856	1,098	989	346	4,982
Canada	276	771	780	886	1,475	1,387	377	5,952
New Zealand	53	273	265	244	323	354	103	1,615
All other territories	551	1,720	2,183	2,832	2,188	1,917	2,238	13,629
Total	8,832	26,234	37,460	41,214	42,026	52,813	24,409	232,988

SOURCE: Commonwealth Immigrants Act, *Statistics* (1 July 1962–31 December 1963, 1964, 1965, 1966, 1967, 1968, monthly), Cmnds. 2397, 2658, 3258, 3594.

In 1968, the Third World population of England and Wales was estimated to number 1,113,000, or roughly 2 per cent of the total population.[23] Thus, by 1930 from the vantage point of the American

[23] This population estimate appears in E. J. B. Rose and Associates, *Colour and Citizenship* (London, 1969), p. 100.

TABLE 3.6: COMMONWEALTH IMMIGRANTS ACT, ARRIVALS BY CATEGORY, 1 JULY 1962 TO 30 JUNE 1968

	Voucher-holders	Dependants	Others/Settlement	Total
West Indies	10,797	58,669	6,383	75,849
India	22,172	68,339	4,995	95,506
Pakistan	21,582	51,836	1,517	74,935
Cyprus	1,807	5,598	1,061	8,466
Malta	3,861	2,249	484	6,594
West Africa	3,241	11,412	738	15,391
East Africa	318	4,181	915	5,414
All others	11,970	30,704	7,544	50,218
Total	75,748	232,988	23,637	332,373

SOURCE: Commonwealth Immigrants Act 1962, *Statistics* (1 July 1962–31 December 1963, 1964, 1965, 1966, 1967, 1968, monthly), Cmnds. 2397, 2658, 3258, 3594.

North and by the late 1960s from the vantage point of the United Kingdom, the issues of race could no longer be considered at one remove; they were no longer 'out there' in the South or the Commonwealth, but in the preceding decades had become domestic political questions of consequence.

II

'It is obvious', Robert Park has written, 'that race relations and all that they imply are generally, and on the whole, the products of migration and conquest.' What we call race relations today, he argued, is the product of *a single mass migration*, consisting, mainly in the nineteenth and early twentieth centuries, of 'the emigration of European peoples and the emigration of extra-European peoples,' which 'have taken place in direct and indirect response to conditions in Europe.'[24]

Stanley Lieberson has distinguished in his 'Societal Theory of Race and Ethnic Relations' between two contrasting types of ethnic and racial contacts that have taken place as part of what Park described as a single mass migration: migrant superordination (the pure colonial case) where a minority migrant population imposes its will on an indigenous majority, and indigenous superordination (the voluntary migrant case) where a minority in-migrates to a situation where it is subordinate, if only temporarily. Lieberson argues that each of these contact situations produces a dynamic of its own. Colonial contact situations typically lead to a numerical decline of the indigenous population, new political boundaries, middleman minorities, and, ultimately, nationalist revolt. The immigrant case, on the other hand, is marked by the increasing assimilation of the

[24] Robert Park, *Race and Culture* (New York, 1950), pp. 100–7.

voluntary immigrants into the ongoing social and political order and by striking cultural assimilation as well.[25]

This typology ignores a third case, of which the American and British racial situations in the periods under examination here are striking examples: the case of the immigrant–colonial amalgam, the case of apparent voluntary migration (in the sense of the absence of overt coercion) that is at least partly the product of a colonial or quasi-colonial contact situation. Put another way, to Lieberson's two cases we should add the case of the secondary migration of Third World peoples to the 'mother country' under the control of the European colonizer; secondary in the sense that this type of racial contact becomes intelligible only when placed in the context of the single European mass migration of which Park wrote.

On the face of it, the movement of American blacks from South to North, 1900–30, and of Third World (non-European, non-Western, non-white) peoples from the Commonwealth to Britain since 1948 are instances of Lieberson's voluntary migrant case. Indeed, much race relations scholarship in the United States and the United Kingdom has adopted this orientation, focusing on acculturation and gradual assimilation. Thus, in the United States, for example, Oscar Handlin has written that blacks, as 'the newest immigrants to a great cosmopolitan city, will come to play as useful a role in it as any of their predecessors,' and Philip Hauser has asserted that the 'acculturation' problems of blacks will extend over 'human generations rather than years.'[26] And in the United Kingdom, Sheila Patterson, for one, has argued that the 'new West Indian migrants to Britain are, in fact, passing through the same kinds of dynamic process in their relationships with the local population as do all other working-class economic migrants.'[27] Not only does this perspective ignore a considerable amount of evidence on the intensity and quality of attitudinal and institutional racism and the obvious point that in contrast to white immigrants the immigrants of colour remain permanently visible (and in this sense, if in no other, remain a permanent minority), but it also ignores the colonial context of the migrations.

And, too, the focus on the acculturation of the 'voluntary' immigrants misses the point, made by van den Berghe among others, that the analysis of racial and ethnic relations,

. . . must not be focused exclusively or even primarily at the cultural level; ethnic relations cannot satisfactorily be accounted for simply in terms of cultural differences, culture contact, and acculturation between groups. It is important to distinguish analytically the structural elements of ethnic relations from the

---

[25] Stanley Lieberson, 'A Societal Theory of Race and Ethnic Relations', *American Sociological Review* (Vol. 26, December 1961), pp. 902–10.

[26] Oscar Handlin, *The Newcomers* (New York, 1962), p. 120; Hauser cited by Sidney Wilhelm, *Who Needs the Negro?* (Boston, 1970), p. 16.

[27] Patterson, op. cit., pp. 8–9.

D

cultural ones. The dynamics of group membership, solidarity, and conflict, and the network of structured relationships both within and between groups, are at least as essential to an understanding of ethnic relations as the cultural dynamics of group contact. People are not only 'carriers of culture'; they are also members of structured groups. In so far as systems of ethnic relations are largely determined by structural asymmetries in wealth, prestige, and power between groups, an inventory of cultural differences gives one a very incomplete picture of group relations.[28]

By selecting comparative research locales that share the features of the immigrant–colonial amalgam, it is possible for us to pursue a research strategy that holds constant both the types of society under examination and the temporal sequences of racial group interaction.

III

There are, of course, undeniable divergences that distinguish the sending societies of the American South and the British West Indies, including, most prominently, the related facts of a majority white population in the Southern United States coupled with a racial stratification system that distinguished only between black and white (without allowing for middle categories) and a minority white population in the West Indies coupled with a classificatory stratification system based on gradations or degrees of colour. By contrast to the rigid caste-like divisions of the Southern United States, West Indians, in Naipaul's telling phrase, have 'a nice eye for shades of black'.[29]

Despite these numerical and classificatory differences, both sending societies shared key common elements. The Third World populations in both locales were 'sociological minorities',[30] if not numerical minorities; that is, in all social spheres, relative to the white population, they were essentially powerless. And Hoetink reminds us that while,

. . . the coloured is not . . . regarded by the dominant white group in the Deep South as a separate social category, and this is where the characteristic difference from the other Caribbean societies lies, it should be kept in mind, however, that the same basic principle obtains in all these societies, namely that it is the white group which decides the grades of the different categories.[31]

In his comprehensive study of Caribbean race relations, he thus classifies

[28] Pierre van den Berghe, *Race and Ethnicity: Essays in Comparative Sociology* (New York, 1970), p. 150.

[29] V. S. Naipaul, *The Middle Passage* (London, 1962), p. 15.

[30] G. Balandier, 'The Colonial Situation: A Theoretical Approach', in I. Wallerstein, ed., *Social Change: The Colonial Situation* (New York, 1966), p. 49. ('The colonial population presents two salient characteristics: its overwhelming numerical superiority and the rigid control to which it is subjected. While a numerical majority, it is nevertheless a sociological minority.')

[31] H. Hoetink, *The Two Variants in Caribbean Race Relations* (London, 1967), p. 47.

the American South with the North West European Caribbean (including, of course, the British West Indies), contrasting their pattern of race relations with the Iberian variant.[32]

M. G. Smith's 'Framework for Caribbean Studies', distinguishes between five meanings of the concept of colour: (1) phenotypical, referring to the individual's racial appearance; (2) genealogical, the biological status of an individual defined in terms of racial purity or mixture; (3) associational, referring to those persons with whom an individual regularly associates on terms of equality, intimacy and familiarity; (4) cultural or behavioural, referring to the extent to which an individual's behaviour conforms to the cultural standards or norms socially associated with his racial group; and (5) structural, which

consists in those factors and aspects of the social process, and the relations between them, that give the society its distinctive form as an arrangement of units and processes. Thus the structural dimension is an abstract analytical category reflecting the distributions and types of power, authority, knowledge, and wealth, which together define and constitute the social framework. When we speak of structural color, we imply an allocation of these variables among color-differentiated groups which obtains presently and reflects historical conditions.[33]

It is the last of the five meanings that will concern us here, because the structural dimension gives social meaning to the phenotypical and the genealogical, and both shapes and limits associational and cultural or behavioural choice. The structural similarities of West Indian and American Southern societies are striking.

Clearly this is so in terms of van den Berghe's well known distinction between paternalistic and competitive race relations. Building on Tönnies's distinction between *Gemeinschaft* and *Gesellschaft*,[34] van den Berghe argues that the most fundamental differences in contexts of race contact situations are differences that relate directly to levels of industrialization and economic development. Thus, paternalistic race relations characteristically are typical of pre-industrial societies; competitive race relations of industrial societies.[35]

Both the American South and the British West Indies closely resemble the paternalistic ideal type, whose basic structural factors include: a non-manufacturing, agricultural, pastoral economy, often of the plantation type; simple or intermediate division of labour along racial lines, with a wide income gap between racial groups; little horizontal or vertical mobility; a caste-like system of stratification with wide gaps in living standards between castes, and a homogeneous upper caste.[36] The most

[32] Ibid., especially parts one and three.
[33] M. G. Smith, *The Plural Society in the British West Indies* (Berkeley, 1965), pp. 60–6.
[34] Ferdinand Tönnies, *Community and Association* (London, 1965).
[35] For an overview, see van den Berghe, *Race and Ethnicity*, Chapter 1.
[36] Van den Berghe, *Race and Racism*, pp. 27–8.

salient components of the racial situation include apparent accommodation in which everyone knows his place; an ethos of benevolent paternalism; ascriptively defined roles and statuses; an elaborate and definite etiquette of behaviour; condoned and frequent miscegenation between upper caste men and lower caste women; and stereotypes of the lower caste as childish, immature, lazy, uninhibited, fun-loving, inferior, but lovable.[37] This pattern of relationships is sanctioned by law, and by dominant collectivity control of the legitimate means of coercion. Indeed, for van den Berghe, 'large-scale production of a cash crop on slave plantations is a common and perhaps the "purest" case of paternalistic relations as shown by the pre-abolition regimes in northeastern Brazil, the Western Cape Province of South Africa, the West Indies, and the Southern United States.'[38]

Both the Southern United States and the British West Indies shared, in the periods of migration, the core elements of what Blauner has called the colonization complex: forced, involuntary contact; 'an impact on the culture and social organization of the colonized people which is more than just the result of such "natural" processes as contact and acculturation'; direct or indirect administration by representatives of the colonizer; and racism ('a principle of social domination by which a group seen as inferior or different in terms of alleged biological characteristics is exploited, controlled, and oppressed socially and psychically by a superordinate group').[39]

In both cases, the population movement was away from colour-ascriptive colonial societies characterized by paternalistic race relations, to the 'mother country', to the North or to England.[40] Though the dominant economic explanations for both migrations, which are well known and need not be repeated here,[41] are essentially correct, they are incomplete, in that in both cases, for the migrants, there was a normative sense of coming home. 'In the sociology of the Deep South,' Hoetink has noted, 'we encounter again the metropolitan, the outsider from the mother country. By "mother country" we have to understand in this

[37] Ibid., pp. 27–34. [38] Ibid., p. 28.

[39] Robert Blauner, 'Internal Colonialism and Ghetto Revolt', Social Problems (Vol. 16, Spring 1969), p. 396.

[40] One of the most striking uniformities in the two cases is that in the early years of contact in the 'mother countries' race relations were fluid, the problems tractable. In 1911, Mary White Ovington described New York's attitude towards the black migrants as 'a capricious mood, varying with the individual, considerate today and offensive tomorrow'. Her description holds for Britain in the 1950s and 1960s. Mary White Ovington, Half a Man: The Status of the Negro in New York (New York, 1911), p. 195.

[41] For examples, see Franklin, op. cit.; Carl Kelsey, 'Some Causes of the Negro Emigration', Charities (Vol. 15, October 1905); Emmett J. Scott, Negro Migration During the War (New York, 1920), p. 13; Donald Henderson, 'The Negro Migration of 1916–1918, Journal of Negro History (October 1921); Peach, op. cit.; R. B. Davison, West Indian Migrants (London, 1962); G. W. Roberts and D. O. Mills, 'Study of External Migration Affecting Jamaica', University College of the West Indies, 1958.

case mainly the North of the United States. The term "mother country" may not be applicable to the old "Yankee" country historically, but it certainly is psychologically.'[42] Thus, Richard Wright wrote of his personal experience: 'With ever watchful eyes and bearing scars, visible and invisible, I headed North full of a hazy notion that life could be lived with dignity.' The North, for Wright, symbolized 'all that I had not felt and seen; it had no relation whatever to what actually existed. Yet by imagining a place where everything was possible, I kept hope alive in me.'[43] For generations, Southern black rationality was sustained, as Ralph Ellison has put it, by the 'almost mystical hope for a future of full democracy—a hope accompanied by an irrepressible belief in some Mecca of equality, located in the North and identified by the magic place names, New York, Chicago, Detroit.'[44]

Similarly, the immigrants to England have not arrived from anywhere; they have come from the British Commonwealth. And they have not moved to any urbanized, industrial locale, but to Britain. In Jerome Hartenfels's novel of West Indian migration, the protagonist, a prospective migrant in his teens muses:

I wanted to get out of the dirt, the noise, and the everlasting oppression of hundreds of human beings crowded too closely upon me and upon each other; and I wanted to get out of being a black boy, out of that unbreakable rule of nature and life. The first problem I hoped to solve by going to England; about the second I was less clear, but it seemed sufficiently interconnected with the first for me to hope my eventual journey to England might solve that too.[45]

As in any voluntary migration, the migrants were self-selected. In a real sense, the 'Children of Empire' were coming home. 'Again and again', John Rex and Robert Moore observe in their study of race relations in Sparkbrook, 'as we read our research notes we find our West Indian respondents protesting they are not different from anyone else. . . . West Indians come to England as to their mother country.'[46]

Following van den Berghe, again, we can take note of the basic similarities between the receiving societies which shared the outstanding characteristics of the 'competitive' ideal-type: a manufacturing, large-scale capitalist industrial economy; a complex division of labour; much horizontal and vertical mobility: factors, in short, which make the paternalist master–servant model inadequate.[47] In political terms, both receiving 'mother countries' were liberal democracies based on what Apter has called the secular–libertarian model which 'essentially accepts society as

[42] Hoetink, op. cit., pp. 62–3.
[43] Richard Wright, *Black Boy* (New York, 1966), pp. 285, 186.
[44] Ralph Ellison, *Shadow and Act* (London, 1967), p. 299.
[45] Jerome Hartenfels, *Lazarus* (London, 1967), p. 16.
[46] John Rex and Robert Moore, *Race, Community, and Conflict* (London, 1967), pp. 156, 100.
[47] Van den Berghe, *Race and Racism*, pp. 29–34.

it is and suggests a framework that will allow modest change over time.' The model

... consists of a set of presuppositions about the way in which representative government ought to operate: (1) There should not be a monopoly of power any more than there should be a monopoly of corporate enterprise. (2) The same rules apply to all; hence, as legal personalities, all are equal. (3) Preference can be realized within a framework of law in which those exercising power are checked by legal means—by control over the executive and so on.[48]

What is significant for us is that both the northern United States and Great Britain in the periods of migration claimed to offer (legally) free and equal citizens the opportunity to participate in the political process. The central question becomes, therefore, participation on what terms, with what structurally limited choice possibilities?

IV

The relatively brief discussion of the selection of comparative locales in this chapter is not meant to exhaust the possibilities of comparisons between the sending and receiving societies in both cases, but rather to make concrete an aspect of the research strategy of the book. No society of course is precisely like any other society; yet the shared features of the immigrant–colonial amalgam make possible a research strategy of limited comparisons.

The thrust of the research, however, is not the detailed justification of similarities of context, but rather to inquire in detail after the political linkages fashioned by the migrants and the polity in the two 'mother countries' in the early, and fluid, periods of mass migration. The student of American race relations stands in relation to his work much as a weaver to his nearly completed but deficient cloth. He wants to unravel the cloth to discover the threads that have been woven deficiently. British race relations, too, are like a complex cloth, but one on which work has only recently begun. But here too something is clearly amiss (one has only to read the headlines), and the weaver wants to locate the deficient threads before continuing to weave the cloth. This study attempts to untangle the political–structural thread, hold it up for examination, and show its relationship to the cloth as a whole.

Thus, our central focus will be on the critical structural decisions made by local and national elites in the critical periods of migration to link the black migrants from the South and the Third World immigrants from the Commonwealth to the polity, since the policy outcome of those decisions both shaped and limited the migrants' choice possibilities, the extent of racial justice, and the degree to which liberal democratic rhetoric and practices were capable of incorporating the politics of race.

[48] David Apter, *The Politics of Modernization* (Chicago, 1965), pp. 33-4.

Part Two

American Patterns, 1900–30

Chapter Four

The Parameters of National Participation

SOME American blacks reacted to the closed political possibilities of the Southern colonial racial system by seeking to establish new and (they hoped) more viable linkages with the national political system. This effort to widen the scope of black political activity by constructing productive, structured national political relationships assumed three dominant forms: an attempt to secure patronage for individuals in exchange for mass support, an attempt to put an end to the reflexive black support for Republican candidates in order to make the black vote (or what remained of it) a bargaining resource, and an attempt to secure protective legislation from the Congress.[1]

These efforts, in this period, all failed. Through case studies of Booker T. Washington's relationship with Presidents Roosevelt and Taft, the Wilson campaign of 1912 and the racial aftermath, and the anti-lynching campaign of the National Association for the Advancement of Colored People, this chapter explores the reasons for failure and their significance.

I

Booker T. Washington's conservative philosophy was the product of the objective situation in the South as the nineteenth century drew to a close. Washington was acutely conscious of what was possible; the 'discouraging conditions at the turn of the century led him to feel that a program of self-help and solidarity, limited political activity, economic and moral virtues, and both industrial and higher education would be thoroughly realistic, whereas an appeal to the moral sense of the nation would avail little.'[2] At the heart of his regional programme was an attempt to reassure the South's white population that his activities were compatible with the racial *status quo*. At Atlanta in 1895, Washington announced to a receptive audience, 'The wisest among my race understand that the agitation of questions of social equality is the extremest folly, and that progress in the enjoyment of all privileges that will come to us must be the result of severe and constant struggle rather than of artificial forcing.' Addressing

[1] For an illuminating discussion of black politics in the North in the period preceding the Great Migration, see Leslie Fishel, Jr., 'The Negro in Northern Politics', *Mississippi Valley Historical Review* (Vol. 41, December 1955), pp. 466-89.

[2] August Meier, *Negro Thought in America, 1880-1915* (Ann Arbor, 1966), p. 215.

himself to the issue of political activity, Washington soothed his listeners by assuring them that 'it is the duty of the Negro—as the greater part of the race is already doing—to deport himself modestly in regard to political claims.'[3]

Washington was not, however, a synthetic 'Uncle Tom' whose reputation and position rested *solely* on white approbation. Quite the contrary. Washington spoke for a significant section of the black population, the conservative middle class. His following was national; black businessmen, lawyers, intellectuals, ministers, doctors, realtors, editors, and politicians —in short, the period's black elite—in varying degrees tended to support Washington. There can be little doubt that Washington commanded an enthusiastic, if not always well-informed, mass following as well.[4]

The strength of Washington's leadership and the moderation of his views made him an ideal political instrument for the Republican party. Most blacks who could vote voted Republican. Every four years the Republican party platform, in ritual fashion, condemned lynching, disfranchisement, and called for congressional action to provide 'equal justice for all men, without regard to race or color'.[5] In fact, however, the party's 'appeal was illusory', its 'most attractive quality was a memory'.[6] Republican pledges were not redeemed because blacks had no where else to turn. 'I carry the Negroes' vote in my vest pocket', Senator Mark Hanna casually remarked, and he was right.[7]

Washington, who accepted the Republican allegiance of black voters as desirable, sought to increase the tangible, material rewards of the relationship. President Theodore Roosevelt, in turn, who wished to continue his party's traditional practice of appointing blacks to minor patronage positions to assure their loyalty and propagandize the group as a whole, sought a means by which he could dispense black patronage and, at the same time, boycott the routine machinery for patronage dispensation, the

---

[3] Quoted in John Hope Franklin and Isidore Starr, eds., *The Negro in 20th Century America* (New York, 1967), pp. 87, 89. Vann Woodward has commented 'that in so far as Washington's pronouncement constituted a renunciation of active political aspirations for the Negro it had an important bearing upon the movement of disfranchisement'. Actually, Washington opposed disfranchisement as such. He favoured, rather, educational and property tests administered equally to blacks and whites. He was not prepared, however, to contest disfranchisement openly lest he antagonize the white community. See C. Vann Woodward, *The Origins of the New South* (Baton Rouge, 1951), p. 323, and Meier, op. cit., pp. 110-318.

[4] August Meier concluded after examining a representative sample of the black elite that 'it is evident that most of them ... were at one time or another (if not all the time) either enthusiastic or lukewarm supporters of Booker T. Washington.' Meier, op. cit., p. 245.

[5] For the Republican party platform statements on race relations from 1896 to 1924 see Kirk Porter, *National Party Platforms* (New York, 1924), pp. 109, 123, 139, 160, 236, and 265. The subject was not mentioned in 1912 and 1916.

[6] Fishel 'The Negro in Northern Politics', op. cit., p. 466.

[7] Quoted by Elbert Lee Tatum, *The Changed Political Thought of the Negro, 1915-1940* (New York, 1951), p. 72.

state party organizations, since most were dominated by Hanna supporters. The unofficial appointment of Washington as Roosevelt's (and later in the decade, as Taft's) black patronage referee and liaison to the black community, allowed both men to promote their ambitions.[8] The Washington–Roosevelt, Washington–Taft relationship was seriously flawed, however, on two counts: both presidents thought blacks inferior and patronized Washington by treating him as an exception, and, as a consequence of Southern black political powerlessness, Roosevelt and Taft became enchanted with the possibility of wooing the white South away from the Democrats, a concern which was more important to them than pacifying a racial group thought inferior and which, on the whole, could not vote.

Roosevelt spoke and wrote often of black inferiority. At a Lincoln Day speech in 1905, the President urged that the 'backward race be trained . . . that it may enter into the possession of true freedom while the forward race is enabled to preserve its civilization unharmed. . . . Race purity must be maintained.'[9] To the novelist Owen Wister he wrote in July 1906, 'I entirely agree with you that as a race and in the mass they are altogether inferior to the whites.'[10] He reaffirmed that view in a letter to his friend Harry Hamilton two years later in which he stated that the Negro race was one of the 'most underdeveloped races'.[11] Hence Washington was perceived as the exception. In a revealing address at the unveiling of the Frederick Douglass Monument at Rochester, New York, in 1899, Roosevelt made explicit his distinction between the black mass and men like Booker T. Washington. He spoke first of 'the worst enemy of the colored race, . . . the colored man who commits some hideous wrong, especially if that be the worst of all crimes, rape.' After endorsing the irrational sexual fears of some whites, Roosevelt commended Washington to his audience as 'a man who is striving to teach his people to rise by toil to be better citizens, by resolute determination to make themselves worthy of American citizenship.'[12] Washington, Roosevelt wrote to Wister, was one of the 'occasionally good, well-educated, intelligent and

[8] See Carl Offord, 'The Republican Party and the Negro, 1900–1939', W.P.A. research paper, The Schomburg Collection, New York Public Library, dated August 1939, p. 13. Kelly Miller, the black president of Howard University aptly described Washington's role as that of 'the consulting statesman of the Negro race. . . . No Negro,' he wrote, 'can expect to receive consideration at the hands of the President unless he gets the approval of the great educator.' Kelly Miller, *Roosevelt and the Negro*, pamphlet printed by the author (Washington, 1907), pp. 8, 11.

[9] Cited in Seth Scheiner, 'President Theodore Roosevelt and the Negro', *Journal of Negro History* (Vol. XLVII, July 1962), pp. 180–1.

[10] Elting E. Morison, *The Letters of Theodore Roosevelt* (Cambridge, Mass., 1951–4), Vol. V, p. 227.

[11] Ibid., p. 1,126.

[12] Theodore Roosevelt, Address at the unveiling of the Frederick Douglass monument at Rochester, New York, 10 June 1899 in *The Public Papers of Theodore Roosevelt* (Albany, 1899), pp. 332, 335.

honest colored men' who should be permitted to vote.[13] The qualities Roosevelt most admired in Washington were essentially those of moderation; Washington did not challenge the President to make good on the promises of the party platforms. 'There is not a better or truer friend of his race than Booker T. Washington'; Roosevelt wrote to the newly elected President Taft, 'and yet he is so sane and reasonable that following his advice never gives cause for just criticism by white people.'[14]

Taft's attitudes were strikingly similar to Roosevelt's. In the second month of his Administration, Taft exclaimed: 'Why, a race that produces a Booker T. Washington in a century ought to feel confident that it can do miracles in time.' Later that year Taft endorsed the Tuskegee programme because it leads 'Negroes along the path which natural taste and early environment marked out for him by assigning the greatest importance to teaching in a practical way agricultural and kindred pursuits rather than those of an urban community.'[15]

The second difficulty with the Washington–Roosevelt, Taft relationship was more significant. As the white South disfranchised its black citizens, the possibility of building Republican strength in the South increasingly intrigued the Party leaders. With the divisive issue of the place of blacks safely (so it appeared) resolved, the South, it was believed, might divide politically on grounds similar to those in the nation as a whole. And there was evidence that in the South an incipient coalition of 'lily-white' party leaders, businessmen, and those opposed to one-party politics on principle was, in fact, emerging:

These elements were not very harmonious, but they had enough in common to enable them to agree upon a sort of standing petition to Republican presidents, renewed from one administration to the next. The petition urged the appointment of white men to Federal offices in the South, the complete abandonment of the threat of Federal intervention on behalf of the Negro, and reassurances of any kind that would overcome the Southern trauma of Negro domination.[16]

[13] Roosevelt to Wister, 27 July 1906, in Morison, op. cit., pp. 226–8.

[14] Theodore Roosevelt to William Howard Taft, 20 January 1909, in the Booker T. Washington Papers, Library of Congress, Washington, D.C.

[15] William Howard Taft, 'Addresses Touching The Negro Problem', in The Schomburg Collection, New York Public Library; 25 February 1909, pp. 33, 11. Roosevelt had also explicitly endorsed Washington's Tuskegee programme. Speaking to a black audience at Tuskegee on 24 October 1905, Roosevelt reminded his listeners that 'no help can so permanently avail you save as you yourselves develop capacity for self-help. You young colored men and women educated at Tuskegee must by precept and example lead your fellows toward sober, industrious, law abiding lives. . . . If you save money, secure homes, become taxpayers, and lead clean, decent, modest lives you will win the respect of your neighbors of both races. . . . The colored people have many difficulties to pass through, but these difficulties will be surmounted if only the policy of reason and common sense is pursued. You have made real and great progress.' In his State of the Union Address of 3 December 1906 Roosevelt declared 'Of course the best type of education for the colored man as a whole is such education as is conferred in schools like Hampton and Tuskegee.' Cited in Franklin and Starr, op. cit., pp. 81–2.

[16] Vann Woodward, op. cit., p. 462.

On assuming office in 1897, President McKinley made clear that he intended to do nothing to inhibit the development of Southern Republicanism. 'It would be my constant aim', he stated, 'to do nothing and permit nothing to be done that will arrest or disturb this growing sentiment of unity and cooperation, this revival of esteem and affiliation which now animates so many thousands in both the old antagonistic sections, but I shall do everything possible to promote and increase it.'[17] To lend substance to his rhetoric, McKinley toured the South twice, but did little to shift the balance of Republican political power in the South from the 'black and tan' to the 'lily-white' organizations.

In fact, McKinley had continued to award political patronage to Southern blacks. In September 1901, Roosevelt summoned Washington to the White House to inform him that there would be departures from previous Republican patronage policies. In a memorandum dictated after their meeting, Washington noted that Roosevelt expected 'to appoint fewer colored men to offices in the South . . . and a certain number of colored men of high character and ability in the Northern states.'[18] Roosevelt's presidency was marked by ambivalent and often contradictory actions regarding blacks. The noted invitation to Washington to dine at the White House, the Crum appointment in Charleston, South Carolina, and the closing of the Indianola, Mississippi, Post Office seemed to hold out the promise in his early presidential years that Roosevelt would do battle with Southern racialism. Increasingly, however, the President channelled Southern patronage to the 'lily-white' Republicans, and in the Brownsville affair appeased Southern opinion. By the end of 1906, some of Washington's closest advisers urged him to break with Roosevelt. T. Thomas Fortune, the influential editor of the Harlem-based New York Age, for example, wrote to Washington on 8 December 1906: 'The President has forfeited the confidence and good esteem of the Afro-American people, and largely of the American people, by the adoption of Southern ideas and methods in dealing with us, and Mr. Scott and I both think you have gone as far with him as you can afford to.'[19] Washington, who consistently sought to get along and make the best of things as they were, ignored Fortune's advice.[20]

Taft, if anything, was even more intrigued by the possibilities of Southern white Republicanism than his mentor. In January 1908, before the commencement of his campaign for the Presidency, Taft informed W. R. Nelson of his impending campaign strategy: 'When a man is running for the presidency . . . he cannot afford to ignore the tremendous

[17] James D. Richardson, ed. Messages and Papers of the Presidents (Washington, 1911), p. 6243.

[18] Memorandum, in Fishel, 'The Negro in Northern Politics', op. cit., p. 487.

[19] Fortune to Washington, 8 December 1906, in Washington Papers.

[20] See Ralph Bunche, 'A Brief and Tentative Analysis of Negro Leadership', 1940, MS. in Schomburg Collection, p. 14.

influence, however undue, that the Southern vote has, and he must take the best way he can honorably to secure it.'[21] After the November election returns showed a substantial Republican vote in some areas of the South, Taft wrote, 'I am greatly interested in the southern question and have only just begun.'[22] By late February the President had made up his mind 'to take a decided step in respect to Southern Negro appointments. I am not going to put into places of such prominence in the South, where race feeling is strong, Negroes whose appointments will only tend to increase this race feeling.'[23] Of 9,876 Presidential appointments made by Taft, only thirty went to blacks.[24]

Taft's appeal to the South was not based on patronage policies alone; on a tour of the South in 1909, he explicitly endorsed black disfranchisement:

When a class of persons is so ignorant and so subject to oppression and misleading that they are really political children not having the mental stature of manhood, then their voice in the government serves no benefit to them. A policy, therefore, which excludes from the ballot both the black and white when ignorant and irresponsible cannot be criticised.[25]

The slow, steady progress which Washington had hoped to achieve had yielded to a rapid deterioration. Washington never secured the bargaining relationship he sought; instead, his position as patronage referee camouflaged the Republican party's retreat from its stated principles in its quest for a new constituency.

II

Led by W. E. B. DuBois and William Monroe Trotter, the NAACP 'radicals' rejected Washington's policy of working within the Republican party in hope of securing significant numbers of patronage positions for blacks, a policy they considered bankrupt. Blacks, they reasoned, were not part of the process of political bargaining because the Republican party was assured of black support. Thus, in 1912, DuBois and Trotter endorsed Woodrow Wilson, the Democratic presidential candidate.[26]

[21] Taft to W. R. Nelson, 18 January 1908, in Henry F. Pringle, *The Life and Times of William Howard Taft* (New York, 1939), p. 347.

[22] Taft to H. W. Anderson, 4 November 1908, ibid., p. 391.

[23] Taft to W. R. Nelson, 23 February 1908, ibid., p. 390.

[24] *The Crisis* (Vol. 5, January 1913), p. 122.

[25] Taft, 'Addresses', in Pringle, op. cit., p. 4, speech delivered in Greenborough, North Carolina, 9 July 1909. Though Taft's comments on the franchise referred to whites as well as blacks, given the locale for his address—a Southern community that systematically disfranchised blacks—the meaning of his endorsement of a limited franchise was clearly understood to refer to the extant racial barriers to voting.

[26] DuBois turned to the Democratic Party as he had in 1908 when he . . . had urged the election of Bryan. At that time he hoped that the weight of the Negro vote would break the exasperating impasse in the Democratic party caused by the "impossible

Indeed, during the campaign, Wilson, who saw the possibility of obtaining unexpected electoral support, made an overt appeal for black votes. The New Jersey Governor pledged to bring about 'justice done to the colored people in every matter; and not mere grudging justice, but justice executed with liberality and cordial good feelings.'[27] On another occasion Wilson declared, 'Should I become President of the United States they [Negroes] may count on me for absolute fair dealing, for everything by which I could advance the interests of their race in the United States.'[28] The *Crisis*, the monthly organ of the NAACP, rejoiced that for the first time black votes were, in part, an unknown factor in a presidential campaign.[29]

Though Taft and Roosevelt outpolled Wilson in the black community, the Democratic nominee did succeed in obtaining a significant number of black votes. In New York City, for example, it was estimated that Wilson received approximately 25 per cent of the black vote. In the nation as a whole, the *Crisis* wrote, 'at least 100,000 black votes went to swell the 6,000,000 that called Woodrow Wilson to the Presidency. . . . We have

alliance of radical socialistic Democracy at the North with an aristocratic caste party at the South". The Democratic party, once freed from its enslavement to the reactionary South, could return to its pre-Civil War creed of the widest possible participation of American citizens in the government.' Charles F. Kellogg, *NAACP: A History, 1909-20* (Baltimore, 1907), p. 156. See also W. E. B. Dubois, 'The Negro Vote', Talk No. 4, *Horizon* (September 1908), and the New York *Age* (2 April 1908).

In 1912, DuBois turned to the Democrats only after considering the endorsement of the new Progressive party. DuBois, writes Link, 'at first greeted Roosevelt's movement with great enthusiasm, had written a proposed plank for the platform demanding the repeal of discriminatory laws and a guarantee of the Negro's right to vote', but Roosevelt rejected his draft, preferring to bid for Southern white votes. Roosevelt's advisers believed that the Progressive party, to have a chance to win, would have 'to divorce itself from the few Negro voters who, in the deep South at least, constituted the backbone of the old Republican party'. Theodore Parker, Roosevelt's leading Southern adviser, thus counselled the candidate, 'this should be a white man's party, recognizing the superior ability of the white man and his superior civilization attained through countless centuries of struggle and endeavor, peculiarly fitting him to lead and direct, as during all of this period the Negro has been perfectly content to remain the ignorant savage devoid of pride of ancestry or civic ambition' (24 July 1912). Southern black delegates were excluded from the Progressive convention. Roosevelt explained, 'The progress that has been made among Negroes of the South during these forty-five years has not been made as a result of political effort. . . . It has been made as a result of effort along industrial and educational lines.' In late August, Roosevelt defended his party's racial policies in an article in *Outlook*, the Progressive magazine, in which he endorsed Negro rights 'so long as he behaves in straight and decent fashion', and called for the 'gradual re-enfranchisement of the worthy colored man'. Link, op. cit., pp. 97, 93-4; Roosevelt to Julian Harris, 1 August 1912, copy in Schomburg Collection; and T. Roosevelt, 'The Progressives and the Colored Man', *Outlook* (Vol. 101, 24 August 1912), pp. 910-11.

[27] See Alexander Walters, *My Life and Work* (New York, 1917), pp. 194-5, and John Hope Franklin, *From Slavery to Freedom* (New York, 1964), p. 445.

[28] Ibid.

[29] The *Crisis* (Vol. 5, December 1912), p. 58.

helped call to power . . . a scholar and a gentleman.'[30] This opinion was shared by a significant minority of the Southern Negro press. 'We believe,' wrote the editor of the Richmond *Planet* in a typical pro-Wilson editorial, 'that he will prove a friend to us in the White House.'[31]

Though DuBois's theory of the pivotal black vote had logical merits, it ignored two aspects of reality. First, in 1912, as in the twelve preceding years of Roosevelt–Taft rule, America's blacks, on the whole, were politically impotent. Henry Blumenthal perceptively noted:

Neither Wilson nor the American people, with the exception of the colored population, treated the Negro question as an important issue in the campaign of 1912. The Demociats did not consider the Negro vote politically significant, for in those states in which Negroes were not disfranchised, they traditionally identified themselves with the Republican party.[32]

In this light Wilson's appeal for black votes can be seen as of marginal importance.

Moreover, in supporting Wilson, the DuBois 'radicals' structured their perception of reality so as to avoid the obvious: Wilson was a Southerner, his party was led by Southerners, and his electoral triumph would be (and was) widely interpreted as symbolizing the return of the South to the Union on the South's terms. 'The truth is', Wilson's most noted biographer has written,

. . . that although he never shared the extreme anti-Negro sentiments of many of his contemporaries, Wilson remained throughout his life largely a Southerner on the race question. He had an extravagant and romantic love for the South which increased in direct ratio to his absence from the region. Not once in his entire career before 1912 had he lifted his voice in defense of the minority race. As President of Princeton University he had, by evasion, prevented Negroes from enrolling. As a matter of fact, Mrs. Wilson felt much more strongly about drawing the color line than did her husband, but both were opposed to social relationships between the races.[33]

The Wilson wing of the Democratic Party was led by Southern Progressives like Josephus Daniels of North Carolina. Though Southern Progressivism shared the national traits of the movement, it differed significantly in one respect—it was 'progressivism for white men only'.[34] Indeed, Daniels, Wilson's campaign manager, who edited the *Raleigh News and Observer*, editorialized one month before the election of 1912,

[30] Ibid., p. 59.

[31] Richmond *Planet* (20 November 1912); cited in ibid., p. 69.

[32] Henry Blumenthal, 'Woodrow Wilson and the Race Question', *Journal of Negro History* (Vol. XLVIII, January 1963), p. 3.

[33] Arthur Link, 'The Negro as a Factor in the Campaign of 1912', *Journal of Negro History* (Vol. XXXI, January 1947), p. 87. Tindall is a bit kinder to Wilson: 'In the best tradition of Southern paternalism, he clearly wished Negroes no harm, but the whole question was peripheral to his concerns and he drifted willingly in the current of the time.' George Tindall, *The Emergence of the New South* (Baton Rouge, 1967), p. 143.

[34] Vann Woodward, op. cit., p. 373.

'The attitude of the South regarding the Negro in politics is unalterable and uncompromising. We take no risks. We abhor a Northern policy of catering to Negroes politically just as we abhor a Northern policy of social equality.'[35] Link argues, in fact, that Wilson only dealt with the race question at all to silence the party's Northern reformers. It is not surprising therefore that with the exception of Arizona, Wilson was unable to poll a majority vote outside of the South.[36]

As late as April 1913, the *Crisis* wrote of Wilson in glowing terms. Though the President had yet to mention the race question in public, the NAACP journal described the new administration as 'the high enterprise of the new day' that would lift the nation 'to the light that shines from the hearth fire of every man's conscience and vision of rights'.[37] But, ironically, in April the racial policies of the new Democratic regime began to assume coherent shape.

On 7 April 1913 a postal clerk in the railway mail service in Arkansas sent a letter to Postmaster-General Burleson:

We feel assured that the service would be very much benefited and the standard of efficiency raised if the races could be segregated, the Negroes placed on lines to themselves. . . . We are compelled to be together night and day . . . each car is provided with one wash basin and one toilet facility and every member of the crew is compelled to use the same in common. . . . We are assured that Negroes cannot object to segregation—it is the best thing for them as well as ourselves.[38]

Burleson raised the matter at the next cabinet meeting, which is dealt with at length in Josephus Daniels's diary:

The Postmaster General brought up a matter that is always the hardest matter to deal with—to wit: policies that are affected by race conditions. In the railway mail service there are a great many negroes who are employed, and it often happens that there are four railway mail clerks in one car and when this happens the white men might often have to do all the work. It is very unpleasant for them to have to work in a car with negroes where it is almost impossible to have different drinking vessels and different towels, or places to wash, and he was anxious to segregate white and negro employees in all Departments of the Government and he talked with Bishop Walters and other prominent negroes and most of them thought it would be a great thing to do.[39] . . . the matter came

---

[35] *Raleigh News and Observer* (1 October 1912); cited in Arthur Link, *Wilson: The Road to the White House* (Princeton, 1947), p. 501.

[36] Ibid., p. 502; Dewey Grantham Jr., *Hoke Smith and the Politics of the New South* (Baton Rouge, 1958), p. 238; and Tindall, op. cit., p. 1.

[37] The *Crisis* (Vol. 6, April 1913), p. 267.

[38] Arkansas mail clerk to Burleson, 7 April 1913, cited in the *Crisis* (Vol. 6, June 1913).

[39] In September 1913 Bishop Walters categorically denied acquiescing in these policies: 'Believe me when I tell you that I have never in any way, shape or form endorsed segregation by the administration and never will.' Washington *Bee* (13 September 1913). See also August Meier, 'The Negro and the Democratic Party, 1875–1915', *Phylon* (Vol. 17, 2nd quarter 1956), p. 190.

E

up generally about negro appointments and how to use them. The President said he made no promises in particular to negroes, except to do them justice, and he did not wish to see them have less positions than they now have; but he wished the matter adjusted in a way to make the least friction. A negro is now register of the Treasury, and Mr. Burleson, the Postmaster General, thought it wrong to have white clerks, men or women, under him or any other negro. Secretary of the Treasury McAdoo doubted whether the Senate would confirm a negro even if the President appointed one for this place, and believed it would be very doubtful.[40]

Though Wilson never issued any executive orders on the subject, by the end of 1913 segregation had quietly been introduced in the Post Office, the Treasury Department, the Bureau of Engraving and Printing, and in other Federal offices. In 1914, applicants for civil service positions were directed to submit photographs. The President's correspondence makes clear that he favoured these developments. Segregation, he wrote to Oswald Garrison Villard in July 1913, had been introduced 'with the idea that the friction or rather the discontent which had prevailed in many of the departments would therefore be removed.'[41] In early September the President informed the black minister who edited the *Congregation and the Christian World*, Rev. H. A. Bridgeman, 'I would say that I do approve of the segregation that is being attempted in several of the departments.'[42]

Wilson's patronage policy complemented his Administration's segregation directives. By the summer of 1913 the trend was unmistakable. In April, William Lewis, a black appointee, had resigned his office as Assistant Attorney General of the United States with special responsibility for Indian claims. That office, on the advice of Attorney-General McReynolds, was promptly abolished by the President on the ground that Indian claims work had been completed.[43] Wilson appointed a white man to succeed W. F. Powell in the traditionally black-held post of Minister to Haiti. A. D. Patterson, who had been proposed by Wilson to fill the position of Register of the Treasury, withdrew at the President's request in face of Southern pressure. After Patterson complied, Senator Vardeman of Mississippi gloated, 'No Negro shall be appointed to any executive office in which there may be subordinate white employees.'[44]

---

[40] E. D. Cronon, ed., *The Cabinet Diaries of Josephus Daniels* (Lincoln, 1963), pp. 32–3; cabinet meeting held on 11 April 1913. Wilson's cabinet had a distinctly Southern complexion. Burleson was a Texas politician, Daniels a North Carolina editor, and Houston, who took leave from Washington University to become Secretary of Agriculture, was born in North Carolina. McAdoo and McReynolds were born and grew up in Georgia and Tennessee, respectively.

[41] Wilson to Villard, 21 July, 1913, in Wilson papers, Library of Congress, Washington, D.C.; cited also in Kathleen Wogelmuth, 'Woodrow Wilson and Federal Segregation', *Journal of Negro History* (Vol. XLIII, April 1959), p. 163.

[42] Wilson to Bridgeman, Wilson papers, 4 September 1913; cited also in Wogelmuth, op. cit., p. 164.

[43] See the *Crisis* (Vol. 6, May 1913), p. 10.

[44] 'The President and the Negro', the *Nation* (Vol. 97, 7 August 1913), p. 114.

By September 1913 there could be no doubt; the President's black supporters of the year before were thoroughly disillusioned. The NAACP in that month, in an open letter, broke with the President:

Sir, you have now been President of the United States for six months and what is the result? It is no exaggeration to say that every enemy of the Negro race is greatly encouraged. . . . They are evidently assuming that their theory of the place and destiny of the Negro race is the theory of your administration. . . . A dozen worthy Negro officials have been removed from office, and you have nominated but one black man for office. . . . Public segregation of civil servants in government employ necessarily involving personal insult and humiliation has for the first time in history been made the policy of the United States government.[45]

III

Philip Peabody, a Boston philanthropist, offered to donate $10,000 to the NAACP in the winter of 1916 to finance an effective anti-lynching campaign. An Anti-Lynching Committee, chaired by William English Walling, recommended that the fund be used for research and a programme of publicity and education which would feature lectures by Southern whites who condemned lynching. This programme did not satisfy Peabody who withdrew $9,000 of his offer; the NAACP, however, succeeded in raising the money for an anti-lynching fund elsewhere.[46]

After a two-year period of vacillation, the NAACP decided that the major thrust of the campaign would be an attempt to induce the Congress to pass legislation that would penalize participants in lynchings. On 6 April 1918, Congressman L. C. Dyer of Missouri[47] wrote to John Shillady, the Secretary of the NAACP 'to invite the attention of yourself and the other officers of your Association to the draft of the Bill that I have prepared with reference to introducing in Congress pertaining to lynching . . .'.[48] Dyer was interested especially in factual information and in getting assistance to find witnesses to testify for his Bill at the House

[45] The *Crisis* (Vol. 6, September 1913), pp. 232–3. The tone of this letter differs strikingly from that of the open letter the *Crisis* wrote in March 1913; '. . . the fight is on, and you, Sir, are in the arena. Its virulence will doubtless surprise you and it may scare you as it scared one William Howard Taft. But we trust not; we think not' (pp. 236–7).

[46] Kellogg, op. cit., pp. 216–18. By the end of 1924, the NAACP had spent approximately $45,000 on anti-lynching activities. See Robert Jack, *History of the NAACP* (Boston, 1943), p. 29.

[47] Dyer and the NAACP had worked together before. After the East St. Louis riot of July 1917, Dyer had prevented the suppression of a Congressional report which had investigated the racial conflict in detail. At that time, he also informed an NAACP official that he was planning to draft a bill to make lynching a Federal Crime. See Kellogg, op. cit., pp. 226–7.

[48] Dyer to Shillady, 6 April 1918, Records of the NAACP (hereafter referred to as NAACP Papers), the Library of Congress, Washington, D.C.

Judiciary Committee hearings. Actually, the NAACP's assistance was much more comprehensive; the strategy and financing to secure passage of the Dyer Bill were provided by the Association.

The Dyer–NAACP anti-lynching partnership almost foundered, however, on the issue of constitutionality. Two months after Dyer had introduced his measure, Walter White, the NAACP's Assistant Secretary, informed Moorfield Storey, the Association's President and one of America's most distinguished attorneys,[49] that he had 'been in correspondence constantly with Mr. Dyer, attempting to arrange a Hearing during the latter part of this month so as to give time for the preparation of an argument on the constitutionality of the bill', and asked Storey, 'will you be good enough to let me know if you can be present at the hearing in August?'[50] In early July Storey replied to White in disappointing terms. He advised the Association not to press too strongly for the legislation, lest Congress be offended; moreover, he found the Dyer Bill unconstitutional 'because it assumed that an *individual* could be punished for depriving United States citizens of the privileges or immunities granted them under the Fourteenth Amendment'. Storey argued that the Supreme Court had already made it clear that this amendment protected individuals from *state* violations of citizens' rights. Storey declined, on these grounds, to testify for the Bill.[51] Dyer revised his measure to provide for the infliction of heavy fines on *counties* in which lynchings occur and required that part of the fine go to the victim's surviving relatives. By the end of 1918, Storey was satisfied that the Bill was constitutional.

Despite a massive publicity campaign and some successes on the state level,[52] the Dyer Bill languished in the House Judiciary Committee until

---

[49] The NAACP had only white presidents, a good indication of the paternal attitude white liberals have traditionally assumed toward blacks in America. Storey's paternalism was undisguised. In a letter to Trotter, for example, on the subject of Wilson's racial policies, Storey noted his 'disappointment at the segregation action', and advised, 'I have urged you to be patient, and believe that I can give you no better advice. The mills of the Gods grind slowly and patience does its perfect work. It is only fifty years since slavery was abolished in this country, and the colored man was made free, but left poor, ignorant, and well-nigh helpless. . . . The prejudice against you today is no stronger than the prejudice which Jews and Irish have overcome. I think it is less bitter and enduring. They have overcome it and so will you.' Storey to Trotter, 16 October 1913, cited in Mark A. De Wolfe Howe, *Portrait of an Independent, Moorfield Storey* (New York, 1932), p. 261.

[50] White to Storey, 3 June 1918. Storey Papers, Library of Congress, Washington, D.C.

[51] Kellogg, op. cit., p. 232; Storey to White, 11 July 1918, Joel Spingarn Papers, Howard University, Washington, D.C.

[52] In May 1919, the NAACP held an Anti-Lynching Conference in New York. The distinguished speakers and supporters' lists included Charles Evans Hughes, former Alabama Governor Emmett O'Neal, and Elihu Root. The conference passed resolutions which urged the Congressional passage of anti-lynching legislation, intensified publicity and fund-raising campaigns, and the organization of state anti-lynching

hearings were finally held in 1920, largely as a *pro forma* exercise in making a record the Republican party could present black voters in the Presidential campaign. Though hearings were held in the Spring of 1920, the Bill was not reported out of committee.

The 1920 Republican party platform promised to eradicate lynching: 'We urge Congress to consider the most effective means to end lynching in this country which continues to be a terrible blot on our American civilization.'[53] In his first State of the Union message, the newly inaugurated President Harding called on Congress 'to wipe the stain of barbaric lynching from the banners of a free and orderly representative democracy.'[54] Harding never again pressed the issue. Attorney-General Harry Daugherty, however, explicitly endorsed the Dyer Bill on 9 August 1921.[55] The House Judiciary Committee favourably reported the Bill on 20 October. The President, despite prodding from the NAACP, remained silent. George Christian, Harding's secretary, assured a worried James Weldon Johnson, the NAACP's Executive Secretary, 'you need have no misgivings as to the President's attitude regarding the Dyer Bill.' He added, though, in terms that indicated the President would not fight for the measure, 'it is true, however, as you are well aware, that a good deal of question has been raised about the constitutionality of the Dyer Bill'.[56]

The House commenced debate on 19 December 1921. The measure's opponents, Southerners in the main, argued that the bill was unconstitutional and that if passed would encourage blacks to violate the law.

Congressman Byrnes (South Carolina) spoke to the first point: 'You cannot cure lawlessness by indulging in it yourselves. This you do when you pass a bill clearly in violation of the Constitution of the United States.' Representative Garrett (Tennessee) insisted that 'this bill ought to be amended in its title to read "A Bill to Encourage Rape".' This theme was at the core of the Southern position. Representative Assell's (Louisiana) rhetoric was typical:

You calmly discuss it here impersonally, but should your wife or daughter be criminally assaulted by an African brute would you be restrained? . . . Let us first seek to remove the cause that provokes the lynching. If this bill is passed in some sections it would not be safe for a white woman to live . . . the trustworthy and dependable Negro of the South has no interest in such legislation. . . . When a black brute assaults a neighborhood girl with infinite promise

committees to secure the passage of state anti-lynching legislation. This last effort met with limited success; in 1919, Tennessee, Kentucky, and Wyoming acted, by legislation, to curb lynching. See Kellogg, op. cit., pp. 230-4.

[53] Porter, op. cit., p. 461.
[54] *The New York Times* (13 April 1922).
[55] Richard Sherman, 'The Harding Administration and the Negro: An Opportunity Lost', *Journal of Negro History* (Vol. XLIX, July 1964), p. 61.
[56] George Christian to J. W. Johnson, undated, NAACP Papers.

in which we all rejoice, when the brute assaults her, crushes out every spark of her hope into the unspeakable hell, men and boys will rush to protect their own home from the peril of the monster at large among them.[57]

The House passed the Dyer Bill on 26 January 1922; the vote, largely along regional lines, was 230–119. Most of the affirmative votes were cast by Republicans. A party record had been made.

The NAACP was aware that there were formidable obstacles to Senate passage of the legislation. The most difficult barrier, James Weldon Johnson believed, was 'having the Bill go to sleep in the Committee on the Judiciary. I believe, just as I believed about the House, that if we ever get the Bill reported out it will pass the Senate just as it passed the House. The Senate,' he thought, incorrectly as later events were to show, 'might not be afraid to let it die in committee, but they would not have the temerity to kill it after it had reached the stage of debate.'[58]

The Bill was referred to a five member sub-committee chaired by William Borah, the Idaho Republican progressive, who was troubled, he wrote Storey, about the Bill's constitutionality: 'I am heartily in accord with your views that this fearful evil ought to be controlled. I have only one question opened up for investigation with reference to the bill and that is constitutionality. . . . If I conclude that it is unconstitutional, I would have to vote against it.'[59] Troubled by this letter which Storey showed him, Johnson went to Washington on 7 March to see Senator Borah. Johnson met Borah again in May when he tried to impress on him 'the fact that an unfavorable report on the Bill would be followed by a deplorable psychological effect upon the colored people, by an impression that would be tantamount to a license to lynching mobs, and by the further alienation of colored voters from the Republican Party.'[60] On 22 May in spite of these efforts, Borah's sub-committee reported adversely on the Dyer Bill; the division was 3–2, Borah voting with the majority.

Johnson visited George Christian at the White House to urge that Harding come out vigorously for the legislation. The President maintained his silence.

The Senate Judiciary Committee, on 30 June, however, favourably reported the Bill to the Senate by an 8 to 6 vote. Though the vote was close and though Borah had voted with the Democratic minority, and Norris the Nebraska progressive had been absent, Johnson was overjoyed; the major hurdle to passage, he believed, had been cleared: 'The fact that we will definitely get a favorable report is highly encouraging', he wrote to Storey, 'I consider that getting the Bill out of the Senate

---

[57] *The Congressional Record*, 67th Congress, 2nd session, pp. 543–8.
[58] Johnson to Storey, 4 February 1922, Storey Papers.
[59] Borah to Storey, 9 February 1922, Storey Papers.
[60] NAACP, *13th Annual Report* (New York, 1923), pp. 10–11.

Judiciary Committee is the accomplishment of the greater part of the job in the Senate.'[61]

The *New York Tribune* was more realistic. Commenting on the Judiciary Committee's report, the newspaper noted that, 'much doubt is expressed whether the bill will ever be passed. Southern Democratic Senators will fight it to the limit. It is not expected a serious attempt will be made to pass it.'[62] A week later, the Washington correspondent of the newspaper provided concrete evidence to substantiate this opinion. On 7 July, at a conference of Republican Senate leaders held at Henry Cabot Lodge's house, the decision was reached to abandon the anti-lynching measure without making an effort to break the expected Southern filibuster.[63] The measure was brought to the floor of the Senate on 21 September, just one day before the Senate was scheduled to adjourn. Senator Shortridge of California spoke for the Bill and proposed that the Senate delay its adjournment so that the Bill might be discussed and voted on. Only eighteen Senators, all Republicans, supported this suggestion. The Senate thus adjourned with no action taken.

The anti-lynching measure was finally taken up by the Senate when it reconvened (after the Congressional elections) in late November. The Southerners, as predicted, filibustered. The filibuster, led by Senator Underwood of Alabama, was unexpectedly brief. On Saturday night, 2 December, a caucus of Republicans decided to implement the agreement reached by the leadership in July to have the Senate abandon the Bill and move on to other pending business.[64]

During the brief Senate debate, James Weldon Johnson appealed, once again, to the President to save the Bill by personal intervention. The President's secretary replied on 8 December:

I can readily understand the disappointment of the colored people over the inability of the Senate to function in the consideration of the Dyer Anti-Lynching bill. I also feel that our colored citizens will justly place the responsibility for this where it belongs, to wit, on the Democratic minority. . . . The President recommended the Anti-Lynching bill to Congress. The Republican House passed it. The Republican majority in the Senate labored earnestly and sincerely last summer and now to bring about its enactment. The bill is blocked by the Democratic filibuster.[65]

The NAACP's strategy in the Dyer Bill fight was *political*. When the issue was up for debate in the House every Congressman received the following letter from James Weldon Johnson which contained the thinly veiled threat of political sanctions:

[61] Johnson to Storey, 1 July 1922, Storey Papers.
[62] *New York Tribune* (1 July 1922).
[63] Ibid. (7 July 1922).
[64] NAACP, *13th Annual Report*, p. 20.
[65] Christian to Johnson, 8 December 1922, NAACP Papers.

For the purposes of record, and particularly that we may advise colored voters (from whom we are receiving many inquiries) may I ask whether or not you favor the Dyer anti-lynching Bill, H.R. 13, which was favorably reported on October 20 by the House Judiciary Committee, and if you will vote for its passage when it is presented for a vote on the floor of the House?[66]

When he visited President Harding's secretary on 15 June 1922, Johnson presented Christian with a memorandum whose key passage read:

If the Senate Committee on the Judiciary should report this Bill unfavorably ... there would follow the political effect of alienating colored voters from the Republican party whose platform contained a pledge for anti-lynching legislation followed by a recommendation from the President in his First Message to Congress calling for the same.[67]

'In the last few months,' Johnson wrote Storey, 'we dropped our legal and ethical arguments and depended solely upon political pressure.'[68]

Groups that threaten political sanctions must, to be effective, make those sanctions credible. The small black vote, limited to the North, simply was not seen as significant enough by the Republican party leadership to pass the Dyer Bill in the face of determined opposition. As a result, the Dyer Bill was used by the Republicans as an opportunity to make a *gesture* of goodwill to black Americans, a gesture that lacked substance. Thus the House passed the Dyer Bill *before* the 1922 Congressional elections; Northern Republicans could solicit black votes on what appeared to be a record of accomplishment. The Dyer Bill, *The New York Times* correctly asserted 'was an inexpensive dotation to the colored vote. . . . For that purpose the enthusiastic demonstration by the House Republicans was necessary.'[69] The Senate, however, delayed action on the measure until *after* the November election; the anti-lynching bill, which was never intended to pass, could then be dropped quietly and the Southern Democrats blamed. Actually to have passed the measure would have endangered the Republican party's continuing attempt to make inroads in the traditionally Democratic South. During the Harding years, Richard Sherman has written, 'there was much talk among Republican leaders of the opportunities for their party in the South. To encourage this new Republicanism meant rebuilding lily-white state organizations at the expense of the traditional black and tan groups.'[70] Clearly that would have been impossible had the Dyer Bill been enacted into law. The price of disfranchisement and political powerlessness continued to be high.

[66] From James W. Johnson, 9 November 1921, NAACP Papers.
[67] NAACP, op. cit., p. 13.
[68] Johnson to Storey, 15 November 1922, Storey Papers.
[69] *The New York Times* (31 July 1922).
[70] See Sherman, 'The Harding Administration . . .', op. cit., pp. 167-8.

IV

All three major attempts by blacks in this period to establish viable national political relationships—the attempt to secure patronage from the Republicans in exchange for mass support, the attempt to make the black vote pivotal by putting an end to reflexive black Republicanism, and the attempt to secure anti-lynching legislation from the Congress— failed, ultimately, because blacks lacked sufficient national political power. The support of the white voting South was valued over the support of the largely disfranchised black minority. Thus, at the national political level, blacks lacked the political assets that could be converted into power. Despite vigorous efforts, in 1930, at the end of the first period of Great Migration as at its outset at the turn of the century, the generalized political capacity of blacks to shape national policy remained low. The uni-directional power relationships that prevailed in the South, those of non-representative, non-responsive, inefficient subjection, were carried over in only slightly muted form at the national level.

There was, however, one political arena in which blacks did possess the political assets necessary for conversion to political power and justly structured political linkages—the cities of the North. There they could vote; in the ethnic-group centred politics of the Northern urban centres they had the potential to enter, as participant-equals, the processes of bargaining, boundary management, and decision-making. It is to an examination of black politics in New York and Chicago that we now turn, for in these locales the key structural decisions were made in the critical and fluid period of migration.

Chapter Five

Parallel Institutions in New York City

WITH the exception of Chicago, no city felt the impact of the black migration from the South more than New York. In 1890, 36,617 New Yorkers (including those in the yet unconsolidated boroughs) were black; in 1900, 60,666; in 1910, 91,709; in 1920, 152,467; by 1930, New York City's black population numbered 327,706.[1] In 1890, one person in seventy in Manhattan (where most of the city's blacks lived) was black; in 1930, one in nine. By 1910, New York's black population was the second highest for any American city; by 1920, it was the largest in the country. In 1890, Harlem was a semi-rural, all-white, upper-class community; in 1930, James Weldon Johnson correctly described Harlem as '*the* Negro metropolis' in America (see Table 5.1.).

TABLE 5.1: BLACK POPULATION OF NEW YORK CITY, 1900–30

Year	Black Population	Total New York City	Per Cent Black	Per Cent Increase of Black Population
1900	60,666	3,437,202	1·8	54
1910	91,709	4,766,883	1·9	51
1920	152,467	5,620,048	2·7	66
1930	327,706	6,930,446	4·7	115

SOURCE: U.S. Census reports, 1900–30.

The movement of New York's blacks from Southern Manhattan to the mid-town neighbourhoods of the Tenderloin and San Juan Hill, and finally to Harlem, and the transition of Harlem from a genteel community to an overcrowded slum have been superbly documented in

[1] Seth Scheiner, *Negro Mecca* (New York, 1965), p. 221; George Edmund Haynes, *The Negro at Work in New York City* (New York, 1912), p. 47. The population for 1890 was computed by adding Scheiner's figure for Brooklyn to Haynes's population statistics for the other boroughs.

TABLE 5.2: NEW YORK CITY BLACK POPULATION BY BOROUGHS

		Per Cent of Total Borough			
Year	Manhattan	Brooklyn	Bronx	Queens	Richmond
1900	2·0	1·2	1·2	1·7	1·6
1910	2·6	1·4	1·0	1·1	1·3
1920	4·8	1·6	0·7	1·1	1·3
1930	12·0	2·7	1·0	1·7	1·6

SOURCE: George M. Furniss, 'The Political Assimilation of Negroes in New York City', unpublished Ph.D. thesis, Columbia University, 1969, p. 21.

Gilbert Osofsky's *Harlem: The Making of a Ghetto*.[2] As a result of the extension of the city's mass-transit subway line to Harlem in 1902, the area rapidly became the target of real estate speculators, white and black, interested in quick profits. The anticipated profits, however, did not materialize. In anticipation of the subway extension, too many houses had been built. As a consequence, many of the buildings remained partially unoccupied and some were without any tenants at all even after the subway line opened. Rents were high and the expected rush to suburban Harlem never occurred. In spite of a well-organized campaign to keep Harlem white, building owners were compelled, as real estate values fell drastically, to rent to blacks. Those who were not prepared to let to blacks sold to landlords who were. Between 1907 and 1914 over 65 per cent of Harlem's buildings changed ownership.[3]

By 1920, 73,000 of Manhattan's 109,000 blacks lived in Harlem. The area's black population more than doubled to 165,000 by 1930 (see Table 5.3). As a result of indecent overcrowding, exorbitant rentals, the sub-division of flats, the practice of taking in lodgers, and landlord neglect, by 1930 Harlem was a slum. An invisible, but very real, wall made it a ghetto as well.[4]

[2] Gilbert Osofsky, *Harlem: The Making of a Ghetto* (New York, 1963). This invaluable, exciting study is the best book to date on Harlem in the period of the Great Migration. It suffers, however, from occasional analytical weaknesses which are most prominent, I believe, in chapter 11 which deals with Harlem's politics. For other accounts of the early development of Harlem as a black community, see James Weldon Johnson, *Black Manhattan* (New York, 1968), 145ff.; Roi Ottley, *New World A-Coming* (New York, 1968), p. 25ff.; and Roi Ottley and William J. Weatherby, *The Negro in New York* (New York, 1967), pp. 183ff.

[3] Ibid., pp. 90–1, 109. Samuel Battle, New York's first black policeman, described this Harlem in flux: 'All of Eighth Avenue was Irish and Seventh Avenue was a mixture of Irish and Jewish. 135th Street to 140th Street, and any place below 133rd Street was Irish, German, and Italian.... This was a transition period, whites to Negroes. There were houses where Italian, Irish, and Jewish lived, but they'd let colored people in if they paid more money.... A lot of people got wealthy as a result.' 'The Reminiscences of Samuel Battle', Oral History Project, Special Collections, Columbia University Library, New York City.

[4] Osofsky, op. cit., p. 136.

TABLE 5.3: BLACK POPULATION IN HARLEM, BY
ASSEMBLY DISTRICTS

			Per Cent Black			
Assembly Districts:[a]	11	13	17	19	21	22
1920[b]	1·6	7·4	0·8	34·8	48·7	3·4
1930[c]	9	29	30	70	70	[e]
1940[d]	29·2	28·4	61·0	95·3	73·2	43·3

NOTES AND SOURCES: [a] Reapportionment of 1917. There was no change in assembly district boundaries from 1917 to 1944. Thus the 1910 figures are omitted as they are not comparable.

[b] U.S. Bureau of the Census, *Fourteenth Census, Population State Compendium for New York*, pp. 62–8.

[c] Estimate by John Morsell, 'The Political Behavior of Negroes in New York City', unpublished Ph.D. thesis, Columbia University.

[d] U.S. Bureau of the Census, *Characteristics of the Population, 1940, New York State*, p. 138.

[e] Not available.

Table adapted from Furniss, op. cit., p. 203.

The movement of large numbers of blacks qualitatively transformed the group's political possibilities. By 1920, blacks approached a majority of the population in Harlem's two central assembly districts; two decades, even a decade, earlier, when blacks lived in scattered (yet homogeneous) areas, even in the assembly districts of their heaviest settlement they did not constitute 20 per cent of the population, and in most districts less than 10 per cent (see Table 5.4). This demographic pattern made effective black political activity difficult. The two major black population movements of the period, from South to North and from lower and mid-town Manhattan to Harlem, fundamentally altered the black population's political *potential*. In his study of Harlem during the period of migration, Osofsky asserted that the potential was realized. He entitled the book's chapter on ward politics 'A Taste of Honey', arguing that,

. . . while the urbanization of the Negro obviously caused great difficulties, it also provided the base for significant political power—political power unprecedented in the history of the Negro in the North. As the Negro population increased in numbers, the cynical and apathetic attitudes that typified the reactions of politicians in the late nineteenth century came to an end. . . . Although the Negro's political progress in New York City was not an unqualified success, there obviously was greater advance in this sphere of community activity than in all the others. While the social and economic position of the city's Negroes tended to remain stable, or, with the Great Depression, even retrogressed, there was significant political mobility. In the 1890s Negroes were an almost powerless minority group; the least influential minority group in the metropolis. Their role, if any, was on the periphery of municipal affairs. Within the next generation, the generation that settled in Harlem, Negroes became an integral part of city government and politics—and politics proved a wedge for economic advancement.[5]

TABLE 5.4: THE ASSEMBLY DISTRICTS MOST HEAVILY POPULATED BY BLACKS, MANHATTAN, 1900-20

Assembly[a] District	Neighbourhood	Per Cent Black[b]
1900		
11	West Side, Thirties	9·1
27	Midtown, Forties	9·0
25	Midtown, Twenties, Thirties	8·0
19	West Side, Sixties, Seventies	7·7
13	West Side, Forties	6·9
1910		
13[c]	West Side, Fifties, Sixties	17·9[d]
21	Central Harlem	14·9
9	West Side, Thirties	9·8
30	East Harlem (and part of Bronx)	6·8
27	Midtown, Thirties and Forties	6·4
1920		
21[e]	Central Harlem	48·7[f]
19	South Central Harlem	34·8
5	West Side, Forties and Fifties	7·5
13	West Harlem; Morningside Hts	7·4
7	West Side, Sixties to Eighties	5·3

NOTES AND SOURCES: [a] 1894 boundaries.
[b] U.S. Bureau of the Census, *Twelfth Census, Statistics of Population.*
[c] 1907 boundaries.
[d] U.S. Bureau of the Census, *Thirteenth Census, Statistics of Population,* Supplement for New York.
[e] 1917 boundaries.
[f] U.S. Bureau of the Census, Fourteenth Census, *Statistics of Population, State Compendium for New York.*
Table adapted from Furniss, op. cit., p. 202.

This statement is inconsistent. If the 'social and economic position of the city's Negroes tended to remain stable', how then is it possible to assert that success at ward politics was translated into economic gains for New York's blacks? But more significant than this logical lapse, as we shall

[5] Ibid., pp. 159, 177. Osofsky is not alone in his celebration of black political advance in New York in this period. Herman Bloch sees 'the emergence of political recognition' for blacks in late nineteenth century New York. John Henrik Clarke has written that, 'from the beginning, politics was a form of Harlem community activity. After 1900 public recognition was made of this fact. Able spokesmen arose at all levels of municipal politics and demanded greater representation for the community,' demands, he argues, that were successfully met. Herman D. Bloch, *The Circle of Discrimination* (New York, 1969), pp. 187–95; John Henrik Clarke, *Harlem: A Community in Transition* (New York, 1969), p. 229.

see, is Osofsky's confusion of group with individual mobility (which can provide the illusion of group success), and of symbolic recognition with group power. In short, I shall argue that Osofsky was wrong: black political powerlessness was the norm for the generation that settled Harlem. Political progress was not 'a wedge for economic advancement' because in this period there was neither. Though the question of causality may be moot, I agree with Osofsky's implicit assumption that political mobility *may* translate into economic and social mobility as well. Thus it might be argued that as a *result* of their political powerlessness the social and economic problems of the city's blacks grew to unmanageable proportions.

I

The three pre-eminent, and related, features of New York politics in this era were the machine, ethnic-group allegiance, and reform. New York's political machines, like those of other large urban centres, were nurtured by the large-scale European immigration of the period, and depended on the particularistic, neighbourhood-oriented political ethos of the new-comers.[6] The party machines were decentralized, with a dual locus of power; central party leadership in the hands of the party 'boss', and neigh-bourhood leadership at the assembly district level in the hands of district leaders. This decentralized party structure permitted geographically concentrated ethnic groups to secure control of significant political units.

The dividing line between party and government had a tendency to blur. Richard Croker, the Democratic Party (Tammany Hall) leader in the 1890s sought to fuse the two: 'All the employees of the city govern-ment', he stated, 'from the Mayor to the porter who makes the fire in his office should be members of the Tammany organization.'[7] Despite the defeat of the Tammany machine in the Mayoralty campaigns of 1901 and 1913 by an alliance of the Republican party and reform–fusion groups whose central tenets were hostility to party machines, efficiency in government, and government by the skilled,[8] from the consolidation of the city in 1898 to the election of Fiorello LaGuardia in 1933, New York, on the whole, was governed by Tammany mayors. There was little

---

[6] For a discussion of the immigrant pattern of political ethics, see Edward Banfield and James Q .Wilson, *City Politics* (New York, 1963), p. 46, and the essays by Michael Parenti, Raymond Breton, and Raymond Wolfinger in Brett W. Hawkins and Robert Lorinskas, eds. *The Ethnic Factor in American Politics* (Columbus, 1970).

[7] Richard Croker, 'Tammany Hall and the Democracy', *Tammany Hall Souvenir of the Inauguration of Cleveland and Stevenson* (New York, 1893), p. 69. Croker delegated authority on patronage directly to Tammany's thirty-five district leaders, thus tremen-dously strengthening them in their districts. This delegation of patronage responsi-bilities accentuated the decentralized political features of the machine.

[8] For a discussion of reform see Theodore Lowi, *At the Pleasure of the Mayor* (New York, 1964), pp. 187–90. See also Banfield and Wilson, op. cit., p. 47.

doubt in the minds of Tammany politicians as to who ruled: in 1932, when John P. O'Brien won a special election to replace Mayor Jimmy Walker after his resignation, O'Brien was asked whom he would appoint as Police Commissioner. He replied, 'I don't know. They haven't told me yet.'[9] Of the 374 salaried cabinet-level appointments made by Tammany mayors Van Wyck, McClellan, Gaynor, Hylan, Walker, and O'Brien, 277 (74 per cent) went to those who had been active in party affairs.[10]

Machines are pre-eminently vote-getting institutions, and in New York blacks could vote.[11] The overwhelming number of New York's blacks voted Republican in the latter third of the nineteenth century in a reflexive gesture of thanks to the party of the Great Emancipator. Tammany Hall attempted to shift the balance. The first Democratic effort to woo black voters was made in 1886 in the Tenderloin section of Manhattan's West Side. John Scannel, the area's District Leader, invited John Nail, a black saloon-keeper and property owner who had moved to the neighbourhood in 1882, to his office. According to Nail, after a brief exchange of pleasantries, Scannel came to the point: 'We want you to head up Tammany among the colored people. You are not to bother with white people, just the colored. We teach you; you teach them.' Nail later commented, 'What was I to do. I had been a Republican. But there were too many ways these fellows could make it hard for you, like licenses, taxes, assessments, etc.'[12]

Nail's efforts on behalf of Tammany were partially successful. The Democratic party increased its share of the area's black vote; Tammany, in recognition of Nail's accomplishment, placed four patronage positions at his disposal—two cart drivers and two street sweepers.[13]

The Nail–Scannel arrangement, on a small scale, presaged the future pattern of black–Tammany relations: a black 'leader', handpicked by the white-controlled machine, delivered votes while avoiding contact with white voters in the area. In return, the 'leader' achieved prestige because

[9] Alfred Connable and Edward Silberfarb, *Tigers of Tammany* (New York, 1967), p. 286.

[10] Wallace Sayre and Herbert Kaufman, *Governing New York City* (New York, 1965), p. 219. See also E. P. Kilroe, 'Scrapbook', Kilroe Deposit, Special Collections, Columbia University Library; George B. McClellan Jr., 'The Grand Tour: An Old Man's Memories', undated MS. in New York Historical Society archives; and Harold Syrett, ed., *The Gentleman and the Tiger: The Autobiography of George B. McClellan* (New York, 1956), especially pp. 20–7, 230–1.

[11] Though there were significant obstacles to black suffrage before 1870, the passage of the Federal Constitution's fifteenth amendment in that year at least nominally guaranteed blacks equal suffrage rights. See Herman Bloch, *The Circle of Discrimination* (New York, 1969), p. 168.

[12] For a record of the Scannel–Nail conversation and a discussion of Tammany activity in the Tenderloin, see Ralph Bunche, 'The Political Status of the Negro', unpublished 7-volume research memorandum for the Carnegie-Myrdal study *An American Dilemma*, MS. in Schomburg Collection, New York City Public Library (Vol. VI), pp. 1335–6. See also Bloch, op. cit., p. 187.

[13] There were at least 1,500 black voters in Nail's district.

of his influence with his white patrons, and personal privilege or, at a minimum, protection from harassment. The black voters which the 'leader' mobilized were awarded a few menial patronage jobs to create an illusion of progress.

Tammany Hall's second, and far more significant, attempt to lure black votes from the Republicans came in 1897 as the product of the reciprocal needs of Boss Croker and a small, but significant, group of middle-class disenchanted black Republicans. In February 1897 the State Legislature approved a consolidation measure to add the boroughs of Brooklyn, Queens, and Richmond to New York City, with effect from 1 January 1898. The government of Greater New York was to be centralized, with most powers vested in the office of Mayor. The consolidation plan was the handiwork of Thomas Platt, the state's Republican leader, who wanted to end Tammany's political control of New York by adding normally Republican boroughs to the city to offset the traditional Democratic majorities in Manhattan and the Bronx. Hence the election of 1897 would be crucial in determining who would rule the new city of three and a half million people.[14]

In 1897, Richard Croker returned to New York after three years in England and Ireland to take personal charge of the campaign. His position as Tammany leader was now precarious; district leaders, angered by his long absence, threatened to oust him if the Democrats lost the November election. Croker was thus compelled to look for votes for his candidate Robert Van Wyck wherever they could be found. It was Croker's good fortune that a group of New York black Republicans who had expected government appointments by President McKinley, whom they had supported in 1896, were prepared to defect when it became clear that the expected patronage would not be forthcoming. These men were particularly galled by what they considered to be a breach of promise by the Republican District Attorney of New York who, they alleged, had promised to appoint James D. Carr, a black Columbia University graduate, to the office of Assistant District Attorney, but declined to do so after the 1896 election. This group of disappointed Republicans decided to approach Croker, who pledged to secure Carr's appointment and give substantial patronage to blacks in exchange for support for Van Wyck. The group's activities were largely confined to San Juan Hill where they produced over six hundred votes for Tammany. Carr was appointed Assistant District Attorney, and Croker, in the expectation that many more blacks could be induced to vote Democratic, decided to formalize Tammany's relationship with the black community.[15]

In January 1898 Croker appointed Edward 'Chief' Lee, a Virginia-born black whom he knew as head bellman of the Plaza and Murry Hill

[14] See Sayre and Kaufman, op. cit., pp. 13–15.
[15] Roi Ottley, *New World A-Coming: Inside Black America* (Boston, 1943), p. 210. In 1896 'the Republican party in order to appeal to Negro voters, established the

hotels, to lead a new party organization—the United Colored Democracy of Tammany Hall (U.C.D.). Lee's position was analogous to his old job as a bellman;[16] he was hired to serve and would be rewarded in the manner chosen by those he served. Lee, who was appointed to the sinecure of Deputy Sheriff of New York County, was promised patronage 'in the most liberal measure' for the U.C.D.[17]

His political power, however, was more illusory than real. From the date of its founding, his political fief, the United Colored Democracy, compromised the position of New York's blacks. The organization, which, on paper, controlled all political and patronage matters that concerned the city's blacks was, in fact, a powerless segregated institution whose primary tasks were winning votes for Tammany and isolating blacks from positions of real political influence.[18]

The U.C.D. was a city-wide organization; thus blacks were unable to compete for political power on the district level, and as was noted, under the machine it was district political control that mattered. The U.C.D., John Morsell has written,

. . . never, at any time, occupied the role of a Democratic club in the organizational structure of county politics. . . . It did not even have the attribute of a geographical designation, as belonging to this or other Assembly district; it was 'for Negroes' whether they voted in the 19th or the 21st or the 22nd or in any other district. Its leaders may, from time to time, have been listened to when central decisions were made on matters affecting their—or their community's interests, but this never approximated the system of consultation and solicitation which is dictated by custom and practicality in the case of leaders of clubs which are on a footing of recognition by the county leadership.[19]

Republican National Bureau in Charge of Matters Affecting Colored People. It also made large and liberal promises of patronage to the colored constituency. The Negroes supported McKinley almost to a man, and the Republican candidate was sent to the White House. But when New York's patronage was distributed, the Negro voters were completely ignored.' Waring Cuney, 'The United Coloured Democracy', W.P.A. research paper, MS. in Schomburg Collection, June, 1939, p. 2. See also Bloch, op. cit., pp. 191, 193.

[16] 'Responsible positions in the service occupations yielded the best wages a Negro could earn, and their occupants formed a second-echelon elite just below the few professionals and college educated individuals. Among these lower-elite positions were headwaiters in major hotels, chief bellmen at the same hotels, head redcaps, Pullman car porters, and dining car stewards.' Furniss, op. cit., p. 57.

[17] Ibid., pp. 2–3.

[18] 'In time', Roi Ottley has aptly noted, 'Lee was referred to as the "Black Croker"— a name he hardly deserved. He was without voice in the councils of Tammany Hall, and only a few crumbs fell to Negroes beyond the appointment of James D. Carr as the first Negro Deputy Assistant District Attorney.' Ottley, op. cit., pp. 210–11. The quality that most endeared Lee to Croker, one observer has noted, was his (perceived) ability to take direction without complaint. See M. Rothman, 'Chief Lee', W.P.A. research paper, MS. in Schomburg Collection, New York Public Library.

[19] John Morsell, 'The Political Behavior of Negroes in New York City', unpublished Ph.D. thesis, Columbia University, 1951, pp. 28–31.

F

By precluding neighbourhood control, potential black political power was thus channelled through the U.C.D. into harmless activity.[20]

A faction of 'progressives', with close ties to the state Democratic organization, led by Robert Wood, which opposed the U.C.D.'s policies of accommodation and sought to change the U.C.D. into a pressure group for civic improvement, ousted Lee in 1911. Tammany responded by simply ignoring the U.C.D. during Wood's four years as leader. Wood died in 1915; Ferdinand Q. Morton, a Lee protégé, was elected to succeed him. Morton purged those who had opposed his candidacy. Once again, the U.C.D. was under absolute Tammany control.[21]

The newly elected Morton, who often spoke derisively of the black masses, proved to be an ideal token leader from Tammany's perspective.[22] 'Morton', Ralph Bunche has written, 'was about all the whites wanted in their Negro leader, He asked Tammany for little, and gave that begrudgingly to his Negro followers.'[23] Because he demanded so little, and deferred to Tammany and Harlem's white district leaders, Morton regained for the U.C.D. the position it had had when Lee was leader, as the dispenser of black patronage.

Under Morton's direction, the United Colored Democracy for the first time produced large numbers of black votes for Tammany. In 1917, John Hylan, the Democratic candidate for Mayor, polled 27 per cent of the black vote. In his 1921 re-election bid, Hylan, advised by Morton, made a direct attempt to obtain black support. In July, the Mayor solicited contributions for the Urban League, noting 'its valued contributions not only to the welfare of our Negro citizens, but to the entire city.'[24] The

---

[20] George Furniss reports that in an interview held in October 1965, Bertram Baker, Brooklyn's first black district leader, noted 'that the white district leaders originally were in favor of the county leader distributing party patronage directly to Negroes via the ethnic auxiliary, despite the fact that the ethnic organization violated the cardinal political machine principle of territorial control by district leaders. Negroes were told that they had to recognize that the average white clubhouse member was prejudiced against Negroes. The white district leaders could not afford to alienate the white members of their clubs by giving club patronage to Negro party workers, although they might wish to do so, the argument continued. By having patronage distributed directly to Negroes by the county leader through the Negro auxiliary, the conflict for the white leader was resolved.' Furniss, op. cit., pp. 268–9.

[21] In 1910, a Democratic state organization was created with James Carr and Robert Wood as the chief assistants to the chairman, Judge James Matthews. This group planned and carried out the takeover of the U.C.D. By 1913, Carr and Wood were quarrelling. Lee supported Wood in order to regain influence in the U.C.D. See August Meier, 'The Negro and the Democratic party', *Phylon* (Vol. 17, 2nd quarter, 1956), pp. 183–4.

[22] My late colleague Wallace Sayre, who served with Morton on the Civil Service Commission under Mayor LaGuardia, remembered Morton as a kind, warm friend, and as a person very much out of touch with the Harlem community.

[23] Bunche, op. cit., Vol. VI, p. 1337.

[24] Copy of letter sent out 8 July 1921, in Hylan Papers, Negro File, Municipal Archives, New York City.

U.C.D. established a Hylan League in Harlem which stressed the Mayor's repeated opposition to the fare increase, from five to eight cents, sought by the city's traction companies. This issue, understandably, was of relevance to the city's black newcomers. Hylan's share of the black vote nearly tripled to 73 per cent.[25]

A fortnight before the election, Hylan wrote Joseph McLane who was active in U.C.D. affairs, 'Your race has too long segregated itself politically. I can think of nothing which will contribute more effectively towards your progress . . . than this removal of the barriers behind which you so long remained in political isolation.'[26] After his election, however, Hylan refused to alter the segregated status of the U.C.D. He was understandably reluctant to tamper with the organizational structure that had produced the impressive black vote.

Ferdinand Morton, not the black community as a whole, was rewarded by the Mayor. There had been considerable agitation by a vocal group of black women for a black Judgeship for Harlem. Morton had withheld his support, thinking the demand politically imprudent. After Hylan's re-election, however, Morton approached Tammany Hall to nominate himself for the position. Tammany, which was as yet unprepared for a black judge, struck a bargain: Hylan appointed Morton to the three-member Civil Service Commission, a cabinet level position.[27]

Morton, from this strategic vantage point, now controlled many city jobs, but, whether because he was only one member of the three-man board or because he refused to exercise his powers to the fullest lest he antagonize his patrons, was unable or unwilling to see that a fair share went to blacks. The successes he had were limited in impact to the small black bourgeoisie of which he was a part, and even for this group his only achievements under Hylan were the appointment of four black physicians of the staff of Harlem Hospital and the establishment of a training school for black nurses. Hylan, in turn, used these low-visibility appointments to claim that in his administration 'appointments to the city service have been made without discrimination of any kind'; Morton's position and the appointment 'by the Medical Board of Harlem Hospital of four members of the colored race to the medical staff', he boasted in a letter to the editor

[25] 'The Negro Vote', W.P.A. research paper, MS. in Schomburg Collection, New York Public Library.

[26] Hylan to Joseph S. McLane, 26 October 1921, in Hylan papers.

[27] Lowi, op. cit., p. 42; Osofsky, op. cit., p. 169. Another version is presented by Furniss: 'In the 1921 campaign, there was pre-election bargaining by Negroes for specific positions. A delegation of Harlem Negroes visited Charles F. Murphy, the Tammany leader, and pledged their support of the Hylan ticket if Murphy would promise to have a Negro judge appointed in the Magistrate's Court. Murphy is said to have "half-promised" to do so. After the election, Murphy apparently offered Ferdinand Q. Morton, the United Colored Democracy leader and an able lawyer, the magistrate post which would have made him the first Negro judge in the city. However, Morton seems to have requested appointment instead as a Civil Service Commissioner.' Furniss, op. cit., p. 230.

of the New York *Afro-American*, 'indicates that recognition of equality of opportunity which this administration has adhered to'.[28] At the dedication of a Harlem square in 1925 in memory of Dorrence Brooks, a soldier killed in the First World War, Hylan again cited this record as he prepared for the city's first intra-party mayoral primary (against James J. Walker), and thanked Harlem's residents for 'the wholehearted cooperation which they have freely extended in the maintenance of law and order and in the promotion of works of civic betterment.'[29]

Walker defeated Hylan in the primary and went on to be elected in November. Like his predecessor, Jimmy Walker paid lip service to the cause of black equality. Speaking at Liberty Hall in Harlem, for example, Walker explicitly denied a report that he had 'caused the ejection of a colored man who was dancing with a white woman and that I had objected to the presence of colored people in the restaurant'. Walker continued, 'I did not believe that the colored people of New York City place any stock in it. I relied on my record of accomplishment on behalf of all the people of New York City, including the colored people.'[30] His 'record of accomplishment', however, was limited to a reorganization of Harlem Hospital which ended the institution's racial restrictions and to Morton's reappointment to the Civil Service Commission.[31] Morton's durability, which was related directly to his usefulness to white politicians, was amazing. When the Republican–Fusion reform movement elected LaGuardia in 1932, Morton left the Democratic party, which was no longer a source of patronage, and was again appointed to the Civil Service Commission. Morton was reappointed by LaGuardia in 1938 and 1944.[32]

The United Colored Democracy was an instrument of political deception. Tammany Hall used it to confer rewards on hand-picked 'leaders', thus convincing them that they were participants, with influence, in the Tammany power structure. These leaders, in turn, pointed to the United Colored Democracy as evidence for Harlem's blacks that meaningful political progress had and was being made. Though Osofsky cites Morton's U.C.D. as evidence for his contention that in this period blacks moved from the periphery to the centre of New York's political

[28] Hylan to George Taylor, 27 July 1925, in Hylan papers.

[29] Copy of speech in Hylan papers.

[30] Speech at Liberty Hall, Harlem, 1 November 1927, copy in James J. Walker papers, the Municipal Archives, New York City.

[31] See Osofsky, op. cit., pp. 169–70.

[32] Ibid., pp. 173–4; Lowi, op. cit., p. 148. A contemporary commented on Morton's leadership of the UCD: 'It cannot be said of Morton that his was a most brilliant leadership. . . . Negroes considered him weak, afraid to demand rights, and lacking in the power to fight for the advantages of political power that would create better working conditions and more pay for the Negro masses. . . . There is no record of his fifteen years in office that shows Morton interested in Harlem's suffering and overcrowded living teeming thousands.' James Gardner, 'Brief History of Ferdinand Q. Morton of New York', W.P.A. research paper, May 1938, MS. in Schomburg Collection.

affairs, he concedes, quite rightly, that 'the UCD's structure *prevented* the emergence of grass-roots ward leaders and centered Negro Democratic influence in the hands of a single, often autocratic, boss.'[33]

As soon as blacks began to vote the Democratic ticket in substantial numbers in local and state elections, 'an inevitable controversy arose between the district leaders of Tammany Hall and the United Colored Democracy over administrative control of the colored Democrats.'[34] George Olvany, who succeeded Charles Murphy as Tammany leader in 1924 sided with Harlem's district leaders the following year by voiding the political status of the U.C.D.,[35] thus reducing the black organization to a civic and social group. Morton, however, secured political recognition for the United Colored Democracy once again in 1930 when Tammany leader John F. Curry channelled most black patronage through Morton's political organization.[36] But with the election of LaGuardia in 1933 and Morton's subsequent defection from the Democratic party, the United Colored Democracy was finally destroyed as a viable political force in New York.[37]

II

The Republican party in New York did not establish an organization comparable to the United Colored Democracy, but it did have a functional substitute—Charles W. Anderson, the party's liaison with the black community, its broker black 'leader' who, in return for personal preferment, delivered votes to the machine.

Anderson became active in Republican district politics in the late 1880s, was elected President of the Young Men's Colored Republican Club, and was appointed to a minor position in a district office of the Internal Revenue Service in 1890. In 1895, Anderson entered the New York State Treasurer's office as a private secretary, and was later appointed chief clerk in the department. In 1898, Theodore Roosevelt, the newly elected Governor of New York, selected Anderson to be supervisor of accounts for the New York Racing Commission.[38] Roosevelt

[33] Osofsky, op. cit., p. 161. Emphasis in original.

[34] 'The Negro Vote', p. 4.

[35] See Cuney, 'The United Coloured Democracy', p. 5.

[36] Morton once told Dr. Sayre that he always viewed the U.C.D. as a temporary expedient to be abandoned as soon as blacks could compete for ward control. The fact that Morton, as late as 1930, fought for the survival of the U.C.D. seems to belie this assertion, for as early as 1917 blacks were elected to state legislative offices. Moreover, by 1930, the black population of central Harlem exceeded 70 per cent. Morsell, 'The Political Behavior of Negroes . . .', p. 26. See also Furness, op. cit., p. 272.

[37] Ultimately, this new arrangement was the undoing of Harlem's white district leaders. Blacks now joined the regular ward Democratic organization, and succeeded in electing a black district leader in 1935.

[38] Osofsky, op. cit., pp. 161-2.

began to channel patronage for blacks through Anderson, much as he later used Booker T. Washington as his national patronage referee. Anderson was made a member of the Republican State Committee where he sat 'as the representative of the Negroes of this State, though representing no district'.[39]

After Roosevelt became President, Anderson sought to maintain their special relationship. In February 1904, a meeting of the Republican State Committee was expected to divide between the supporters of Senator Platt and those of Governor O'dell. Anderson, in a letter marked confidential, urgently sought the help of Booker T. Washington, 'I am friendly with both men', he wrote, 'but am anxious to do as the President would have me. Can you find out which way he is leaning? I do not want to support the one side only to discover afterwards that the President would have had me support the other.'[40]

Anderson's continuing obeisance to Roosevelt and his position as an intimate of Booker T. Washington paid off handsomely in 1905.[41] In late December 1904, Washington met the President to discuss a suitable Federal appointment for Anderson.[42] At the end of an hour's discussion, they agreed that Anderson should be offered a choice of either U.S. Marshal in New York or Collector of Internal Revenue for the second district. Washington counselled Anderson to accept the Collectorship, noting that 'it is possible that some of the newspapers and small fry politicians might make a great outcry over the fact that a Negro was put in a place where he would have to arrest white people'.[43] Anderson, who 'always found that in the last analysis the Doctor Washington's judgement is usually right', accepted the revenue post. His control of black politics and patronage in New York City's Republican party was now absolute.[44]

Like Ferdinand Morton, Anderson was isolated from and often disparaged the mass of his people whose views he claimed and was

[39] New York *Age* (9 March 1905). In this post, Anderson followed William B. Derrick, minister of the Bethel African Methodist Church in Greenwich Village, who was selected by the white Republican leadership as the black representative at large on the Republican State Committee in 1889. New York *Age* (19 October 1889).

[40] Anderson to Booker T. Washington, 21 February 1904, in Booker T. Washington papers, Library of Congress, Washington, D.C.

[41] 'Outside of his secretary, Emmett Scott', August Meier has written, 'no one was closer and more useful to Washington than Charles W. Anderson'. August Meier, *Negro Thought in America, 1880–1915* (Ann Arbor, 1966), p. 254.

[42] Washington and Roosevelt had first corresponded on the matter of a Federal position for Anderson in June 1904. Washington suggested that something be done for Anderson, and on 14 June the President's secretary replied that that suggestion 'is peculiarly acceptable to the President'. Washington papers.

[43] Washington to Anderson, 23 December 1904, Washington papers.

[44] Anderson to Emmett Scott, 19 April 1910, Washington papers. Roosevelt wanted to appoint a black to a major Federal post to offset Southern criticisms of the Crum appointment. White Southerners had argued that the President would not dare to make a comparable appointment in the North. See the New York *Age* (9 March 1905).

thought to articulate.[45] His racial views were close to those of his mentor, Booker T. Washington. Of W. E. B. DuBois and the other blacks active in the Niagara Movement who demanded political equality and racial integration, Anderson wrote, 'We do not belong to that group to whom nothing is desirable but the impossible.'[46]

As a patronage referee, Anderson's practices closely followed the examples of Lee and Morton of the U.C.D. He described the candidates he hoped to appoint as meeting the 'test of honesty, capability, discretion, and at the same time possess gentility of deportment and address. This last consideration,' he wrote, 'is not to be sneezed at. . . . Given ability and honesty, no small part of the success of a colored man in public office is due to discretion and gentlemanly deportment.'[47]

Anderson spent almost as much time battling against black militants as he did fighting for patronage.[48] He referred often to the Niagara and NAACP leadership as 'the enemy', 'our enemies', and 'our Boston opponents', and attempted to distinguish between 'the good dogs and the mangy curs'. When writing of DuBois and Trotter, Anderson begged Washington's pardon 'for wasting so much time on such cattle'.[49]

Anderson's antipathy to blacks who shunned his advice to be patient, prove their worthiness through industry, thrift and Christian behaviour, and accept tokenism as a substitute for equality, extended beyond rhetoric. Those who held patronage positions were liable to be removed. A good example is the case of Hubert Harrison, a West Indian Socialist party member and a black nationalist. On 10 September 1911, Anderson wrote Washington:

Do you remember Hubert H. Harrison? He is the man who wrote two nasty articles against you in the New York 'Sun'. He is a clerk in the Post Office. The Postmaster is my personal friend, as you probably know. Harrison has had charges preferred against him and I think he is liable to be dismissed from the service. If not dismissed, he will get severe punishment. Can you see the hand? I think you can. Please destroy this that it may not fall under another eye— unless it be Emmett's [Scott]. I will attend to Harrison. If he escapes me he is a dandy.[50]

---

[45] Furniss notes that Anderson lacked a significant personal following, and was often hooted down derisively by Harlem blacks when he attempted to speak at political rallies. Furniss, op. cit., p. 188. Also see Osofsky, op. cit., p. 162.

[46] Anderson to Scott, 1 November 1905, cited in ibid., p. 165.

[47] Anderson to Washington, 9 December 1905. Washington papers.

[48] Anderson assured Washington that 'the Atlanta crowd' would not get 'ahead him', that 'I am working day and night now and am keeping on the job . . . my endeavour is to lose no man on our side, however much I disagree with him personally, and gain a recruit from the other side, whenever and wherever possible.' 29 December 1910, Washington papers.

[49] Anderson to Washington, 16 January 1904 and 17 February 1907. Washington papers.

[50] Anderson to Washington, 10 September 1911, Washington papers.

Three weeks later Anderson wrote again:

I am sure you will regret to learn that Mr. Hubert H. Harrison has been dismissed from his position as clerk in the New York Post Office. I am certain that you will also regret to hear that he is blaming me for his dismissal. . . . He is now stumping for the Socialist party, and will probably have plenty of time in the future to learn that God is not good to those who do not behave themselves.[51]

Patronage was not only, perhaps not even primarily, to be used to secure group mobility, but as a weapon in the Washington–DuBois ideological controversy.

Osofsky pointed to Anderson to demonstrate that 'the situation began to change in the early twentieth century',[52] but Anderson's role, like that of the U.C.D., was deceptive, for it seemed to denote progress. Actually, the Republican party used Anderson as a safety valve; wasn't the manner in which he was treated by the party proof enough that Republicans meant what they said about equality? Whenever a black was needed to round out the ethnic and racial balance of official committees, the city, when under Republican–Fusion rule, turned to Anderson. He served on Mayor Mitchel's committee of welcome for Marshal Joffre and members of the French High Commission, on the commission that welcomed Prime Minister Nitti of Italy, and on the committee that received the bodies of American marines killed on Vera Cruz, to name only a few.[53]

New York's press habitually referred to Anderson, patronizingly, as 'the Negroes' best', as 'an honor to his race'.[54] 'Charles W. Anderson', wrote the New York *World*, 'is a striking example of the Negro fading into the everyday life and the most advanced customs of a great American metropolis.'[55] Anderson, the individual, clearly had achieved striking success; but the group he claimed to lead, equally clearly, had not. When Anderson became the Republican party's broker black 'leader', the city's blacks were increasing in number, in geographic concentration, hence in potential political influence. Anderson, however, acted as a buffer to isolate his party's white leadership from the pressures of blacks who

---

[51] Anderson to Washington, 30 October 1911, Washington papers. Harrison did not repent of his views. In 1917, two years after Washington's death, he wrote, 'until this rising generation of Negroes can shake off the tramels of such time-serving leaders as Mr. Washington . . . there can be little hope of change.' In 1919, he was active in the Harlem Lafayette Theatre strike, and, in 1921, joined the predominantly West Indian radical, nationalist, and later Communist, African Blood Brotherhood. Hubert Harrison, *The Negro and the Nation* (New York, 1917), pp. 46–7, and Cruse, op. cit., pp. 75, 45. Morton also punished black militants who held patronage positions. See Osofsky, op. cit., p 173.

[52] Ibid., p. 161.

[53] Listed in *Amsterdam News* (11 March 1931); in *File of Newspaper Clippings on Charles W. Anderson*, the Schomburg Collection.

[54] New York *World* (8 July 1921), in ibid.

[55] Ibid.

demanded fundamental changes in the racial *status quo*. As a consequence, the Republican party, protected from organized pressure for structural and institutional changes, never had to choose either to match its rhetorical zeal for black rights with meaningful action (at the risk of alienating other ethnic groups), or lose black votes.

Anderson was a Federal employee and depended on Booker T. Washington's access to Roosevelt and Taft to maintain his job and influence. With Wilson's election, and subsequently as blacks in the Federal service were dismissed in large numbers, Anderson's position became increasingly precarious. At first, Anderson believed that DuBois's supporters would secure his removal. 'The black Democrats', he wrote Washington just after Wilson's victory, 'are crowing very loudly and have already divided the offices now held by colored Republicans among themselves.... A half-dozen of them are pointed for my place.'[56] By March 1913, as Wilson's racial policies became unambiguous, Anderson began to despair: 'As for me', he wrote to Scott, 'I am sitting tight and making no effort to be retained. I am confident that if my record will not sustain me, no other influence I could bring to bear could. . . . I am afraid we are up against the real thing, at last.'[57] President Wilson, however, found Anderson, who never publicly voiced disagreement with the Administration's policies, useful to maintain in office, for a while longer, because Wilson had decided to intervene in New York City politics to punish Tammany Hall for having supported Clark Champ at the Democratic Convention of 1912. Wilson successfully urged the Republican party in New York to accept the Fusion party candidacy of a Democratic reformer, John Puroy Mitchel.[58] Thus Anderson was informed that he 'would be retained', he told Washington, 'if I could *absolutely guarantee* that I could deliver the colored vote in this city to Mr. Mitchel'.[59] Though Anderson insisted that he believed his apparent success in staying on 'will not be real', he worked 'day and night to elect Mr. Mitchel and the entire Republican ticket'.[60] Mitchel's election enabled Anderson to continue to dispense black Republican patronage. In 1915, he finally resigned his Federal post at the Administration's request.[61] Within a few months, Republican Governor Whitman appointed Anderson to a supervisory position with the State Agricultural Department; in 1923, Anderson returned to the Internal Revenue Service when President Coolidge appointed him Collector for the third (Harlem) district of New York, a position he held until his retirement in 1934.[62]

---

[56] Anderson to Washington, 8 November 1912, Washington papers.
[57] Anderson to Scott, 14 March 1913, Washington papers.
[58] See Lowi, op. cit., pp. 176–7.
[59] Anderson to Washington, 13 September 1913, Washington papers.
[60] Anderson to Washington, 16 October 1913, Washington papers.
[61] Curiously enough, a testimonial dinner for Anderson was chaired by John Nail, Tammany's first black 'leader'.
[62] See Osofsky, op. cit., pp. 166–8.

III

Edward Lee, Ferdinand Morton, and Charles Anderson justified the nature of their political activity by asserting that in realistic fashion they achieved what blacks really needed, not status-oriented gains like full integration or social equality but jobs for the masses. 'As usual', Anderson insisted, 'the oldtime politicians are giving us recognition, but the reformer and sociologist and race-worker is giving us pleasant talk. As for me, I would rather have less praise and more jobs.'[63] In municipal elections, Anderson's Republican machine and the U.C.D. bid for black votes with claims of patronage successes. The rhetoric of patronage reached its most strident pitch in the campaign of 1913. Anderson authored a widely circulated campaign leaflet entitled, *Attention! Colored Voters: Some Facts You Should Remember: Some Facts You Should Not Forget*, which cautioned, 'The colored voter should stand with his friends in this campaign,' and asked, 'Where do these friends stand and whom are they supporting?' The pamphlet's tone was almost threatening:

Remember: Postmaster Morgan has 411 colored men drawing salaries of $360,000 per year. POSTMASTER MORGAN is supporting Mr. MITCHEL.
Remember: The Collector of Customs has under him 170 colored men with salaries ranging from $840 to $2,200 per year. THE COLLECTOR OF CUSTOMS is Hon. JOHN PUROY MITCHEL.
Remember: The two collectors of Internal Revenue in Manhattan have 10 colored employees at salaries ranging from $1,000 to $2,500 per year. The TWO COLLECTORS are supporting Mr. MITCHEL.
Remember: The U.S. Marshall has a colored deputy in his office. The U.S. MARSHAL is supporting Mr. MITCHEL.
Remember: District Attorney Whitman has a colored Deputy Assistant District Attorney. DISTRICT ATTORNEY WHITMAN is supporting Mr. MITCHEL.
Remember: Borough President McAneney has a colored Inspector of Water Meters and a colored Inspector of Highways and other colored employees. BOROUGH PRESIDENT McANENEY is supporting Mr. MITCHEL.
Remember: The Postmaster of Brooklyn has 100 colored clerks and carriers under him. POSTMASTER VOORHEES is supporting Mr. MITCHEL.
Remember: Comptroller Prendergast has a colored clerk and a colored bank messenger. THE COMPTROLLER is supporting Mr. MITCHEL.[64]

Of the 697 patronage positions mentioned in the leaflet, 692 were Federal posts, only five were municipal in origin. Since the Republican party had ruled the consolidated city for only two of its sixteen years of existence, and since Anderson's influence depended on his national ties to the Republican presidents, these striking figures of national success and municipal patronage failure are not surprising. But even the national

---

[63] Anderson to Washington, 11 January 1910, Washington papers.
[64] Copy in Washington papers.

figures, when examined closely, prove disappointing. Of the 692 Federal jobs, 511 were in the postal service, yet in Chicago, whose black population was only half of New York's, in 1910 there were 566 black postal employees.[65]

The United Colored Democracy was able to counter the Republican–Fusion campaign claims with the correct assertion that the bulk of municipal patronage given to blacks came from the beneficence of Tammany Hall. In a pamphlet colourfully entitled *Tammany Hall versus Fusion or Organized Democracy against Disorganized Autocracy and Bastard Reform*, the U.C.D. argued forcefully that while the Republican–Fusion Alliance had been responsible for distributing city patronage worth $4823 a year, 'through the kindness of Tammany Hall, Colored citizens are receiving nearly $600,000 a year from the treasury of the city'.[66]

It is clear, then, that the standard of success set by the period's black politicians themselves was based on patronage achievements. Judging these men by their own standards, to what extent did they succeed?

In the 1913 U.C.D. campaign tract, the organization listed 'nearly all of the positions held by Colored citizens in this city under the Democratic party since 1897'. The list, which is the most complete and accurate available for the period, deserves detailed scrutiny, for it sheds considerable light on the scope and extent of black patronage (see Table 5.5).

Between 1897 and 1913, as New York's black population grew from over 60,000 to almost 150,000, United Colored Democracy activity produced fewer than 850 city patronage jobs for blacks, the overwhelming number of which were for unskilled heavy labour, the type of employment which was possible for blacks to obtain in the economy's private sector. Moreover, of the 850 municipal positions, over 600 were in the Street Cleaning Department which was seriously understaffed because of recruitment difficulties. These positions alone accounted for over $470,000 of the $600,000 earned by blacks in the public service.[67] A breakdown of black public employment in 1910 by classes is revealing (see Table 5.6). Only one black, an Assistant Corporation Counsel, was employed in a position that was exempt from civil service regulations. Thirty-five were in positions filled by competitive or non-competitive examinations, while the vast majority, 475, were employed as menial labourers.[68] This distribution remained fairly constant. By 1930, only

[65] H. F. Gosnell, *Negro Politicians: The Rise of Negro Politics in Chicago* (Chicago, 1967), p. 302.

[66] United Colored Democracy of Tammany Hall, *Tammany Hall versus Fusion or Organized Democracy against Disorganized Autocracy and Bastard Reform*, 1913 election pamphlet, copy in Schomburg Collection, pp. 6–7.

[67] Ibid., p. 8.

[68] George Snowden, 'The Growth of Negro Office Holders and Employees in the Government of New York City, since 1898', unpublished M.A. thesis, New York University, 1935, p. 47.

TABLE 5.5: DEMOCRATIC PARTY BLACK PATRONAGE, NEW YORK CITY, 1897–1913

Board of Education	70 female teachers
	6 male teachers
	1 assistant musical director
Borough Presidents' Offices	
a. The Bronx	1 messenger
b. Manhattan	1 inspector of highways
	1 inspector of vaults
	1 foreman
	5 corporation inspectors
	1 clerk
	1 cleaner
	1 elevator attendant
c. Queens and Richmond	several labourers
Bridge Department	1 engineman
	1 marine stoker
	1 marine sounder
	1 stenographer
	1 watchman
	6 labourers
City Chamberlain's Office	2 messengers
Commissioner of Licenses	1 inspector of licences
Coroner's Office, Brooklyn	1 clerk
Corporation Counsel's Office	1 assistant corporation counsel
	1 confidential attendant
Department of Charities	1 messenger
Department of Health	4 sanitary inspectors
	1 clerk
	7 inspectors of disinfectant
	several nurses
	1 typewriting copyist
Department of Sewers	2 labourers
Department of Water Supply	1 assistant engineer
	2 inspectors of water meters
	1 inspector of hydrants
	3 clerks
	1 messenger
District Attorney's Office	1 assistant district attorney
	1 diary clerk
	2 messengers
District Attorney's Office, Brooklyn	1 clerk
Dock Department	2 stenographers
	2 clerks
	6 marine stokers
	30 labourers
Finance Department	1 law clerk
	2 clerks
	1 messenger

Fire Department	1 deputy inspector of combustibles
	1 clerk
	1 driver
	1 inspector of oils
	1 first-grade fireman
Mayor's Office	2 sealers of weights and measures
	1 executive clerk
Park Department	12 labourers
Police Department	2 patrolmen
Register's Office	2 copyists
Register's Office, Brooklyn	1 clerk
Sheriff's Office	1 assistant deputy sheriff
	3 cleaners
Street Cleaning Department	2 detail foremen
	1 inspector of mud scows
	1 inspector of garbage
	(over) 600 drivers and sweepers
Surrogate's Office	1 messenger
Tax Department	1 deputy commissioner of taxes
	2 clerks
	1 messenger
Tenement House Department	1 clerk

SOURCE: United Colored Democracy of Tammany Hall, *Tammany Hall versus Fusion*....

TABLE 5.6: BLACK PATRONAGE, BY CLASSES OF PUBLIC
EMPLOYMENT, NEW YORK CITY, 1910

Class	Number
Exempt	1
By examination	
a. competitive	30
b. non-competitive	5
Labourers	475
Total	511

SOURCE: adapted from figures provided by Civil Service Commissioner Ferdinand Q. Morton, 1934; in George Snowden, 'The Growth of Negro Office Holders . . .', p. 47.

TABLE 5.7: EXEMPT BLACK PATRONAGE, NEW YORK CITY,
1898–1930

Office	1st Appointment	Number
Assistant District Attorney	1898	7
Assistant Corporation Counsel	1910	4
Civil Service Commissioner	1922	1

SOURCE: Snowden, op. cit., p. 37.

twelve blacks had been appointed to exempt-municipal positions; of these, eleven were either chosen to be Assistant District Attorneys (seven) or Assistant Corporation Counsels (four), positions which had become 'black jobs'. The remaining exempt appointee was Ferdinand Q. Morton[69] (see Table 5.7).

In 1910, 1·9 per cent of the city's and 2·6 per cent of Manhattan's population was black, yet just under 1 per cent of the city's 52,978 employees were black. In the second decade of this century, as the proportion of black residents in New York increased to 2·7 per cent and in Manhattan to 4·3, the percentage of black employees increased only to 1·7. Thus despite the drop in European migration and the massive movement of blacks to the city, the gap between population and patronage employment remained stationary.[70] In the next decade, the rate of growth of black municipal employment, compared to white, actually declined: in 1920, 973 of every 100,000 whites worked for the city, compared to

TABLE 5.8: BLACK PATRONAGE IN MUNICIPAL DEPARTMENTS, NEW YORK CITY, 1934–5

Department	Total Employees	Black Employees	% Black
Accounts	121	0	0·00
Buildings	206	3	1·41
Correction	973	14	1·30
Docks	556	17	3·05
Finance	1,435	21	1·41
Fire	7,714	11	0·15
Health	2,588	141	5·43
Hospitals	13,200	781	5·09
Law	524	4	0·07
Licences	73	0	0·00
Markets	295	3	1·05
Parks	3,571	71	1·09
Plant and Structure	3,400	40	1·01
Police	19,725	127	0·64
Sanitation	14,950	649	4·31
Taxes	387	3	0·08
Tenement House	442	18	4·01
Water, Gas, and Electricity	3,326	25	0·07
Welfare	596	33	5·05
Works	11,028	367	3·33
Total	85,107	2,294	2·69

SOURCE: Snowden, op. cit., p. 44.

69 Ibid., p. 37.
70 Compiled from figures in ibid., p. 49, and in Scheiner, op. cit., p. 222.

655 of 100,000 blacks, a difference in the number per 100,000 of 218. In 1930, however, 1,239 whites per 100,000 were in city positions compared to 849 per 100,000 blacks—the differential gap between the two groups had widened to 390. Hence, while the absolute number of Negro city workers had increased in the 1920s from 983 to 2,627, in relative terms the black population's share of available patronage was declining.[71] As late as 1935, only 2·7 per cent of New York City government jobs went to blacks, though the black population then composed approximately 11 per cent of the city total (see Table 5.1). This relative quantitative decline, moreover, was not matched by a qualitative increase. Of the 254 black employees of the Board of Transportation in 1935, for instance, 185 (73 per cent) were employed as porters; there were no blacks in supervisory positions[72] (see Table 5.9).

IV

The most significant independent variable for the student of race politics is the relative power of racial groups to make and carry out decisions and non-decisions; our central question, therefore, is not whether blacks in New York could participate in the city's politics (they could), nor are we

TABLE 5.9: BLACK EMPLOYEES BY POSITION AND NUMBER, BOARD OF TRANSPORTATION, NEW YORK CITY, 1935

Position	Number Employed
Clerk	4
Junior electrical engineer	4
Light maintainer	1
Mechanical draftsman	2
Porter	185
Power cleaner	1
Pump maintainer	1
Shop helper (railroad)	14
Station agent	38
Stenographer and typist	2
Trackman	1
Trunk repairman	1
Total	254

SOURCE: William Jerome Daley (secretary, Board of Transport) to George Snowden, 23 April 1935; in Snowden, op. cit., p. 69.

[71] Snowden, op. cit., p. 49.
[72] Ibid., p. 69. Moreover, John Morsell wrote, 'it is possible to infer with some assurance that the United Colored Democracy's extra-curricular status did not entitle it to any of the low-level patronage—captains, inspectors, clerks, etc.—which are the normal accompaniment of demonstrated control of votes.' Morsell, op. cit., p. 30.

concerned here with shifts in electoral behaviour in the period of migration, but rather, with the terms of participation, with the critical structural decisions that limited and shaped behavioural possibilities. It is precisely this order of questions that has been neglected in previous analyses of black politics in this period (of which Osofsky's work is the leading example).[73] This neglect has produced conclusions about political success based on the study of the behaviour of individual black leaders that are misleading.

The political honey that Osofsky asserted was tasted by New York's blacks, was spooned to a few, but only to a few. The political linkages fashioned in the migration period were the product of a white elite strategy (perhaps not always consciously felt or expressed) of social control that structurally linked blacks to the polity in a manner strikingly different from the decentralized machine links of other ethnic groups.

White Democratic and Republican political leaders wanted, and sometimes very badly needed, black votes, but on terms that did not disturb the racial *status quo* which benefited, psychologically, economically, and politically, a great many New Yorkers. The method used by Tammany and the Republicans has been discussed above: blacks, excluded from the segregated district political clubs (at least until the late 1920s) were linked to the party organizations through city-wide structural buffers—the United Colored Democracy organization and Charles Anderson's functional equivalent. In Halpern's classificatory terms, these relationships were an amalgam of buffering, subjection (since power capabilities were uni-directional), and isolation (in that blacks were isolated from the main stream party structures). Neither the U.C.D. nor the black Republican leadership was representative beyond the symbolic level. They were not formally representative, in that territorial community procedures for leadership selection were absent. The black leaders were chosen by the white party elites, not by the community—territorial or racial—they claimed to represent. They were not descriptively representative, in that their class composition differed strikingly from that of the represented; nor, as we have seen, were they responsive in terms of orientation or efficacious in delivering patronage rewards (their own standard of success).

These liaison or buffer leaders were given a taste of honey, the illusion of political access and some visible patronage. But these political rewards, they knew, came not as the product of independently organized territorial control, but from the white party leadership. The result, of course, was to detach the recognized black leaders from the mass of the black population. If position, for the black leadership, rested not on a mass base from below but was conferred from above, then what was conferred could always be retracted. Thus, both black elites and mass in New York City in the

---

[73] See also, Scheiner, op. cit., and Robert Brisbane, *The Black Vanguard* (Valley Forge, Pa., 1970), especially Chapter 6, for two other leading examples.

critical period of migration, like their Southern brothers, were political objects, not participant-equals. To speak, as does Osofsky, of political linkages with the capacity to transform, of blacks forming 'an integral part of the city government and politics', is to speak the language of illusion.

G

Chapter Six

Black Politics and Political Power in Chicago[1]

FOR many Southern blacks, the place names North and Chicago were interchangeable. In Hattiesberg, Mississippi, a potential migrant remarked, 'Chicago for a while seemed to be everything. You could not rest in your bed at night for Chicago.'[2] Chicago, publicized in the pages of Abbott's *Defender*, famous for its industries, schools, and mail order houses, was the natural geographical terminus for migrants from the border states of Kentucky, Tennessee, and Missouri, and the deep-South states of Mississippi, Georgia, Alabama, and Louisiana.[3] In 1900, of the 1,698,575 citizens of Chicago, only 30,150 were black. By 1930, the city's population had just about doubled to 3,376,438, but the black population had increased eight-fold to 233,903 (see Table 6.1).

TABLE 6.1: THE BLACK POPULATION OF CHICAGO, 1890 TO 1930

Year	Total Population	Black Population	% Black
1890	1,099,850	14,271	1·3
1900	1,698,575	30,150	1·9
1910	2,185,283	44,103	2·0
1920	2,701,705	109,458	4·1
1930	3,376,438	233,903	6·9

SOURCE: U.S. Census reports, 1890–1930.

[1] Chicago's black ghetto, in all its features, has probably been more intensively studied than any other. Nevertheless, in comparison with other American cities to which blacks migrated, the study of race relations in Chicago suffers from a dearth of available primary material and personal manuscripts. For this reason, this chapter relies more than I would have liked on secondary source material.

[2] Emmett J. Scott, *Negro Migration During the War* (New York, 1920), p. 26. Chapter 5 in Scott's work deals with the economic and social conditions of Chicago's black migrants.

[3] Ibid., p. 102. See also, for detailed figures, Allan Spear, *Black Chicago* (Chicago, 1967), pp. 13, 143, and the *Chicago Defender*, especially the issues of February through May 1917 which document the 'Great Northern Drive'.

In Chicago the possibilities for black political power based on ward organization were more promising than in any other American city as a result of three related factors: the city's ethnic heterogeneity, its factional politics based on ethnic coalition-building, and the size of its electoral boundaries which created self-contained, ethnically homogeneous political units.

G. W. Steevens, the English journalist, described Chicago in 1897 as 'the most American of American cities, and yet the most mongrel; the second American city of the globe, the fifth German city, the third Swedish, the second Polish, the first and only veritable Babel of the age.'[4] In 1890 three-quarters of the population either had been born abroad or had parents who had been; and it was only in the 1890s that the New Immigration from Eastern and Southern Europe began to make an impact. In 1920, only 642,871 of the city's 2,701,705 residents were native whites of native parentage. Well over a million whites were the second generation children of immigrants, and nearly a million themselves were foreign-born.[5] Chicago was, indeed, 'a mosaic of foreign language cities' with over twenty-five distinct ethnic communities[6] (see Table 6.2).

As a consequence of the mosaic pattern of ethnic settlement in Chicago, the city's political parties, to win elections, had to put together electoral majorities composed of blocs of ethnic groups; as a result, the ethnic group, *as a group*, functioned as a pressure group that could bargain and threaten sanctions. In turn, the opportunity for ethnic communities to enter the political process acted to solidify group consciousness and to perpetuate the division of the city, demographically and politically, into ethnic components.[7]

---

[4] G. W. Steevens, *The Land of the Dollar* (New York, 1897), in Pierce, op. cit., p. 396.

[5] Charles Merriam, *Chicago: A More Intimate View of Urban Politics* (New York, 1929), p. 134.

THE POPULATION OF CHICAGO AND ITS DECENNIAL INCREASE IN POPULATION, BY RACE AND NATIVITY, 1900 TO 1930

Year	Native White	% Inc.	Foreign Born	% Inc.	Black	% Inc.
1900	1,081,720	—	586,705	—	30,150	—
1910	1,357,840	25·5	783,340	33·4	44,103	46·3
1920	1,783,687	31·4	808,560	3·1	109,458	148·2
1930	2,275,674	27·9	866,861	6·2	233,903	113·7

SOURCES: adapted from O. and B. Duncan, *The Negro Population of Chicago* (Chicago, 1957), p. 24, and St. Clair Drake and Horace Cayton, *Black Metropolis* (New York, 1962), Vol. I, p. 8.

[6] Ray Ginger, *Altgeld's America* (New York, 1958), p. 96.

[7] For an illuminating discussion see Theodore Lowi, *At the Pleasure of the Mayor* (New York, 1964), Chapter 2, especially p. 44. Chicago's ethnic politics are discussed in Caroll Wooddy, *The Chicago Primary of 1926* (Chicago, 1926), pp. 184–5.

TABLE 6.2: NATIONALITY GROUPS IN CHICAGO (INCLUDING SECOND GENERATION), COMPRISING AT LEAST 1% OF CITY TOTAL, 1920

Nationality	Number	Percentage
American (white, native parentage)	642,871	23·8
Polish	319,644	11·8
German	285,216	10·6
Russian	230,668	8·6
Swedish	154,051	5·7
Irish	145,919	5·4
Italian	129,815	4·8
Czech	116,115	4·3
Negro	109,458	4·1
Austrian	72,531	2·7
English	67,907	2·5
Canadian (excepting French)	62,006	2·3
Hungarian	61,847	2·3
Norwegian	53·891	2·0
Lithuanian	43,274	1·6
Danish	29,450	1·1
Greek	27,017	1·0

SOURCE: Chicago Association of Commerce, in Merriam, *Chicago*, p. 135.

Chicago's ethnic enclaves largely coincided with the political unit of the ward. Compared with New York's, Chicago's wards (fifty after 1921) were small and compact, hence for the most part ethnically homogeneous. The multitude of national groups in Chicago had, as a result of this institutional feature of the city's politics, a political base from which to bargain, to attain access to the decision makers, or become decision makers themselves. The politics of Chicago were the politics of boundary management and direct ethnic group bargaining.[8]

In terms of numbers, the city's black population was one of many ethnic groups. As many blacks moved into the city from the South, blacks quickly gained numerical control of a number of political wards. In New York, blacks could vote but, as we have seen, were effectively excluded from ward politics; in Chicago, blacks could not only vote, but almost from the onset of the migration, could, in realistic fashion, fight for

[8] The ethnic nature of Chicago politics was illustrated in microcosm in the nineteenth ward where Alderman Johnny Powers, the Irish boss, campaigned under the name Johnnie De Pow after the neighbourhood became predominantly Italian. Henry Pelling, 'Labour and Politics in Chicago', *Political Studies* (Vol. 5, February 1957), p. 24. For a discussion of the political polarities of direct bargaining and boundary management see Manfred Halpern, 'Conflict, Violence and the Dialectics of Modernization', a paper presented to the 64th Annual Meeting of the American Political Science Association (6 September 1968), pp. 15–16. See below, Chapter 2, Part III.

political control of at least two of the city's political subdivisions as well.[9]

The potential for effective black political action in the city's decentralized pluralistic politics was augmented by the pivotal position of the small, but rapidly growing, black vote assumed in the factional struggles of the Republican party. Unlike New York, where the only political alternative to the reform controlled Republican–Fusion alliance was Tammany Hall, in Chicago the Republican party was split into factions, one of which came to depend on black support. The two major factions in the Republican party were the reform-minded, middle-class oriented group led by Governor Charles Deneen[10] and a more traditional machine group, based on patronage and a powerful organization, headed by Senator William Lorimer.[11] The crucial position of the black vote in Republican party politics is perhaps most clearly evident in the mayoralty campaign of 1915 when Judge Olson, the Deneen candidate, was challenged by William Hale Thompson, who ran as the candidate of Fred Lundin, a Swedish politician, who had taken over the Lorimer organization after Lorimer was unseated by the Senate, on bribery charges, in 1912.

Bill Thompson, who inherited the wealth and prestige of his father, an 'old settler' who had amassed a fortune in real estate, comprehended and skilfully exploited the ethnic politics of his city. In his early races for minor political office, at the turn of the century, he had run, with effect, not against his opponents, but against the King of England to attract Irish, German, Swedish, and Italian votes.[12] In his 1915 primary contest with Judge Olson, Thompson again was able to use ethnic animosities to win votes. He appealed, successfully, to the city's Germans, Austrians, and Irish by cleverly identifying himself with the claims of a man fortuitously named Robert Thompson, a former American consul in Germany, who had exposed the misstatements of fact in the British war propaganda German atrocity stories. Candidate Thompson soon found himself besieged with speaking invitations from German groups and was made an honorary member of the German–American Alliance.[13] Thompson's campaign also took advantage of religious cleavages by assuming an anti-Catholic tone, in Protestant wards, to appeal to the same groups which later in the 1920s were to support the Ku Klux Klan— small businessmen, lower-level clerical workers, and semi-skilled workers

[9] see Elmer William Henderson, 'A Study of the Basic Factors in the Change in the Party Alignment of Negroes in Chicago, 1932–1938' (unpublished M.A. thesis, University of Chicago, 1939, pp. 10–11, and James Q. Wilson, *Negro Politics, the Search for Leadership* (New York, 1960), p. 27.

[10] Charles Deneen: Governor of Illinois 1905–13, U.S. Senator 1925–31.

[11] William Lorimer: U.S. Senator 1909–1912 was unseated on bribery charges in 1912. On Republican party factions see H. F. Gosnell, 'The Chicago Black Belt as a Political Battleground', *American Journal of Sociology* (Vol. 40, November 1933), p. 339.

[12] Lloyd Wendt and Herman Kogan, *Big Bill of Chicago* (New York, 1953), p. 51.

[13] Ibid., pp. 94–5.

who feared and resented the competition, economic and political, of the city's European immigrants, many of whom were Catholic.[14] Thousands of leaflets were distributed in Protestant neighbourhoods which claimed that the election of Judge Olson (whose wife was Catholic) would guarantee papal control of the Chicago public school system.

Lundin and Thompson recognized, too, that the black vote, largely located in the second ward, might be significant. Thompson, with his old black associate Rev. Archibald Carey, toured the black belt often, repeating the pledge, 'I'll give your people the best opportunities they've ever had if you elect me.'[15] Thompson's decision to bid for black votes proved crucial, for the predominantly black second ward provided him with the margin of victory.[16]

The black vote, though not decisive in the inter-party election, added significantly to Thompson's majority. The ethnic–religious cleavages of the primary campaign dominated Thompson's effort to defeat Robert Sweitzer, the Democratic candidate. Sweitzer was a German Catholic; in Polish wards, Thompson was anti-German. In the German and Irish wards, he was an anglophobe. In WASP wards he was a reformer; in immigrant wards, he pledged to fight the prohibition movement and provide jobs.[17] To blacks he also pledged employment, and, in patronizing fashion, an open ward: 'I'll give you people jobs. And if any of you want to shoot craps go ahead and do it. When I'm Mayor the police will have something better to do than break up a friendly crap game.'[18] The nativist, anti-papist appeals against Sweitzer also had their impact in the black belt. In white neighbourhoods, however, 'Thompson men went around calling upon the great God Public to strike down Sweitzer, the Pro-Negro, the carpetbagger.'[19]

The decisive potential of the black vote was made clear, again, in Thompson's narrowly successful re-election bid in 1919. Running once more against Sweitzer and a strong independent candidate, State's Attorney Maclay Hoyne, Thompson's plurality was only 21,622. In the black belt, Thompson received 15,569 votes to 3,232 for Sweitzer; had those figures been reversed, Sweitzer would have been mayor.[20]

By 1920, the pivotal nature of the black vote had been clearly demon-

[14] For an illuminating examination of the Chicago Ku Klux Klan see Kenneth T. Jackson, *The Ku Klux Klan in the City* (New York, 1967), p. 126.

[15] Wendt and Kogan, op. cit., p. 95.

[16] The city wide primary vote was: Thompson 87,333; Olson 84,825; and Hey 4,283. In the Second Ward the vote was: Thompson 8,633; Olson 1,870; and Hey 47.

[17] See Lloyd Lewis and Henry Justin Smith, *Chicago: The History of its Reputation* (New York, 1929), pp. 374–5.

[18] Wendt and Kogan, op. cit., pp. 103–4.

[19] John Bright, *Hizzoner Big Bill Thompson* (New York, 1930), p. 59. Thompson's margin of victory was 147,000 votes: Thompson 398,538; Sweitzer 251,061; others 28,326.

[20] See Lewis and Smith, op. cit., p. 394. Thompson 259,828; Sweitzer 238,206; Hoyne 110,851; others 81,917.

strated. By that year, 10 per cent of the Republican primary vote was black, which represented a potential plurality change of 20 per cent.[21] This large bloc of voters remained loyal to Thompson throughout his political career. In the second ward, the heart of the black belt, Thompson's share of the primary vote in the four mayoral primaries in which he participated and won never fell below 80 per cent. With the exception of 1927, when his plurality was 35·7 per cent, Thompson would have been defeated without black support.

II

Before the onset of the Great Migration, the Republican party in Chicago appointed blacks to a few minor political offices. These posts were not the product of political bargaining (only approximately 1 per cent of the city's population was black from 1850 to 1890), but were handouts to insure against black defection to the Democrats.[22] 'For the most part,' Spear has noted, 'Negroes received only political crumbs. Without a political organization rooted in their own community, Negro politicians lacked the leverage to demand more.'[23] The black politicians who were rewarded with political office had backgrounds which, in some cases, were strikingly similar to those of the United Colored Democracy politicians in New York. John Buckner, a black Republican elected to the Illinois House of Representatives, for example, had worked for white politicians, as a head waiter at private parties before his selection as a candidate in 1894. He later commanded the all-black ninth regiment of the Illinois militia, and served in the patronage posts of deputy collector, deputy sheriff, deputy state game warden, deputy in the office of the county clerk, and as a state parole officer.[24] This pre-machine period also saw the emergence of black politicians who employed the rhetoric of racial militancy. John G. Jones, elected to the Illinois House of Representatives in 1912, spoke out often, with intensity, against segregation and the development of separate black community institutions. In 1889, he protested against the founding of an all-black Y.M.C.A., and in 1891 against the establishment of the black Provident Hospital. He spoke vigorously for the small black professional

[21] Henderson, op. cit., p. 10.

[22] Both Carter Harrison and his son Carter Harrison II sought black support. Harrison II, who distributed conspicuous black patronage (he appointed Robert Mitchel and S.A.T. Watkins assistant city prosecuting attorneys), was reported to have stated his belief that 'the Negro will divide his vote if the proper intelligence is displayed in seeking it.' In 1885, Harrison I received 50 per cent of the minuscule Negro vote; his son, in 1897, received 65 per cent. However, the Democrats never, in this period, nominated a black to run for elective office, and, as the black Democratic organization divided into factions and the migration swelled the city's ranks of Negro Republicans, the Democratic party swiftly declined as an attractive political alternative. Drake and Cayton, op. cit., Vol. I, p. 345; Henderson, op. cit., p. 3; and Spear, op. cit., p. 125.

[23] Ibid., p. 119.

[24] Drake and Cayton, op. cit., Vol. I, p. 345.

class in Chicago which sought to integrate into the white professional groups of the city.

But with the large increase in the number of black migrants at the turn of the century, black professionals with political aspirations correctly understood that racial rhetoric could be used to weld together a powerful black political machine which would be able to win concessions from its white allies. The new black elite, predominantly composed of business-men and lawyers, rejected, implicitly, the quest for integration, but sought instead to succeed, in business and in politics, with the migrant masses as their consumers and voters.[25] Unlike their predecessors, the new black political leaders 'were professional politicians, who made their reputations in politics and devoted all of their talent and energy to political careers'.[26] These men correctly understood that the construction of a black political machine, in parallel fashion to the construction of other ethnic machines, would give them the ability to bargain, not as suppli-cants, but as leaders with a power-base. They fused the self-help, racial unity philosophy of Booker T. Washington to the rhetoric of race pride and militancy.

Though the new political leadership was largely secular, in its early period of development the black political machine was led by one of the community's leading religious spokesmen, Reverend Archibald Carey.[27] Carey was raised in Georgia, where both his grandfather and father had been literate slaves and had participated in Reconstruction politics. He attended Atlanta University, and came to Chicago in 1896 at the request of his African Methodist Episcopal Church bishop (whom he would later succeed) who asked Carey to go north to save a struggling A.M.E. church. Carey was an intensely political minister. He often invited local politicians and Illinois Congressmen and Senators to address his congregation. Carey was uniquely well placed to politicize the masses; the most influential figure in the black community was the successful minister.

Carey used his church as a substitute for a political clubhouse. Unlike most black churches, which were other-worldly, Carey's Institutional Church and Social Settlement reproduced the welfare activities of the white clubhouses. Its services included a kindergarten, a day nursery and, most significantly, an employment bureau, as well as other social activities.[28] Carey's political power was based on his ability to deliver black votes. In 1900, he had supported Thompson in his aldermanic campaign; in 1902, Thompson saw to it that a playground was built

[25] For an informative, extended discussion of the new leadership see Spear, op. cit., Chapter 4.

[26] Ibid., p. 78.

[27] On the role of political clerics, see William T. Hutchinson, *Lowden of Illinois* (Chicago, 1957), p. 268.

[28] Joseph A. Logsdon, *The Rev. Archibald J. Carey and the Negro in Chicago Politics*, unpublished M.A. thesis, the University of Chicago, 1961, p. 11, and Spear, op. cit., p. 95.

across the street from Carey's church. 'When I got the ordinance for the first kiddies playground,' Mayor Thompson told a black belt political meeting in 1931, 'Bishop Carey got me to put it across the street from his church at 24th and Wabash. I got the ordinance. Thompson was responsible for that and the Negroes got the playground and Bishop Carey was responsible for that.'[29] As his political influence grew, Carey was able to find employment for his church members in municipal patronage positions.

By 1910, Carey had developed an independent church-based political machine. Its independence was dramatically demonstrated in 1911 when Carey supported Carter Harrison II, a Democrat, for re-election as Mayor, and again in 1912 when he endorsed Edward Dunne, the Democratic candidate for Governor. In return, the Mayor appointed Carey to the Moving Picture Censor Board (1914), and, more significantly, Dunne selected him to lead a committee which was to take charge of a celebration of the fiftieth anniversary of the 13th Amendment to the Constitution. This appointment was rather more than token or ceremonial; the legislature appropriated $25,000 for the event which placed a considerable amount of patronage under Carey's direct control. Moreover, Carey's church was selected as the celebration committee's headquarters. This appointment made Carey the most influential leader in the community.[30]

His dominant political position was strengthened by Thompson's election as Mayor in 1915. The pulpit of Carey's church provided Thompson with a political platform in the black belt that was denied his rivals. From the pulpit as well, Carey promoted the image of Thompson as 'the second Lincoln'. When the fiftieth anniversary celebration was held in September 1915, Carey stated effusively that, 'there are three names which will stand high in American history—Abraham Lincoln, William McKinley, and William Hale Thompson.'[31] After Thompson's election, Carey and Edward H. Wright, a black politician (see below), were appointed to the corporation counsel's office. For the next five years, Logsdon has noted, 'Carey probably held the most authority in the Negro community over the distribution of patronage.' He and Wright, after 1915, were 'the most powerful leaders in the Negro community'.[32]

Wright, in contrast to Carey, was a full-time politician. He came to Chicago from his native New York in 1884 at the age of twenty, and immediately began to organize blacks for the Republican party. He was rewarded with minor patronage jobs as a clerk and book-keeper, and in 1896, was elected to the fourteen-member Cook County Commission to fill the traditional black post (Wright was the third black county

[29] 25 March 1931, in Harold F. Gosnell, *Negro Politicians: The Rise of Negro Politics in Chicago* (Chicago, 1967), p. 50.

[30] Logsdon, op. cit., p. 18.

[31] *Chicago Defender*, 18 September 1931; also cited in Gosnell, op. cit., p. 51.

[32] Ibid., pp. 51, 56.

commissioner). His alliance with the Lorimer–Lundin–Thompson party faction was the result of a long-standing feud with Charles Deneen. After his election to the commission Wright withheld an appropriation from Deneen's office of State's Attorney to compel the appointment of F. L. Barnett, a black lawyer, as an assistant to Deneen.[33] At the end of his second term, Wright was denied renomination by the Deneen faction. In 1910, he unsuccessfully contested the second ward city council seat, and continued to campaign for black aldermanic representation until Oscar De Priest's election in 1915. With Carey, Wright dispensed patronage for the Thompson administration.

Until 1920, though black politicians had created a potent political organization and had achieved electoral successes, the black belt's party machinery remained in the hands of the area's white leaders—Congressman Martin Madden and Alderman George Harding. Madden, the second ward's Republican committeeman, decided not to seek re-election to that position in 1920. Mayor Thompson secured the nomination of his faction for Wright, who easily defeated the Deneen candidate. As the elected, official ward leader, Wright was, formally, an ethnic leader among equals.

By 1920, the black machine's successes at capturing major patronage positions and the ward machinery were reinforced by striking electoral successes. Oscar De Priest, a former Alabama house-painter who had made a fortune in real estate and helped organize the Negro Business League in Chicago, and who had succeeded Wright on the County Commission in 1904, was elected in 1915 as the city's first black alderman. In 1910, Wright had run in the Republican primary, finishing third in a four-way contest, with 18 per cent of vote; in 1912, though the black population of the ward had doubled to almost 50 per cent, Madden and De Priest's opposition ensured Wright's defeat once again. Two years later, Wright supported a black realtor, William Cowan, for alderman. De Priest supported Madden's white candidate, but elicited a promise from him that in the near future a black candidate would be nominated for one of the ward's two aldermanic posts. Cowan's 45 per cent share of the vote in 1914 convinced Madden that a black nominee would win in 1915. De Priest, who had been loyal to the organization, and who had quietly but assiduously cultivated the support of civic organizations, religious and professional groups, and the district's precinct captains was the logical choice.[34]

[33] Ibid., pp. 154–5; another version appears in the *Chicago Defender* (8 October 1932).

[34] After his election, De Priest argued that in the second ward, for the time being, blacks should leave the ward's second council seat in white (Alderman Harding's) hands. Blacks, he asserted, were satisfied with one of its group's members in the council for the ward; if other blacks wanted to be aldermen, he advised, they should run from other wards. Clearly, De Priest's alliance with Madden remained close. See *Chicago Defender* (15 January 1916).

This city success was complemented by the election of two state senators, Robert Jackson in 1912 and Sheadrick Turner in 1914. Thus by 1920 it was possible to talk of a powerful black South Side political machine. The machine's electoral successes reached a climax in 1928 with De Priest's election to succeed Madden in Congress. De Priest became a national symbol of the possibilities of organized black political action in the North.[35]

Politics, wrote Cayton and Drake in their classic study of black Chicago, 'became an important, perhaps the most important, method by which the Negro sought to change his status.'[36] Contemporary observers pronounced that method a striking success. Chicago, Ralph Bunche claimed in 1929, 'has become the "seventh heaven" of Negro political activity. The state of Illinois,' he continued,

Cook County (of which the midwestern metropolis comprises the major part), and Chicago boast a greater degree of Negro political participation and influence than any city, county or state in the nation. The toga of Negro political leadership adorns the Illinois Negro. His influence is vitally felt at every election. His vote is often the conclusive determinant in hot races for political office. His reward for support of the successful candidate is the usual consideration condoned by contemporary American political practice.[37]

H. F. Gosnell, whose 1935 study of Chicago black politics remains unsurpassed in comprehensiveness, began by noting what cannot be denied: 'The Negroes in Chicago have achieved relatively more in politics during this period than have the Negroes in other cities of the United States. They have been more aggressive along political lines than have Negroes in New York City.'[38] In his recent study of the early years of the black belt, Allan Spear similarly concluded, 'By 1920, Negroes had more political power in Chicago than anywhere else in the country. They held more appointive and elective offices and exercised greater influence on the dominant political organization than their counterparts in New York, Philadelphia, or Baltimore.'[39]

III

That blacks were able to participate on the elite and mass electoral levels in Chicago politics during the migration period is not in doubt. Yet, as was noted in Chapter 2, to state that participatory behaviour is possible leaves the most important question unanswered—participation on what

[35] 'The seat in Congress', Roi Ottley has written, 'was a symbol of Negro achievement. It stood for the recapturing of a banished hope. It means that the Negro was part of the National government.' Roi Ottley, *The Lonely Warrior: The Life and Times of Robert Abbott* (Chicago, 1955), p. 346.
[36] Drake and Cayton, op. cit., Vol. I, p. 343.
[37] Ralph Bunche, 'The Thompson–Negro Alliance', *Opportunity* (March 1929), p. 78.
[38] Gosnell, op. cit., p. 11.
[39] Spear, op. cit., p. 191.

terms and with what structural constraints? The limits and possibilities of participation and political choice are defined by the nature of the political relationships fashioned between the group and the polity. For that reason, we must inquire if the black–polity relationships in Chicago had the capacity (to paraphrase Manfred Halpern) to produce change and justice through political collaboration and conflict. In probing the nature of the structured linkages, it is important, among other concerns, to ask: How descriptively representative were the black leaders? What were their aspirations and how did they relate to the group's social, economic, and political needs? In terms of the leadership goals, can we measure their success? With which whites, representing which interests, were the black politicians allied? To what extent did black political activity in Chicago promote or challenge the racial *status quo*? Since blacks in Chicago did achieve more politically in the migration period than blacks in any other Northern city, an examination of these questions provides an opportunity to examine the limiting case of relative success.[40]

The city's black politicians lived, as did most of Chicago's blacks, on the South Side but were far from typical residents of the area. Most of the politicians were lawyers, businessmen, or clergymen; yet in 1920, when 36 per cent of black males worked as manufacturing labourers, and 28 per cent in domestic and personal employment (mainly porters, servants, and janitors), there were only ninety-five black lawyers, 528 store-owners and retail dealers, and 215 clerymen (the vast majority apolitical) in Chicago. In percentage terms 0·2 per cent of blacks in Chicago's labour force were lawyers, 1·2 per cent were businessmen, and 0·5 per cent clergymen.[41] The black elite was thus very small, and unlike New York's, the black belt's political, civic, and business elites overlapped and converged. James Wilson has argued persuasively that one of the pre-eminent features of black Chicago's political life in the Thompson years was the element 'of compatible elites . . . the individuals active in these matters tend to be the same, or at least share common sets of values and motives.'[42]

The black belt's leading social institution, the Appomattox Club, which was founded by E. H. Wright in 1900 as a social club for black politicians, soon became the favourite meeting place of the interlocking black bourgeois elite. The club rarely expressed a corporate view, but one occasion when it did, semi-officially, is instructive. In this period, black workers in the post office, especially in the railway mail service ('the preferred branch of the postal service')[43] qualified for middle-class status; many joined the Appomattox Club. In 1911, club members founded

---

[40] See Robert Brisbane, *The Black Vanguard* (Valley Forge, 1970), pp. 115–16.

[41] U.S. Fourteenth Census, 1920, Vol. 4, pp. 1076–9; also in Spear, op. cit., 152–3.

[42] Wilson, op. cit., p. 312.

[43] Henry McGee, 'The Negro in the Chicago Post Office', unpublished M.A. thesis, University of Chicago, 1961, pp. 7–8.

the Phalanx Forum, a social organization for black postal workers. When the Wilson administration introduced segregation into the service and purged black workers, the National Alliance of Postal Employees, which acted as a militant trade union to protect black jobs, was organized (1913). The Phalanx Forum, however, with the advice and consent of the Appomattox Club, fought the National Alliance and sought instead to use the political connections of the Appomattox Club members to protect the postal employees.[44]

The business-oriented black elite, hostile to trade unions, discouraged black unionization. White businessmen had encouraged black migration to Chicago because they needed cheap labour. Black politicians, in turn, helped provide them with that labour. Rev. Carey, for instance, used his church's employment service to place Southern migrants 'with the Pullman company, with firms in the stockyards, and in wealthy households [as] domestic and personal servants.'[45] 'I believe that the interest of my people,' he stated bluntly in 1924, 'lies with the wealth of the nation and with the class of white people who control it. Labor and capital cannot adjust themselves by rival organizations; they must work together.'[46] Blacks were used as strike-breakers in the stockyards in 1894, 1904, and 1921, and most conspicuously in the steel strike of 1919. ('Negro workers were imported and shifted from plant to plant . . . besides the comparatively small number of avowed strikebreakers . . . it is evident that the great numbers who flowed into the Chicago and Pittsburg plants were conscious of strikebreaking.'[47] In the meat industry, blacks joined an all-black company union, the American Unity Labor Union. Black mass anti-labour activity and the willingness 'to act as "scabs" could be explained only too easily', notes Henry Pelling, 'in view of the known discriminatory practices of so many unions.' Only three Chicago unions in 1920 were open to blacks on terms of full equality.[48] Pelling ascribes the disappointing record of the Chicago labour movement as a whole to the divisive ethnic factor, one element of which was anti-black discrimination. Significant here, however, is the fact that while ethnic groups in Chicago founded their own unions, some militant like Sidney Hillman's Jewish Amalgamated Clothing Workers, blacks, with the exception of Kelley's Union (a black waiters' trade union) did not form their own unions but rather, if admitted to white unions at all, were segregated in subordinate locals.[49] The anti-union business perspective of the Appomattox Club black elite was at least partially instrumental in the failure

[44] Ibid., pp. 16–17, 31.

[45] Logsdon, op. cit., p. 17.

[46] Chicago *Whip* (29 March 1924). See also Logsdon, op. cit., p. 80 and Gosnell, op. cit., p. 320.

[47] Interchurch World Movement, *Report on the Steel Strike of 1919* (New York, 1920).

[48] Pelling, pp. 31–2. The three unions were the Hod Carriers, the International Ladies Garment Workers Union, and the Flat Janitors.

[49] Ibid., pp. 33, 31, and Spear, op. cit., p. 39.

of blacks to exploit the possibilities of militant trade union activity. As a result, Chicago's racial cleavage was exacerbated by overlapping with the city's class divisions.[50]

Indeed, some of Chicago's leading black politicians had made fortunes by crude forms of business exploitation. Oscar De Priest, for example, whose People's Movement stridently exployed the rhetoric of racial solidarity, made his fortune by the technique known as 'block-busting'. In 1908, De Priest opened a real estate office on the fringe of the black belt. He purchased buildings of flats that were occupied by white families and then rented vacant apartments to Negroes. The building's whites usually soon moved out, the building became all-black, and rents were promptly raised. Profits were high. De Priest used his profits to invest in securities, more real estate, and to finance his political career.[51]

The black political machine, as we have seen, had considerable bargaining potential; Carey's support of the Democrats in 1911 and 1912 illustrated the possibilities. But the potential for a continuing politics of direct bargaining and boundary management was not realized, for after 1915, the machine ceased to bargain independently between factions and parties but became instead a dependent element in the Thompson–Lundin electoral coalition, an element which, though courted and sometimes rewarded, could be taken for granted. The leadership, which was well rewarded for its support, was thus detached from the mass; its role thereby changing from one of bargaining agent and spokesman for the group to that of a broker or buffer, soliciting votes for the white machine while providing the appearance of striking racial–political progress. Subtly, yet surely, what had been a relationship between white and black politicians whose terms had been defined, at least in part, by both sides, was transformed into a relationship whose terms were defined for the black leadership by the city's dominant Republican white politicians. Thus, in Halpern's terms, the emergent structured linkage was an amalgam of subjection and buffering.

As in New York, the differences between elite and mass black patronage are striking. Mayor Thompson made De Priest his floor leader in the City Council and later was instrumental in getting him the 1928 Republi-

---

[50] I think Baran and Sweezy are quite right in pointing at the business community in their analysis of the social forces and institutional mechanisms that have kept blacks at the bottom of American society. They write, convincingly, of 'a formidable array of private interests [which] benefit, in the most direct and immediate sense, from the continued existence of a sub-proletariat. . . . Employers benefit from divisions in the labour force which enable them to play one group off against another, thus weakening all. Historically they note, 'no small amount of Negro migration was in direct response to the recruiting of strikebreakers. In aiding this business class, the Appomattox Club elite helped institutionalize Northern racism'. Paul Baran and Paul Sweezy, *Monopoly Capital: An Essay on the American Economic and Social Orders* (London, 1968), pp. 257–8.

[51] See Gosnell, op. cit., p. 169.

can congressional nomination. Carey, Wright, and Louis B. Anderson (who succeeded De Priest as the second ward's alderman in 1917) were appointed to the corporation counsel's office at high salaries. Other political loyalists were given patronage posts as well. Politics, Carey often asserted, was a means in the struggle to win recognition for blacks.[52] In this, clearly, individual blacks were strikingly successful.

The recognition of individual politicians by the Thompson machine no doubt appealed to the black masses as a whole recently arrived from the South, and to a large degree explains the huge majorities amassed by Thompson–Lundin candidates in black belt wards. Moreover by 1920, perhaps motivated by the Mayor's distribution of symbolic black patronage, Chicago's Negroes had registered to vote in higher proportions than white voters. 'On the basis of figures for the Second Ward, which over a period of time had the highest proportion of Negroes, it was estimated that 72 per cent of the eligible Negro voters were registered... as compared with 66 per cent for the entire city.'[53]

For the masses, however, the patronage rewards of political alliance with the Thompson–Lundin faction were more disappointing than a glance at the aggregate figures would indicate. In 1920, 224 municipal jobs (1·5 per cent) were held by blacks, a figure close to their 2 per cent of the population.[54] In 1920, after five years of Thompson rule, 959 blacks worked for the city, a dramatic increase to 4·2 per cent, a figure higher than the blacks' 4·1 per cent of the population, and almost in line with their 4·9 per cent of the work force.[55] A 1930-2 survey found that 6·4 per cent of the patronage (nominally civil service) positions in Chicago were held by blacks, which almost matched their 6·9 per cent of the population.[56] From these figures, Wilson has concluded that 'Negroes held more or less their share of the jobs available from both the machine's patronage and the classified public service (which itself was subject to political influence).'[57]

A closer look at the patronage figures, however, is revealing. In 1930,

[52] Logsdon, op. cit., p. 23.

[53] PROPORTION OF ADULT CITIZENS AND ELIGIBLE VOTERS REGISTERED IN SECOND WARD AND IN CITY OF CHICAGO, 1920 AND 1930

	City		Second Ward (1921 lines)	
	1920	1930	1920	1930
Total adult citizens	1,367,515	1,906,366	50,185	31,947
Estimated eligible voters	1,331,000	1,858,000	45,000	29,000
Percentage of adult citizens registered	64·7	66·3	64·7	71·4
Percentage of estimated eligible voters registered	66·4	68·1	71·6	77·4

SOURCE: Gosnell, op. cit., p. 374.

[54] Spear, op. cit., pp. 33, 35.

[55] Ibid., pp. 152–3.

[56] Gosnell, op. cit., p. 259.

66·6 per cent of the city government's porters and cooks, 27 per cent of its janitors, 17·4 per cent of its messengers, errand, and office boys and girls, and 11·7 per cent of its garbage men and scavengers were black, but under 2 per cent of the city's carpenters, electricians, engineers, firemen, detectives, accountants and street cleaners. Moreover, in the city service there were no black boilermakers, builders, blacksmiths, machinists, painters, canvassers, salesmen, designers, draughtsmen, photographers, electrical, mechanical, and mining engineers, waiters, collectors, credit men, purchasing agents, shipping clerks and weighers.[58] As Gosnell has commented, 'It is only when the kinds of positions held by Negroes are examined that the real situation comes to light. The proportion of Negroes in such jobs as janitors, janitresses, and laborers has exceeded the population ratio, but the proportion in clerical and professional occupations is far below that ratio.'[59]

Thompson and his black allies often proclaimed that patronage was distributed to blacks on a non-discriminatory basis. When he introduced the Mayor at the fiftieth anniversary celebration of the 13th Amendment, Rev. Carey asserted that though the city had discriminated in the past, Mayor Thompson's policy was to appoint 'American citizens who have earned their positions. By his appointments, Mayor Thompson is merely recognizing the worth of a people.' The Mayor picked up this theme in his address: 'Prejudices do exist against Negroes. . . . But to deny equal opportunity to the Negro in this land would be out of harmony with American history, untrue to sacred history, untrue to the sacred principles of liberty and equal rights, and would make a mockery of our boasted civilization and justice and render meaningless the word opportunity.'[60] The rhetoric notwithstanding, with Gosnell we can conclude that 'to Mayor Thompson directly the Negroes in the classified service do not owe a great deal.'[61]

Even in the visible symbolic positions, the black rate of patronage increase was, on the whole, slower than that for other ethnic groups. Mayor Thompson's highest level black appointment was his selection of Carey to the three-man Civil Service Commission (1928). Carey died under indictment for bribery,[62] and no black was appointed by subsequent mayors to take his place. As late as 1935 blacks had

. . . not yet won the headship of a city department and at no time have they received in the patronage positions as a whole rewards which were commensurate with their voting strength. Even Mayor Thompson failed to name a colored man to

[57] James Wilson, Introduction to Gosnell, p. x.
[58] Gosnell, op. cit., pp. 377–8.
[59] Ibid., pp. 238–9.
[60] Cited in Bright, op. cit., pp. 87–8.
[61] Gosnell, op. cit., pp. 238–9.
[62] *Chicago Defender* (28 March 1931).

the Board of Education, the Board of local improvements, or a city cabinet position.[63]

Moreover, the Mayor and the Republican machine did little to ensure fair treatment for those blacks who were appointed to the public service.[64] The fire department segregated its black firemen; other departments tended to cluster blacks in particular bureaus. The merit promotion system was often disregarded where blacks were concerned. The few blacks who were promoted on merit tended to have political connections, but 'even political influence has not been able to carry the colored employees of the city beyond a certain point'. There was an invisible ceiling above which blacks could not ascend; as late as 1935 there were no black police captains, fire marshalls, head clerks, or school engineers, though there were blacks who qualified in terms of merit and seniority. One black fire captain, for instance, took the lieutenants examination, passed, but was asked to waive his right to appointment. Had he not acquiesced he probably would have been fired. The man was appointed lieutenant in the all-black fire company twelve years after passing the test.[65]

The alliance with the Thompson–Lundin faction which brought the black elite attractive patronage jobs not only compromised mass patronage, but brought blacks 'a whole lot of bad government'.[66] The Thompson machine used patronage, not improved city services, to maintain the allegiance of its followers. But the black masses' greatest area of need was improved public services. The black–Thompson alliance did nothing to improve the shocking condition of the black belt's housing, schools, recreational facilities, and welfare services. In fact, the Thompson–black alliance may actually have led to a deterioration in living conditions as a result of the collusion of the Mayor with the underworld which permitted vice to flourish in black neighbourhoods. The black underworld's ties to Thompson were made clear when Daniel Jackson, the czar of the black belt underworld and the leader of its strongest syndicate, replaced E. H. Wright as the second ward's committeeman by the appointment of the Mayor in 1927. The militant 'new-Negro' newspaper the Chicago *Whip*, written by race-conscious, activist intellectuals, which persistently criticized the 'big fake-politicians who for a "mess of pottage" have preached submissiveness to the black masses', persistently scored the political–underworld ties: 'Is vice immunity the only plum that Negro Aldermen can secure in the way of

---

[63] Gosnell, op. cit., pp. 156, 201–2.

[64] Gosnell notes that many of the appointees were light-skinned, especially the white-collar workers. One official told him, 'A Negro with a light skin will fit better into an office. He won't be so different. The department heads lean towards this type of person.' p. 226.

[65] Ibid., pp. 226–36.

[66] Bunche, op. cit., p. 80.

H

patronage? . . . Would the voters of the Secord Ward prefer to have open and protected vice to playgrounds and free milk stations?' On another occasion the *Whip*'s editorial stated: 'His [Mayor Thompson's] black friends permitted and most likely converted the once fashionable South Side into a cesspool. It reflects on the Mayor.'[67]

IV

The structured relationships that defined the terms of black political participation in Chicago limited black political achievement. Much like the situation in New York, despite greater potential and more concrete positional achievements, the linkages in Chicago were neither descriptively representative, responsive, nor efficient on two levels. Black access to the competition for political power was limited by the black machine's dependent relationship to the Thompson–Lundin faction of the Republican party. As a consequence, the Thompson–Lundin faction was responsive to the small black elite, and even with respect to the elite, compared to other ethnic groups, the level of responsiveness was low. From the perspective of the black elite the relationship with the Thompson–Lundin faction had limited utility; from the mass perspective, hardly any utility at all.

The non-representative, non-responsive, inefficient nature of the political linkages holds too at the level of black leadership–group relationships. As a result of their individualistic orientation to politics, the leaders of the black machine assumed the structural role of buffers between the black population and the city's white political leadership. In his introduction to the first edition of Gosnell's *Negro Politicians*, Robert Park extolled Chicago's black politicians for their individualistic orientation:

There has emerged a robust and vigorous middle class, often of the mental type of Booker T. Washington, and of the men of the Negro Business League which he organized. These men have more or less the attitudes of pioneers, men who have grown up on an advancing frontier—in this instance a racial frontier.

The Negro politicians who have risen in ward politics . . . seem to be, in most every case, of this type. They are not infrequently men of superior education and they are active in promoting the interests of the race as they see them, *but they act on the principle that the best way to solve the problem of the race as a whole is for each member to solve the problem as an individual.*[68]

[67] Chicago *Whip* (24 June 1919; 13 December 1919; and 10 February 1923).

Hutchinson writes: 'Although the Mayor often professed to be the Negroes' friend and felt assured of their votes, he did little to improve the appalling living conditions within much of their district or to protect them from exploitation by unscrupulous members of their own race and by whites. Machine politicians close to City Hall fostered or protected vice of all kinds within the enclave and on the 'frontier' on its edge'. Hutchinson, op. cit., Vol. II, p. 404.

[68] Robert Ezra Park, *Race and Culture* (London, 1950), p. 176. Italics added.

Here was the crux of the leadership issue: the black politicians had the potential to exercise group power on behalf of solutions for the group; instead, the generalized capacity of the group, based on the assent of the votes of the masses, was used to obtain individual solutions. American liberal ideals proclaim individual opportunity, yet as Cruse has pointed out, 'the individual in America has few rights that are not backed up by the political, economic and social power of one group or another.'[69] Black political power in Chicago was used to wrest political rewards for the few, but even for the few the gains were limited, 'To run for any state office higher than Senator from the Black Belt just wasn't done.'[70] And for the masses, the political gains were almost non-existent.

Pivotal black electoral strength which could have been used to extract concessions from the city, and which could have placed blacks at the decision-making level in city affairs was channelled into activity which placed black politics, to use Wilson's phrase, on the periphery of power. The black political machine was co-opted into the Thompson organization and lost its independence. 'Most of the funds for financing the political organizations in the Second and Third Wards came from the white leaders, and the colored leaders who failed to recognize this sooner or later came into difficulties.'[71]

Once black political independence was lost, the maintenance needs of the black machine dictated that it be issue-free. Issues and agitation are divisive and tend to jeopardize existing electoral alignments. The Carey–Wright–De Priest machine, allied as it was to the 'ins' in Chicago politics thus had built-in conservative features: political agitation for change, political challenges to the racial *status quo* could not be permitted for they would place the (rewarding) alliance in jeopardy. The machine had not only a stake in the ghetto, for the ghetto was the source of its votes, but, despite its militant rhetoric, also had a stake in the racial *status quo*.[72] The

[69] Harold Cruse, *The Crisis of the Negro Intellectual* (New York, 1967), pp. 7–8.
[70] Drake and Cayton, op. cit., p. 80.
[71] Gosnell, op. cit., p. 110. The question of black–white coalitions is dealt with perceptively in Stokeley Carmichael and Charles Hamilton's *Black Power*. They write that all too often 'coalitions involving black people have been at the leadership level; dictated by terms set by others; and for objectives not calculated to bring major improvement in the lives of the black masses.' This description is an apt one of the Thompson–black alliance in Chicago. It is worth considering Carmichael and Hamilton's argument that a viable coalition cannot 'be effected between the politically and economically secure and the politically and economically insecure.' Carmichael and Hamilton, op. cit., p. 60.
[72] Indeed, some black politicians went out of their way to reassure their white counterparts that they were satisfied with the 'progress' being made. In early January 1916, a dinner for Chicago's leading politicians included Rev. Carey as one of the guests. The *Defender* reported: 'Dr. A. J. Carey was among the select few who attended the dinner, representing the hundred thousand Negroes in Chicago. He made one of the principal speeches and was vigorously applauded. He reminded those present that the Negroes of Chicago had contributed much to the success of the Thompson administration and on behalf of the entire race of Chicago thanked the administration for the liberal

politics of the black belt provided a way out for some, but not a way up for the mass. Black political collaboration with the Thompson faction in Chicago's political conflicts produced continuity, but neither change not justice.[73]

representation which his people have been given by the notable appointment of colored men to places in the city government' (8 January 1916).

[73] It is interesting to speculate that perhaps one of the tragic ironies of Chicago's black politics was the fact that the city's Negroes were so closely allied with the 'ins' in city politics. In the 1920s the blacks were solidly Republican; by the mid-1930s Chicago's blacks were equally strongly Democratic. In his brilliant study of New York patronage, Theodore Lowi argues that 'it is the minority, or the majority in the making, party that is the source of innovation. It absorbs the new, no-access interests; its electoral weakness makes it permeable, whereas the electoral strength of the majority party (regardless of whether it is classed Democratic or Republican) makes it a consolidative, essentially conservative force. . . . The minority party, most significantly, is likely to be more vulnerable to the people, groups and ideas that are motivated by new needs and novel problems.' Chicago's blacks needed access and had new needs and problems. That the black alliance with the Democrats in the 1930s was formed only after the Democrats became the majority party and did not predate the change in Chicago's electoral allegiances, may, therefore, have been crucial for the patterns which developed later as the Dawson machine was co-opted by Kelley, Nash, and Daley. Chicago, of course, isn't New York; these reflections are thus only speculative, and would need more detailed study for confirmation. Lowi, op. cit., pp. 23, 175–211.

Chapter Seven

Northern Political Linkages: An Overview

I

'SOCIAL control', Joseph Roucek has written, 'occurs when one group determines the behavior of another group, when the group controls the conduct of its own members, or when individuals influence the responses of others.' Thus, social control can operate on three levels: 'group over group, the group over its members, and individuals over their fellows. In other words, social control takes place when a person is induced or forced to act according to the wishes of others, whether or not in accordance with his own individual interests.'[1] Social control, in short, implies uni-directional power relationships.

For blacks in the South at the turn of the century, social control by whites was unambiguous. Economic exploitation and black poverty were aspects of a pervasive (structured) racial system of relationships; its essential element was black powerlessness. As a slave, the black man had been utterly without control over the crucial aspects of his life; in Elkins's words, he could 'look to none but his master, the one to whom the system had committed his entire being; the man upon whose will depended his food, his shelter, his sexual connections, whatever moral instruction he might be offered, whatever "success" might be possible within the system, his very security—in short, everything.'[2] After emancipation and reconstruction, Southern blacks found that, in terms of power and social control, little had changed. The exploitative, authoritarian nature of the plantation, the feudal-like dependence of the black farm-labourer on his white landowning master was still very much the rule at the turn of the century. Southern black poverty was part of a profound alienation, the product of powerlessness. As Richard Wright put it, 'Days come and go, but our lives upon the land remain without hope. We do not care if the barns rot down; they do not belong to us anyway. No matter what

---

[1] Joseph Roucek, *Social Control* (New York, 1956), p. 3.
[2] Stanley Elkins, *Slavery* (Chicago, 1959), p. 43.

improvement we make upon the plantation, it would give us no claim upon the crop.'[3]

Economic powerlessness was bound up with and related to social and political powerlessness. An elaborate social code, enforced partially by law but primarily by custom and often capricious in operation, developed to ensure that in white–black relationships, blacks would be the objects, not participant-equals. The social powerlessness of slavery had given way to the social powerlessness of caste.[4]

Disfranchisement of blacks, rendering them politically impotent, was the natural guarantor of this colour-ascriptive system of colonial relationships.[5] Nothing had frightened white Southerners during Reconstruction more than black participation in politics on terms that both in potential, and at times in fact, made possible the bi-directional power linkages of boundary management and direct bargaining.[6] By 1877, as the last Federal troops left the South, white supremacist parties were in control throughout the region. Directed by conservative planters and businessmen, on the whole, these parties, in some states, courted black support on the tacit condition that blacks accept their subordinate position. This limited appeal to the black population depended on white unity to protect the racial–systematic arrangements. By 1890, however, fundamental class divisions threatened this arrangement.

The Populist farmers' movement which divided the white South to the alarm of the conservative ruling elite appealed to blacks to unite with them in an alliance of interest. 'You are made to hate each other,' Tom Watson, the Georgia populist told a black and white audience, 'because upon that hatred is rested the keystone of the arch of financial despotism which enslaves you both.' To blacks he pledged an end to the colour line 'if you stand shoulder to shoulder with us in this fight.'[7]

The planters and businessmen fought back by using the weapon of race to destroy the bi-racial partnership of the populists:

The eyes of his old captains were ominous and accusing upon him. From hustings and from pulpits thousands of voices proclaimed him traitor and nigger-loving scoundrel, renegade to Southern Womanhood, the Confederate dead, and the God of his fathers; champion of the transformation of the white

---

[3] Richard Wright, *12 Million Black Voices: A Folk History of the Negro in the United States* (New York, 1941), p. 57.

[4] For a discussion, see Vernon Lane Wharton, *The Negro in Mississippi, 1865–1890* (Chapel Hill, 1947), p. 233.

[5] For a discussion of the core elements of the colonization process, see Robert Blauner, 'Internal Colonialism and Ghetto Revolt', *Social Problems* (Vol. 16, Spring 1969).

[6] See Paul Lewinson, *Race, Class, and Party* (New York, 1932), pp. 46–60. For a discussion of this terminology, adapted from the work of Manfred Halpern, see below, Chapter 2, pp. 44ff.

[7] Cited in C. Vann Woodward, *The Strange Career of Jim Crow* (New York, 1957), p. 45.

race into a mongrel breed. . . . There could be but one outcome . . . the common white of the South did in overwhelming tide abandon his advance upon class consciousness and relapse into his ancient focus.[8]

The Populist movement ended in frustration; many white Populists embittered by their defeat turned on their former black allies. The black man, Watson was now asserting, 'has no comprehension of virtue, honesty, truth, gratitude, and principle'. He now condoned lynching: 'We have to lynch him occasionally, and flog him, now and then, to keep him from blaspheming the Almighty, by his conduct, on account of his smell and his color.'[9]

The lesson of the Populist experience was not lost on the South; potential black political power had to be eliminated. Thus, after the collapse of the bi-racial Populist movement, the Southern racial system was codified by the passage of legislation which systematically dis-franchised Southern blacks. From 1890 to 1910 eight Southern states amended their constitutions to eliminate black electoral participation, while the remaining Southern states, by restrictive statutes, acted, just as effectively, to prevent Negro voting.[10] In Louisiana, for example, a new State Constitution aimed at preventing black voting was adopted in 1898. In the two succeeding years, the number of blacks eligible to vote declined 96 per cent, from 130,344 to 5,320. By 1904, only 1,718 blacks remained on Louisiana's electoral rolls.[11] And by 1913, the Jackson Mississippi *Daily News*' assertion 'that the door of hope is forever closed to the Negro in so far as participation in politics is concerned'[12] seemed beyond contradiction.

As Worsley notes, in both colonization and decolonization, force, though not always used, 'has always been the *ultimate* sanction'.[13] In the South, racial divisions were enforced through law and custom, but ultimately the system depended on the intimidation of blacks through the use of force, legal and extra-legal. In 1900, the year that roughly marked the beginning of the Great Migration, at least 103 lynchings were recorded in the South; over 1,500 blacks were lynched in the first two decades of the century.[14] Some of the offences the lynched were charged with included writing a letter to a white man, voodooism, testifying for another black, testifying against whites, swindling, throwing stones, and the use of inflammatory language; the most common charges were

[8] W. J. Cash, *The Mind of the South* (New York, 1941), pp. 170–1.

[9] Cited in C. Vann Woodward, *Tom Watson: Agrarian Rebel* (New York, 1938).

[10] Arthur Link, 'The Negro as a Factor in the Campaign of 1912', *Journal of Negro History* (Vol. XXXI, January 1947).

[11] Lewinson, op. cit., pp. 79–97, 214.

[12] Cited in George Tindall, *The Emergence of the New South, 1913–1945* (Baton Rouge, 1967), p. 165.

[13] Peter Worsley, *The Third World* (London, 1967), p. 21.

[14] Herbert Aptheker, ed., *A Documentary History of the Negro People in the United States* (New York, 1951).

rape and murder.[15] Most lynch victims were hanged or shot, but often other means, grotesque in their horror, were employed. The humiliations and tortures were often incredible. In Waco, Texas, in 1916, Jesse Washington, a retarded adolescent, was burned at the stake in the public square while thousands watched and cheered. In South Georgia in May 1918, after three innocent men had been hanged for murder, the lynch mob 'strung up the pregnant widow of one by the ankles, doused her clothing with gasoline, and after it burned away, cut out the unborn child and trampled it underfoot, then riddled her with bullets.' Of the 416 blacks lynched between 1918 and 1927, forty-two were burned alive, sixteen burned after death, and eight beaten to death and cut to pieces.[16]

If, ultimately, the Southern relationships of uni-directional power were maintained by the threat or use of force, on a day-to-day basis they were maintained by a combination of institutional enclosure and a pervasive cultural imperialism that mutilated traditional black African values, mores, and institutions and substituted unattainable white-biased goals.[17] Hence, in Halpern's terms, Southern racial relationships were an oppressive mix of isolation, subjection, and emanation.[18]

The large numbers of blacks who migrated to the North were not simply moving away from poverty and conditions of economic deprivation. They were moving away from the web of relationships—economic, social, and political—which formed the system that contrived to limit and shape their choices, made them objects powerless to control their own lives.[19] This system they moved away from was essentially colonial: 'The Negro's position in American society at the turn of the twentieth century', Harlan has written, 'was, after all, roughly analogous to that of Negroes in the African colonies. Both groups were politically disfranchised, socially subordinated, and economically exploited.'[20]

In light of their powerlessness enforced by the imposing threat of violence, the only tangible means of protest Southern blacks had was migration to the North. A migrant, newly arrived in Chicago, wrote his brother to tell of integrated schools and the right to vote—'I just begin to feel like a man'.[21] A perceptive observer noted in 1912 that the migrants 'long for a larger liberty for themselves and their children . . . they

[15] E. B. Reuter, *The American Race Problem* (New York, 1920), pp. 369–72.

[16] Charles F. Kellogg, *NAACP* (Baltimore, 1967), p. 218; Tindall, op. cit., pp. 171–2.

[17] On deculturation and colonialism, see Philip Mason, *Patterns of Dominance* (London, 1970), p. 274.

[18] For a discussion, see above, Chapter 2, pp. 44ff.

[19] For further discussion, see above, Chapter 3, pp. 77ff.

[20] Louis R. Harlan, 'Booker T. Washington and the White Man's Burden', *American Historical Review* (Vol. 72, January 1966), p. 441.

[21] Anonymous, Chicago to Hattiesberg, Mississippi, 13 November 1917, Carter Woodson Collection of Negro Papers and Related Documents, The Library of Congress, Washington.

come North to gain this and escape the proscriptions.'[22] W. T. Andrews, a noted black editor and lawyer, insisted at the South Carolina Race Relations Conference in February 1917—the height of the migration— that a strict economic interpretation was shortsighted:

In my view the chief causes of the Negro unrest and disturbance are as follows: the destruction of his political privileges and curtailment of his civil rights; no protection of life, liberty, and property under law; Jim Crow cars; residential and labor segregation; no educational facilities worthy of the name in most Southern states. These, I believe, are the most potent causes which are now impelling the Southern Negro to seek employment and find homes in the Northern and Western sections of the country.[23]

The migrants, in short, were consciously breaking connections and repudiating, by leaving, existing unsatisfactory linkages, in the (almost mystical) hope of fashioning, in the North, new linkages that could transform their capacities to control their lives.

II

The new political linkages the black migrants fashioned in the North were undoubtedly more successful (from the perspective of the group) than those they had left behind in the South. In the North, blacks could participate in politics (at a minimum, they could vote), segregation was not sanctioned by law, and lynching was virtually non-existent. Yet the migrants' aspirations were not collectively realized; the Northern black– white political relationships established in the critical period of migra- tion—assessed in terms of the criteria discussed in Chapter 2, and in comparison with the European ethnic immigrant experience—were far from satisfactory. New, more indirect, but almost equally powerless quasi-colonial patterns of racial dominance and social control replaced the Southern colonial system.

Though the institutional arrangements in New York and Chicago differed in that blacks in Chicago organized a territorially-based machine while New York's black population was linked to the polity more in- directly through parallel institutions, the structural similarities (structure defined 'as the relationships in a social situation which limits the choice process to a particular set of alternatives')[24] are striking. Blacks did not join the North's politics of ethnic collaboration and conflict, which most often took the forms of boundary management and direct bargaining, as participant-equals. Instead, as a result, largely, of the critical decisions

[22] George Edmund Haynes, *The Negro at Work in New York City* (New York, 1912), p. 33.
[23] Cited in Emmett J. Scott, *Negro Migration During the War* (New York, 1920), pp. 173–4.
[24] David Apter, 'A Comparative Method for the Study of Politics', in David Apter and Harry Eckstein, eds., *Comparative Politics* (New York, 1963), p. 732.

made by the relevant local white political elites, blacks were linked to the polity through buffer institutions with uni-directional power capabilities. The South Side machine in Chicago, and the United Colored Democracy in New York were extensions of the white party organizations, appendages to be used when convenient and to which power could be conferred when necessary.

The absence of productive justice yielded the absence of distributive justice. The structure of black political recruitment, which effectively limited black access to the competition for positions of political authority, produced relationships marked by collaboration that was one-sided, its terms unilaterally directed. Almost inevitably, blacks, largely excluded from decision making positions and to whom local political elites were largely unaccountable, were denied an equitable share of the cities' political resources and rewards: patronage, governmental services, and contracts.

At a minimum, this pattern of black participation called into question the articulated democratic principles of the American North. In much contemporary discussion of democracy, formal criteria have come to replace representation as the defining characteristics of a democratic polity;[25] for example, this is clearly so in terms of Lipset's derivative definition (adapted from Schumpeter):

Democracy in a complex society may be defined as a political system which supplies regular constitutional opportunities for changing the governing officials, and a social mechanism which permits the largest possible part of the population to influence major decisions by choosing the contenders for political office.[26]

Counterposed to this emasculated formalist approach, is Wright Mills's view that 'in essence, democracy implies that those vitally affected by any decision men make have an effective voice in that decision', so that 'all power to make such decisions be publicly legitimated and that the makers of such decisions be held publicly accountable.'[27] In this view, democracy is defined not by electoral organization and choice alone, but by representation, in all its dimensions[28] (including the formal, socially descriptive, substantive, and actual).

Seen in these terms, at best, uneven formal representation was achieved by blacks in New York and Chicago, in that they could vote for competing candidates and could on occasion (more so in Chicago than New York) influence the selection of candidates. But even on the formal level, representation was inadequate; black party leaders in New York, and to a

[25] Richard Hamilton, 'Theories of Society and Democratic Politics', forthcoming Chapter 1 to his *Class and Politics in the United States*.
[26] Seymour Martin Lipset, *Political Man* (New York, 1963), p. 27.
[27] C. Wright Mills, *The Sociological Imagination* (New York, 1961), p. 188.
[28] For a discussion, see above, Chapter 2, Section III.

lesser but still significant extent in Chicago, were selected not by the black community but by the local white political elites. Neither in New York nor Chicago were black–white political relationships socially descriptively representative in two senses: blacks' access to decision-making positions was not proportional to their numbers, and, secondly, the group's political representatives were not descriptively representative of the group as a whole.

On the dimensions of responsiveness (substantive representation) and efficacy (actual representation), the linkages fashioned in the migration period were wanting as well. From the perspective of the mass of the black migrants, their recognized leaders were most often symbolically responsive at best, and, compared to the European ethnic-group politicians, ineffectual in achieving their own patronage goals.

III

The European immigrants' political experience contrasts strikingly with that of the black migrants from the South. For the European immigrants who came in the late nineteenth and early twentieth centuries, the ethnic conflicts of the politics of the North, paradoxically, had an integrating effect. The practical nature of the competition of the machines acted to channel these conflicts into means of adjustment and acceptance; the new political linkages gave direction to social change. In this fashion, for instance, the Irish leaders of Tammany Hall brought Italians, Jews, and Germans into decision-making positions in the Democratic party. 'As each new nationality arrived in the city', Fred Greenstein has written, 'politicians rapidly accommodated to it and brought it into the mainstream of political participation. Parties were concerned with the vote of the immigrants from the time of their arrival.'[29] The very existence of the machines, throughout the North, depended on success in tapping fresh sources of support. Each new group had to be wooed. 'The selfish quest by the politicians for electoral support and power was transmuted by the "invisible hand" into the major force integrating the immigrant into the community.'[30]

For these immigrants, political mobility, at times, was related to class and status mobility in direct fashion. Irish immigrant wealth, for example, on the docks, in transport, and in construction, was often

[29] Fred I. Greenstein, 'The Changing Pattern of Urban Party Politics', *The Annals of the American Academy of Political and Social Science* (Vol. 353, May 1964), p. 8.

[30] Elmer E. Cornwell, Jr., 'Bosses, Machines and Ethnic Groups', in Lawrence Fuchs, ed., *American Ethnic Politics* (New York, 1968), p. 203. In 1911, Henry Jones Ford similarly observed that the political machines were 'probably the secret of the powerful solvent influence which American civilization exerts upon enormous deposits of alien population thrown upon this country by the torrent of immigration'. Ford, *Rise and Growth of American Politics* (New York, 1911), p. 306.

directly the product of political favours which included lucrative municipal contracts.[31] The urban economy needed unskilled labour. Many of the available jobs were filled by political appointments, direct or indirect. 'Aqueducts and streets the city built for itself; trolley, gas, telegraph and electric lines were laid by companies franchised by the city; and every structure, as it went up, was inspected by the city.'[32]

It is possible, of course, to overstate the impact of politics on the mobility opportunities of the European immigrants. Some national groups got more out of politics (the Irish, for instance, more than the Italians); ethnic-group political machines tended to define class grievances as ethnic ones, thus dividing the poor against each other. Too often, the machines achieved real gains only for the few while doling out turkeys to the many. Moreover, the New Deal and the organization of the C.I.O. in the 1930s probably had more to do with European immigrant group mobility than earlier political factors.[33]

Despite these qualifications, however, it is right to conclude that the political linkages the European immigrants fashioned before 1930 were significant. The machines were integrative mechanisms, and did provide power and socio-economic benefits to the communities they served. By 1930, significantly, as the black ghettoes consolidated, the European immigrants' ghetto walls were crumbling.[34] For the immigrants, the significance of political action was not an abstraction: 'They could see the evidence themselves, knew the difference it made in their own existence.'[35] Similarly, the author of the classic Street Corner Society inquired rhetorically, 'Does anybody believe that the immigrants and their children could have achieved their present degree of social mobility without gaining control of the political organizations of some of our largest cities?[36]

A brief look at the structural differences in the positions of black and white ethnic politicians in the migration period is instructive. The European immigrant politician's strength was rooted in his ethnic–territorial community; in Gans's phrase, he was 'their ambassador to the outside

[31] See Daniel Bell, 'Crime as an American Way of Life', The End of Ideology (New York, 1962), p. 142.

[32] Oscar Handlin, The Uprooted (New York, 1951), p. 210.

[33] For a discussion of the limitations of the machines, see 'Black Power: A Discussion', Partisan Review (Vol. 35, Spring 1968), especially Paul Feldman's contribution, pp. 201–4.

[34] 'In summarizing the findings about Negro–European immigrant housing patterns, we may observe that although at one time certain specific immigrant groups in a city have been somewhat less segregated from Negroes than from native whites, or more segregated than Negroes were from native whites, the general summary figures indicate that Negroes and whites have moved in opposite directions, i.e., declining segregation for immigrants and increasing segregation for Negroes.' Stanley Lieberson, Ethnic Patterns in American Cities (Chicago, 1963), p. 132.

[35] Oscar Handlin, The Uprooted (New York, 1951), p. 211.

[36] William F. Whyte, 'Social Organization in the Slums', American Sociological Review (Vol. 8, February 1943), p. 37.

world',[37] and as the community representative he performed two functions, each important. The first was symbolic (a function successfully fulfilled by some black politicians too) because the immigrant politician, or at least most, remained identified with his ethnic community, his triumphs were the group's triumphs, his successes built the group's self-esteem. But the leader's success in fulfilling this function was largely dependent on his second tangible function: that of effectively representing the group to bring about tangible community improvements.[38]

In short, the white ethnic politicians, as a result of the decentralized structure of the machine and their independent, or at least quasi-independent, territorial community base, were able to be effective substantive representatives who practiced the politics of reciprocal obligations and loyalties; their obligations extended downwards into their communities as well as upwards to the machine organization as a whole. Black politicians, on the other hand, detached from the masses, were primarily obligated to the white-run machines. In the main, the black politicians, not selected by the group as a whole, and, in terms of class and status hardly typical black migrants, sponsored substantively unresponsive programmes calculated to bring rewards to the leadership-elite. And even these unresponsive aims were not always achieved.

The reasons for this style of black leadership are not difficult to fathom. Given the critical structural decisions made by local white political elites, the choices open to black politicians were severely circumscribed. They were trapped in an emasculating cycle of limitations; given the uni-directional power limitations with which they were confronted, most black politicians of the period were understandably (though, I would argue, in retrospect, wrongly) convinced that only by accepting the institutionalized white-imposed limitations could they act effectively on behalf of their people. 'It is difficult, if not impossible', Kenneth Clark has written, 'to behave as one with power when all one's experience has indicated that one has none.'[39] Moreoover, there were tangible rewards for not challenging the structural limitations, the rewards of patronage and prestige. If he was prepared to meet the tests of 'sanity, soberness, safe-ness, and temperateness in utterance',[40] to get along, show proper humility, and respect established racial boundaries of conduct, the black politician could move away from the masses, towards white-defined success and respectability. For the powerless, even pseudo-power can be a heady wine.

[37] Herbert J. Gans, *The Urban Villagers* (New York, 1962), pp. 163-80.
[38] See William F. Whyte, *Street Corner Society* (Chicago, 1961), pp. 247-52.
[39] Kenneth Clark, *Dark Ghetto* (London, 1965), p. 156.
[40] Ralph Bunche, 'A Brief and Tentative Analysis of Negro Leadership', 1940, MS. in Schomburg Collection, New York Public Library, p. 74.

IV

Blacks arrived in the North in a period of rapid, convulsive change. The character of New York and Chicago was profoundly altered by the influx of European immigrants, predominantly from Eastern and Southern Europe. Chicago's population doubled between 1900 and 1930; New York's almost quadrupled between 1890 and 1930, partially, of course, as a result of the extension of the city's boundaries by the amalgamation of the boroughs in 1898. Both cities, in these years, rapidly expanded as major centres of industry, banking, investment, and trade.[41]

Potentially, the black newcomers could have been one more poverty-stricken immigrant group competing for the scarce resources of class, status, and political power. Like the blacks, the European immigrants lacked prestige, money, property, and, in far larger numbers than the blacks, even minimal literacy.[42] The European ethnics, like the blacks, were the targets of nativist and racialist hostilities.[43] Indeed, it might logically have been expected that the Southern black migrants would easily fit into the pattern of machine politics for they too were immigrants in the sense of social, economic, and political dislocation, and the machines depended on immigrant support, representing the approach to politics Banfield and Wilson have called 'the immigrant ethos'.[44] Thus the politics of the period, the politics of fluid ethnic alliances conceivably might have

---

[41] For Chicago to 1893, see Bessie Louise Pierce, *A History of Chicago*, 3 vols. (New York, 1937, 1940, 1957), and, for the following years, Emmett Dedmon, *Fabulous Chicago* (New York, 1953). Chapter 1 of Wallace Sayre and Herbert Kaufman's *Governing New York City* (New York, 1965) succinctly summarizes much material on the growth of New York.

[42] In 1920, for the United States as a whole, 22·9 per cent of blacks over the age of 10 were illiterate; the comparable figure for foreign born whites was 13·1. Significantly, however, in the areas to which the black migrants came, the European immigrant illiteracy rate exceeded that for blacks:

BLACK AND EUROPEAN IMMIGRANT ILLITERACY COMPARED FOR THE REGIONS OF NEW ENGLAND, THE MIDDLE ATLANTIC, AND THE EAST NORTH CENTRAL STATES, 1920

	Blacks (%)	*Foreign-born Whites* (%)
New England	7·1	14·0
Middle Atlantic	5·0	15·7
East North Central	7·3	10·8

SOURCE: U.S. Department of Commerce, Bureau of Foreign and Domestic Commerce, *Statistical Abstract of the United States, 1930* (Washington, 1930),p. 32.

[43] See John Higham, *Strangers in the Land* (New York, 1955) for a first-rate study of American nativism.

[44] Edward Banfield and James Q. Wilson, *City Politics* (New York, 1963), p. 46.

been conducive to black political integration on bi-directional power terms.

The failure of this possibility to materialize can be understood only by reference to the pervasiveness and intensity of anti-black attitudinal racism. It is useful to distinguish between folk prejudice, politically relevant prejudice, and its structural-systemic expression. The latter, which has been the subject of the previous chapters, is the product of the other two dimensions. In these terms, the history of race politics in the cities of the North in the period of migration is the history of the translation of attitudinal folk racism into institutional racism.

Like most of us, the Southern black migrants tended to see history in terms of images; the North, for them was the North of Lincoln, the Abolitionists, the Freedman's Bureau, the Radical Republicans—a North of hope. This pattern of images, however, was seriously distorted, the hope misplaced, for in the North in the late nineteenth and early twentieth centuries, anti-black racism was part of the region's conventional wisdom.

The period's journalism and literature mirrored the anti-black norm. To cite only a few typical examples, the *Atlantic* informed its genteel readers that blacks comprised 'a race alien, animal, half-savage, easily mad, sullen or aroused to fury'.[45] Mencken, the country's most popular journalist, told a wider audience that a black's

... brain is not fitted for the higher forms of mental effort; his ideals, no matter how laboriously he is trained or sheltered, remain those of a clown. He is, in brief, a low-caste-man, to the manner born, and he will remain inert and inefficient until fifty generations of him have lived in civilization. And even then, the superior white race will be fifty generations ahead of him.[46]

Henry Adams habitually referred to blacks as 'niggers', while Henry James, who was enamoured of the South, by his own admission, was repulsed by blacks.[47]

Social Darwinists and their intellectual opponents, fundamentalist preachers and liberal theologians, imperialists and anti-imperialists, all shared the conviction of black inferiority. William Graham Sumner, for instance, insisted that 'no man has ever asserted that "all men are equal" meaning what he said. . . . Thomas Jefferson . . . was not talking about Negroes'.[48] E. A. Ross, the distinguished Wisconsin sociologist and a leading critic of Sumner's Spencerian viewpoint, argued that the tone of American society was lowered by the presence 'of several millions of an inferior race'.[49] In the debate over the new U.S. territories in the Pacific

[45] Quoted by Rayford Logan, *The Negro in American Life and Thought: The Nadir, 1877–1901* (New York, 1954), p. 241.

[46] Quoted by John P. Roche, *The Quest for the Dream* (New York, 1963), p. 12.

[47] See Thomas Gossett, *Race: The History of an Idea in America* (New York, 1965), p. 283.

[48] Harris E. Starr, *William Graham Sumner* (New York, 1925), pp. 62–3.

[49] Gossett, op. cit., p. 169.

acquired in the Spanish–American war and inhabited in the main by brown-skinned peoples, 'the anti-imperialists, like the imperialists, saw the world from a pseudo-Darwinian point of view. They accepted the inequality of man—or, to be more precise, of races—as an established fact of life.'[50] In 1899, for example, Senator John W. Daniel (Democrat, Virginia), in an anti-imperialist speech on the Senate floor, asserted that 'there is one thing that neither time nor education can change; you may change the leopard's spots, but you will never change the different qualities of the races.'[51] Twenty years earlier, Lasch notes,

. . . such arguments would have called forth angry rejoinders from the North. That the South's recourse to them at the end of the century did not revive the old controversy over Reconstruction revealed the extent to which Northern liberals had retreated from the implications of their emancipation of the Negro.[52]

It would have been surprising had these Northern racist attitudes not found systemic political expression. Politicians, who are inclined to opt for security, tend not to be much in advance, in their public rhetoric and actions, of perceived social norms. 'If people want a sense of purpose', Harold Macmillan once remarked, 'they should get it from their archbishops. They should not hope to receive it from their politicians.'[53] White Northern politicians made their critical structural racial decisions largely because of their perceptions of the racial attitudes of most of their constituents, including those of many of the European immigrants who, by berating blacks, were able to achieve the comforting sense of belonging to the majority.

V

Today's politics of racial confrontation, chaos, and despair in the Northern cities of the United States underscores the enormity of the failure to establish bi-directional, representative political linkages in the fluid period of migration. Lowi was quite right to stress in his study of patronage in New York that,

. . . the vanguard of an ethnic minority is of fundamental importance to the campaign of the group for representation. The manner in which precedents are broken largely determines whether new precedents are established; *a poor first representation can easily set back the cause of a new minority by many years.*[54]

For the European ethnics, urban political mobility translated into social and economic mobility; on the individual level, from 1900–10,

[50] Christopher Lasch, 'The Anti-Imperialists, the Philippines, and the Inequality of Man', *Journal of Southern History* (Vol. 24, August 1958), p. 321.

[51] *Congressional Record*, 55th Congress, 3rd session, p. 1424 (1899).

[52] Ibid., p. 319.

[53] Cited in Henry Fairlie, *The Life of Politics* (London, 1968), p. 16.

[54] Theodore J. Lowi, *At the Pleasure of the Mayor* (New York, 1964), p. 41. Italics added.

the proportion of college graduates among city commissioners was 73 per cent for native American Protestants, but only 56 per cent for Germans, 41 per cent for the Irish, and 36 per cent for the Jews.[55] Comparable figures obtained for the following two decades. For blacks, on the other hand, Furniss noted,

. . . what is more striking about the educational pattern of the Negro political elite . . . is how few Negro leaders experienced high mobility through politics, even in the Early period. Among the Early leaders, two-thirds had some post-high school education. In contrast, among the 58 Irish appointees as city commissioners between 1898 and 1910, 50% did not attend college and 39% of the 58 were not even high school graduates. . . . Negroes have not found politics an alternative to the educational system as a channel of social mobility. If anything, politics has served as an adjunct to that system.[56]

Fully 87 per cent of Furniss's sample of 101 top black leaders between 1915–39 entered politics from professional, technical, proprietary, and managerial occupations. 'Considering the fact that politics has served as a channel of social mobility for new ethnic groups,' he concluded, 'it is noteworthy that social mobility . . . was a *prior* condition for Negro political progress.'[57]

In New York City, rule by a native-born Protestant elite gave way to the politics of machine control in the late nineteenth century. After the First World War, the machines slowly began to disintegrate. The process rapidly accelerated with the election of a reform mayor, Fiorello LaGuardia in 1933, and with the national welfare programmes of the New Deal. The politics of New York entered a new phase marked by increasingly fragmented, relatively impotent, party organizations, and the development of independent, but not apolitical, bureaucracies which have become new centres of power.

In the machine period, when the party organizations provided the best access routes to positions of political control and mobility, blacks were on the periphery of party affairs. Furniss has calculated that blacks, in 1910, had secured only 5 per cent of the top patronage positions in New York City proportional to their population (100 per cent would indicate that their proportion of patronage positions equalled their proportion of the city's population); as late as 1930, they had secured under 20 per cent of the positions at the top to which they were entitled by reference to the size of the population. By contrast, Italians—who in this period fared least well among the European ethnics—in 1930 controlled 27 per cent of the higher echelon jobs they were entitled to by reference to their population.[58] Between 1900 and 1950, only one black, Congressman Adam

[55] George Furniss, 'The Political Assimilation of Negroes in New York City', unpublished Ph.D. thesis, Columbia University, 1969, p. 390.
[56] Ibid., p. 386.
[57] Ibid., pp. 391, 413.
[58] Ibid., p. 109.

I

Clayton Powell, Jr., was elected to a first-rank decision-making post. To date, in municipal elections for the city's three leading offices of Mayor, Comptroller, and President of the city council, blacks have yet to be nominated by either of the major parties.

Ironically, with the demise of New York City's political machines, blacks have begun to win a more equitable share of lower and middle level party positions; one black, J. Raymond Jones, even became the leader of Tammany Hall (1964), while others have served as Borough President of Manhattan. By 1960, blacks controlled 21 per cent of the borough's district leaderships, though only 14 per cent of Manhattan's population was black.[59] Though the party system is now more open to black participation on bi-directional power terms than ever before, party activity is far less rewarding. It is significant that only *after* the traditional party machines lost their primary position of influence were blacks permitted to participate on terms of near equality. 'The unfortunate thing', Cornwell notes, 'is that American parties have decayed as organizations to the point that they can make far less contribution to this process of adjustment than they could and did in the past.'[60] The new foci of power in New York are the centralized, over-institutionalized, bureaucracies, and there the city's blacks remain essentially without power.

Among America's cities, Chicago is the exception to the prevailing rule of atrophied urban party organizations. There, the dominant structured linkage fashioned between 1900 and 1930, which linked a dependent black sub-machine to the city-wide organization, has endured virtually unchanged, though the relationship is now a Democratic party one. Blacks are still excluded from political decision-making positions. Baron's recent study of Cook County (1965) found that though blacks comprised 20 per cent of the county's population and 28 per cent of Chicago's, 'in government, out of a total of 1088 policy-making positions, Negroes held just 58', about 5 per cent. Like the Carey–Wright organization of the Thompson years, the late Congressman William Dawson's black sub-machine 'basically settled for lesser patronage positions and political favors rather than using its considerable strength to make or change policy'.[61] On the important issues of the schools and urban renewal, for instance, the Dawson sub-machine remains mute.

Thus, while social control of blacks by whites in the South was direct and unambiguous, the situation was more complex in the cities of the North. There, in the critical period of migration, white political elites and a detached black political leadership constructed uni-directional

[59] Elmer E. Cornwell, Jr., 'Bosses, Machines, and Ethnic Groups', in Lawrence Fuchs, ed., *American Ethnic Politics* (New York, 1968), p. 213.

[60] Ibid., p. 216.

[61] Harold Baron, 'Black Powerlessness in Chicago', *Trans-Action* (Vol. 4, November 1968), pp. 28, 33.

buffer institutions and arrangements that shaped and limited the terms of black participation in politics. As a result, the migrants to the North, unlike the European ethnics, were left outside of what Gamson calls the 'competitive establishment' of adequately represented groups and authorities.[62] Without adequate recognition of this key structural feature of race politics of the period, serious analysis of twentieth-century black political behaviour in the North is impossible.

[62] William Gamson, 'Stable Unrepresentation in American Society', *The American Behavioral Scientist* (Vol. 12, November–December 1968), p 19.

Part Three

British Patterns, 1948–68

Chapter Eight

Pre-Political Consensus and Fundamental Debate

THE movement of large numbers of black colonized, and formerly colonized, migrants to the United Kingdom after the Second World War coincided with the liquidation of the British Empire, and, consequently, with a fundamental redefinition of British political relationships with Third World peoples. In 1948, the Empire's citizenship provisions were redefined and codified by the passage of the British Nationality Act which divided British citizens into two classes: citizens of independent Commonwealth countries, and the remainder, lumped together under the rubric 'citizen of the United Kingdom and Colonies'. Two decades later, in 1968, the citizenship arrangements of 1948 were commonly acknowledged to have lost even their symbolic content.[1] Thus, the migration of Third World people to the mother country was linked in both time and space to Britain's colonial and post-colonial arrangements.

Despite the intimate connection between the migration and the colonial experience, to date even race relations scholars who reject the pure immigrant model have failed to deal with the British situation as a complex amalgam of the immigrant and colonial cases. Thus, for example, *Colour and Citizenship: A Report on British Race Relations*,[2] the most comprehensive study of British race relations yet published which rightly stresses the interaction of the racial majority and minority, downgrades the significance of the colonial factor and, as a result, fails to analyse incisively the origins, aims, and structure of the linkages of the immigrants and the polity. The study deals at length with the origins, passage, and effects of immigration control and anti-discrimination legislation; but it has little to say about the network of national and local institutions established to manage the politics of race, which, I argue below, give domestic expression to classic colonial patterns of social control.

[1] For a discussion of the citizenship issue, see Donald Rothchild, 'Politics of Commonwealth Immigration: The Kenya Asian Crisis', unpublished paper.

[2] E. J. B. Rose and Associates, *Colour and Citizenship: A Report on British Race Relations* (London, 1969).

Many aspects of British race relations deserve, and to some extent have received, extended treatment.[3] Demographic, religious, educational, economic, family, and associational issues, policies, and practices provide potentially fascinating areas of inquiry. Based on a concern with the neglected colonial–immigrant amalgam and with a first-order concern for structure, however, this section addresses itself to the critical structural decisions made by British political elites in the period of migration. It examines the emergence, nature, and possible consequences of the racial–political institutional relationships that link the immigrants to the polity through national and local buffering institutions in a manner strikingly different from the way in which white Englishmen are linked to the polity, thus producing a politics of race that contrasts sharply with the country's institutionalized politics of class, and replicates aspects of the classic colonial pattern of indirect rule.

I

British politics, Samuel Beer asserts, have entered the collectivist age, but, one is tempted to add, the liberal collectivist age.[4] The political model which saw the rational, independent individual as the source of action has been replaced by a politics of rational independent groups. The liberal assumptions of rationalism, independence, and tolerance have carried over into the group politics of the mid-twentieth century.[5] Thus the 'rational' conflicts of class can be managed and institutionalized. Indeed, the increasing institutionalization and coherence of the politics of class is the most salient feature of twentieth-century British political history.

From the turn of the century to the First World War, as the country faced substantial labour unrest, the Labour party resembled a pressure group, and the trade union movement grew rapidly, class cleavages appeared to threaten the transformation of the polity itself. These fears, or hopes, were not borne out. To paraphrase George Woodcock, the Labour movement moved out of Trafalgar Square into the committee rooms. The Parliamentary Labour party was absorbed into the political system as it assimilated traditional political attitudes and broadened its class base. The unions developed into a 'rational' interest to be tolerated consulted, and conciliated. By participating in direct bargaining and boundary management, the Labour movement made possible a stable,

---

[3] See A. Sivanandan, ed., *Coloured Immigrants in Britain: a Select Bibliography* (London, 1969).

[4] Samuel H. Beer, *Modern British Politics* (London, 1965), especially pp. 69–102, 319–90.

[5] For both a critique and an elaboration of Beer's work, see Paul Peterson, 'British Interest Group Theory Re-examined: The Politics of Comprehensive Education in Three British Cities', *Comparative Politics* (Vol. 3, April 1971).

coherent, manageable politics of class.[6] Though fundamental relations of property and power were not altered, the development of an institutionalized politics of class defused class conflicts.[7]

However managed and defused, class is still at the core of the British political dialogue. As a result, for the mid-twentieth-century British politician, class issues have presented few unknowns. In discussing issues of class, he knows, broadly, what is expected of him; his rhetoric and behaviour conform on the whole to relatively clearcut norms. For the typical politician, on the other hand, domestic racial issues, when first raised, were worrying, confusing, incoherent, anomic. Consequently, most British politicians have been anxious to depoliticize race, to make the politics of race coherent by creating policies and institutions *outside* of the usual political arenas that are capable of eliminating race once and for all as a public political issue, thus permitting them to deal with the more congenial, well-defined issues of class.

In his analysis of British elite reactions to domestic crisis in 1829–32, Allan Silver noted that 'at critical historical points, the consequences of social change are met by political elites recruited only in part, if at all, from groups that reflect or embody the emerging future.'[8] During the critical structural period of migration to Britain, the critical structural decisions were made by political elites recruited *not at all* from the Third World migrants. To account for their actions, it is necessary, as Goldthorpe has suggested, to transcend 'a functionalist frame of reference and to think, rather, in terms of the purposive actions of individuals and groups in pursuit of their ends'.[9] Without simplifying the diversity of their actions and ends, I would suggest that the central dynamic of British elite reaction to Third World migration has been an attempt to structure the politics of race to take race out of conventional politics.

Seen in these terms, the attempt to produce a coherent politics (or non-politics) of race has passed through three distinct, yet chronologically overlapping, stages: (i) pre-political consensus (1948–61) when, in Deakin's phrase, race 'only touched the periphery of political debate',[10] as both parties were in substantial agreement if not on what to do at least on what not to do. (ii) Fundamental debate (1958–65) when the parties, largely because of internal imperatives, reacted differently to the politicization of race. The pre-political consensus broke down as they

---

[6] For a discussion of direct bargaining and boundary management, see Chapter 2, Section III.

[7] For an illuminating discussion, see Stuart Hall, et al., *New Left May Day Manifesto, 1967* (London, 1967).

[8] Allan Silver, 'Social and Ideological Bases of British Elite Reactions to Domestic Crisis in 1829–1832', *Politics and Society* (Vol. I, February 1971), p. 179.

[9] John H. Goldthorpe, 'The Development of Social Policy in England, 1800–1914', *Transactions of the Fifth World Congress of Sociology* (London, 1967), p. 55.

[10] Nicholas Deakin, 'The Politics of the Commonwealth Immigrants Bill', *The Political Quarterly* (Vol. 39, January–March 1968), p. 26.

differed over immigration control legislation. In potential and in fact, race became a potent partisan electoral issue. And (iii) political consensus (1965 to the present), when the front benches of the two major parties developed a new consensus, politically arrived at, to depoliticize race once again.

II

During the period of pre-political consensus, the issues of race were raised only sporadically in the House of Commons, and never by the Government or Opposition front benches. In November 1954, a Sheffield Labour M.P., John Hynd, asserted that 'we should examine very carefully whether there is not some way by which it [immigration] can be better regulated, even if it is not necessary in any way to restrict it'.[11] Three years later, in November 1957, five London Labour M.P.s (Albert Evans, Eric Fletcher, E. T. Parkin, G. W. Gibson, and Marcus Lipton) who represented constituencies with large numbers of black immigrants discussed the difficulties, especially with regard to housing, that had been exacerbated by the migration and by the absence of government action.[12] In April 1958, Harry Hynd, the Labour M.P. for Accrington and a leader of the small Labour party lobby favouring immigration controls, initiated a debate on a motion signed by members of both parties calling for 'reconsideration of the arrangements whereby British subjects from other parts of the Commonwealth are allowed to enter this country without restriction'.[13] On the Conservative back benches, Cyril Osborne and, after 1955, Norman Pannell, were virtually alone before 1958 in seeking to limit immigration from the Commonwealth.[14]

In addition to the advocates of controls and positive government programmes to promote integration and deal with social deficiencies, two Labour M.P.s, Reginald Sorenson in 1950 and Fenner Brockway in 1956, introduced legislation designed to combat racial discrimination. That, in essence, was the sum of public activity in Parliament before the summer of 1958 concerned with immigration and race relations.[15]

On 5 December 1958, David Renton, the Joint Under-Secretary of State for the Home Office, rose to reject a private member's motion proposed by Cyril Osborne which urged 'Her Majesty's Government to take immediate steps to restrict the immigration of all persons, irrespective of

---

[11] *Hansard*, House of Commons (5 November 1954), Vol. 532, col. 821.

[12] *Hansard*, H. of C. (22 November 1957), Vol. 578, col. 743-75.

[13] *Hansard*, H. of C. (3 April 1958), Vol. 585, col. 1415.

[14] See Deakin, 'The Politics of the Commonwealth Immigrants Bill', op. cit., pp. 27-35, and Paul Foot, *Immigration and Race in British Politics* (London, 1965), pp. 128ff.

[15] For a discussion of the Sorenson and Brockway bills, see Keith Hindell, 'The Genesis of the Race Relations Bill', in Richard Rose, ed., *Policy-Making in Britain* (London, 1969), pp. 184-5.

race, colour or creed, who are unfit, idle or criminal; and to repatriate all immigrants who are found guilty of a serious criminal offence in the United Kingdom'.[16] Despite the disclaimer, there was little doubt that Osborne had Third World immigrants in mind; just a month earlier Osborne had stated, 'It is time someone spoke out for the white man in this country, and I propose to do so', and called for the control of immigration, 'particularly of coloured immigrants'.[17] Renton, speaking for the Government, deplored any step that would breach 'the principle of the open door upon which most of us agree', stating that:

. . . this country is proud to be the centre of an inter-racial Commonwealth which, my Hon. Friend agrees, is the greatest assortment of peoples of all races, creeds and colours the world has ever seen. As a result of that, we have always allowed any of the people in what was the Empire and is now the Commonwealth to come to this country and to go from it as they please.[18]

And, Renton concluded, 'both the Government and, I am glad to record, the Opposition front bench do not see the necessity for any general control of immigration'.[19]

This shared party position developed logically out of the essentially paternal view of the Empire and Commonwealth held in common by those who differed over the future of Britain's colonial possessions.[20] Britain, both Labour and Conservative members argued, was the centre of the Commonwealth; immigration from the Commonwealth must not, therefore, be restricted. As Henry Hopkinson, the Minister of State for Colonial Affairs had put it in 1954, 'we still take pride in the fact that a man can say *civis britannicus sum* whatever his colour may be, and we take pride in the fact that he wants and can come to the Mother Country.'[21] Much as Harold Macmillan justified decolonization in paternal terms (he spoke in 1960 about 'the development of nations in the world to which we already stand in the relationship of parents', and argued that decolonization was 'the logical result—indeed the triumph— of Britain's Imperial policies'),[22] his Government and the Labour party appealed to the Commonwealth ideal to resist the politicization of race and preserve the pre-political consensus.

This, then, was the essence of the pre-political consensus: colour would not be treated as a relevant political category. That there were any problems of discrimination, prejudice, integration, and social deficiencies, was implicitly denied. The dominant political attitude, Adair notes, 'was

---

[16] *Hansard*, H. of C. (5 December 1958), Vol. 596, col. 1552.
[17] Foot, *Immigration* . . . , op. cit., p. 129.
[18] *Hansard*, H. of C. (5 December 1958), Vol. 596, col. 1579–80.
[19] Ibid., col. 1587.
[20] See Dan Horowitz, 'The British Conservatives and the Racial Issue in the Debate on Decolonization', *Race* (Vol. XII, October 1970), pp. 169–85.
[21] *Hansard*, H. of C. (5 November 1954), Vol. 532, col. 827.
[22] Horowitz, 'The British Conservatives . . .', op. cit., p. 182.

that there was no great problem and that things would right themselves in the end.'[23]

Deakin has argued that the 'outwards appearance of indifference . . . is deceptive and . . . strictures on the role of Government in the early and middle fifties are not entirely just', citing the meetings of an *ad hoc* inter-departmental civil service committee and unused contingency plans for the control of immigration.[24] In fact, the 'outwards appearance of indifference' was not deceptive. Marcus Lipton, who approached the Colonial Office and Home Office repeatedly in the 1950s to seek integrative assistance for his Brixton constituency, has asserted that the inter-departmental committee 'was one of those committees that exists and never acts; it never did anything'.[25] Similarly, Reginald Maudling, from the vantage point of the Tory front bench, recalls that the committee was 'not very high-powered or significant', and that the existence of control plans did not mean that the Government seriously considered restrictive action before 1960–1; the plans were drafted because 'after all, that is what the Civil Service is for'.[26] Through the 1950s, R. A. Butler too thought 'the problem was in hand', and was confident that the few minor difficulties that did exist would be dealt with by the inter-departmental committee. Looking back in March 1968, Butler noted that most politicians wanted to leave the issues of immigration and race relations alone, and evaluated the following assessment by Adair as 'a just criticism'.[27]

No positive steps were taken to ensure that the problems which must arise in a situation of this kind did not get out of control and mitigate against good race relations. No attempt was made to educate either immigrants or British about each other; nothing was done to assist the immigrants on their arrival and to help them in their adaption to life in a strange environment. Social deficiencies in housing and education were allowed to go unchecked and the exploitation of immigrants continued unabated.[28]

The Labour Party in the early and middle 1950s uttered the usual platitudes about discrimination, but did little to either educate the public or bring the issues of colour to public attention through political debate. Though the Commonwealth Sub-Committee of the National Executive declared its opposition to racial discrimination in 1955 and a resolution deploring racial discrimination was passed at the 1956 party conference, the Opposition, before the summer of 1958, did not go beyond calls for new committees, conferences, and studies.[29] There was little mention of

[23] Anthony Adair, 'Immigration Control and Integration', *Contemporary Review* (April 1966), p. 177.

[24] Deakin, 'The Politics of the Commonwealth Immigrants Bill', op. cit., pp. 35–6, 44.

[25] Interview with Marcus Lipton, M.P., at the House of Commons (6 March 1969).

[26] Interview with Reginald Maulding, M.P., at the House of Commons (20 February 1969).

[27] Interview with Lord Butler, Trinity College, Cambridge (2 March 1968).

[28] Adair, 'Immigration Control and Integration', op. cit., p. 177.

[29] See Foot, *Immigration* . . . , pp. 166–8.

racial questions at Shadow Cabinet or National Executive meetings except, as Ray Gunter has put it, for 'occasional perfunctory mentions of racial equality'.[30]

III

The pre-political consensus did not last. Largely as a result of the violent racial clashes that erupted in London and Nottingham in the summer of 1958,[31] the issues of race moved from the periphery to the centre of political debate. A Labour M.P. noted astutely in the Osborne private member's motion debate of December 1958, 'I feel this debate originates out of what happened at Notting Hill Gate and Nottingham, and try as we will, we cannot divorce ourselves from those events, for I am certain if those incidents had not occurred we would not have a debate on this issue.'[32] Butler remembers having feared at the time that 'the violence might spread over England, much like it has in America'.[33] Though the 1958 disturbances were not race riots on an American scale, and were over-sensationalized by the press, the fact that whites and blacks clashed violently in English city streets brought the issues of race to public attention. Before the summer of 1958, Ray Gosling has observed, 'the country was in a state of racial innocence: its experience with people of black, brown or yellow skin was colonial, tolerant, and often smug. Now all that was changed. Notting Hill and Nottingham have become loaded words.'[34] The non-political consensus that had kept race out of politics was upset. Colour was now relevant politically, and, respectable or no, it would be dealt with politically.

The immediate reaction of the political elite, however, was to try to preserve the pre-political consensus. Speaking for the Government, the Home Secretary deplored racial violence and insisted, 'We have no intention of allowing extremist elements to take advantage of any situation.'[35] The Labour party endorsed the Brockway Bill, and in late September issued a statement abhorring,

. . . every manifestation of racial prejudice and particularly condemns those instances which have recently occurred in this country. . . . Unless people of different races and colours can learn to live in harmony, the future for our children in this rapidly shrinking world will be one of extreme danger.[36]

[30] Interview with Raymond Gunter, M.P., at the House of Commons (21 January 1969).

[31] For an account of the violence, see James Wickenden, *Colour in Britain* (London, 1958), pp. 23–35.

[32] *Hansard*, H. of C. (5 December 1958), Vol. 596, col. 1564.

[33] Butler interview.

[34] Ray Gosling 'Twistings in that Poor White Boy', *New Society* (29 November 1962), p. 9.

[35] Butler speech at Stambourne, Essex: *Manchester Guardian* (7 September 1958).

[36] Labour Party, 'Racial Discrimination' (September 1958).

These statements were not a prelude to action to reduce social tensions. As Deakin aptly put it, 'once a representative element of the unemployed or under-employed youth who were responsible for the "rioting" had been sentenced to a long term in goal and liberal opinion had purged itself with suitable expressions of disgust, very little further was done',[37] and not for the lack of specific policy proposals. In 1960, for example, Anthony Richmond, one of the small number of British scholars to write about domestic racial problems in the 1950s, proposed a detailed programme which included legislation to prohibit racial discrimination in public places, dispersal of immigrant school-children, an educational programme to minimize white racial prejudices, expanded welfare services for immigrants, special educational and recreational facilities for adult immigrants, and a programme of community development to rehabilitate the 'twilight' areas of immigrant settlement.[38]

The Government chose not to act. 'To the liberal', writes Plamenatz, 'colour prejudice is unpleasant, and in Britain we are most of us to some extent liberals. But all men—and liberals no less than others—are apt to turn away from what is unpleasant.'[39] For politicians, moreover, race questions were not only unpleasant, but in political terms were anomic and unpredictable.

Thus in September 1958, Butler declared: 'We should not take rush decisions in an atmosphere of unrest. Some of the difficulties as those concerned with housing involve the local authorities and these we shall discuss with those principally concerned.'[40] Yet the local authorities were reluctant to act. Though voluntary committees in Leeds, Nottingham, and Paddington assisted the immigrant newcomers, local governments did little lest they appear to give priority treatment to immigrants and arouse the ire of their constitutents. Local authorities were expected to grapple with the problem unaided, yet local politicians viewed local action as a political threat. In 1955, for example, the General Purposes Committee of the Lambeth Borough Council recommended that representation be made to the Home Secretary noting:

. . . that, whilst the Council was anxious at all costs to avoid anything which might lead to racial difficulties, the Council nevertheless stated categorically that whatever it might do as a local authority on behalf of colonial immigrants, such action might well be regarded by the public within the borough as giving quite unfair consideration and priority to the claims and difficulties of these people.[41]

[37] Nicholas Deakin, 'Immigration and British Politics', *Crucible* (May 1965), p. 83.
[38] A. R. Richmond, 'Applied Social Science and Public Policy Concerning Racial Relations in Britain', *Race* (Vol. I, May 1960), pp. 25-6.
[39] John Plamenatz, 'Strangers in Our Midst', *Race* (Vol. VII, July 1965), p. 12.
[40] *Manchester Guardian* (7 September 1958).
[41] Minutes of meeting, 26 January 1955, reprinted in Lambeth Borough Council, 'Immigration from the Commonwealth' (24 November 1965).

In June 1959, replying to a question in the House, Butler reiterated the Government's position:

I am satisfied from consultations which I have had with my colleagues mainly concerned and from consultations which have taken place with local authorities, voluntary bodies, the official welfare organizations and the police that everything possible is being done and that every effort will continue to be made in areas where there is a large coloured population to encourage their effective integration into the community.

He rejected demands for a special inquiry, noting that 'standing arrangements exist, in both Ministerial and official levels, for the effective coordination of the work of the Departments concerned.'[42]

IV

The search for a coherent politics of race between the summer of 1958 and 1962 was primarily a search for coherence *within* each party. Though the ideological differences dividing the parties had narrowed in the 1950s, their hierarchies of interests and social priorities, as well as their membership's social characteristics remained distinct.[43] As a result of these differences, as well as the differences in perspective between governing and opposition, the reactions of the Conservative and Labour parties to the politicization of race differed strikingly. Thus, when the Government announced in the Queen's Speech of October 1961 that it intended to introduce legislation to control immigration from the Commonwealth, the Labour party demurred and vigorously resisted the Bill.

In making policy, the Conservative government had to take into account the views not only of the parliamentary party, but also those of the party's constituents, public opinion as a whole, and the civil service. Within the parliamentary party, a small, but vocal group of backbenchers was clamouring for controls. After the general election of 1959, this group's ranks, led by Cyril Osborne and Norman Pannell, were reinforced by the election of a number of Midland Tory M.P.s whose conservatism was of the lower middle-class variety which contrasted sharply with the well-mannered upper middle-class Toryism of Southern England.[44]

In July 1960 and again in May 1961, members of the Conservative control lobby met with the Home Secretary to argue the case for legislation. In his survey, Paul Foot attributes the passage of the Commonwealth Immigrants Act largely to the activities of these M.P.s.[45] Not surprisingly members of the control lobby too opt for this interpretation. Harold Gurden, for example, who represents the Birmingham constituency of

[42] *Hansard*, H. of C. (4 June 1959), Vol. 606, col. 369.

[43] For a discussion, see Beer, op. cit.

[44] See L. J. Sharpe, 'Brixton', in Nicholas Deakin, ed., *Colour and the British Electorate 1964* (London, 1965), p. 22.

[45] Foot, *Immigration* . . . , pp. 129–38.

Selly Oak, and who was a convert to the control cause after attending a meeting in 1958 organized by his constituents who favoured immigration restrictions, is convinced that his lobbying efforts were instrumental in persuading Butler to favour controls; 'I let him know we meant business, and raised the issue at a meeting of the 1922 committee where I found more party support than opposition. We had sunk our teeth in the issue and would not let go. Butler knew we meant business. I think that is why he came around.'[46]

This interpretation is only partially accurate. Butler has forcefully denied that pressure from the control lobby convinced either him or the Cabinet to bring in legislation: 'I was used to pressure from this group in the party. I took their views for granted.'[47] But the activities of the Conservative parliamentary control advocates were indirectly significant in convincing the Government to curb immigration in two respects. Ironically, their activities had the effect of increasing substantially the numbers of immigrants, many of whom came to beat the mooted ban, and, secondly, they had the effect of influencing Tory constituency opinion and the views of the general public.

Until 1960, the rate of immigration into the United Kingdom varied directly with the state of the British economy. In 1960, 1961, and the first six months of 1962, when immigration curbs were advocated, proposed, and passed, there was, Peach notes:

. . . a major break with the trend. In 1961 the employment index declined slightly but immigration from the West Indies showed a great increase. In the first two quarters of 1962 it was evident that the economy was depressed to the levels of the first two quarters of 1958 and 1959. Immigration reached the highest recorded rate for those quarters.

Moreover, 'for the first time since 1955, a rising number of migrants was associated with a declining proportion of males'; 57·8 per cent of the 1960 West Indian migrants were male, 47·14 per cent in 1961, and only 42·8 per cent in the first half of 1962.[48] The large increase in the number of migrants in 1960–2 was largely an increase of women and children who came to join their families before immigration was restricted. The rush to come reflected the migrants' uncertainty about the future, an uncertainty contributed to by the Osborne–Pannell control lobby.

The control lobby was also influential indirectly in that their efforts helped shape local party and general public opinion. 'The lobbyists arguing for control', writes Deakin, 'became siren voices offering a solution where the Government could only proclaim with diminishing conviction the indivisibility of British citizenship.'[49] In March 1955, the

---

[46] Interview with Harold Gurden, M.P., at the House of Commons (6 March 1969).
[47] Butler interview.
[48] Ceri Peach, *West Indian Migration to Britain: A Social Geography* (London, 1968), pp. 46–7.
[49] Deakin, 'The Politics of the Commonwealth Immigrants Bill', op. cit., p. 45.

Central Council of Conservative and Unionist Associations called on the Government to extend the law on deportation (which applied to aliens) to immigrants from the Commonwealth.[50] Three and a half years later, the 1958 Conservative party conference reacted to the previous summer's violence by passing a resolution, opposed by the Government, calling for controls on immigration. Constituency pressures reached their climax at the 1961 party conference at Brighton. Just under three weeks before the Queen's Speech, the conference debated and overwhelmingly passed one of the thirty-nine motions tabled that, in some form, advocated restrictive legislation.[51]

By 1960-1, general public opinion had crystallized in favour of controls. A survey conducted in 1960, based on a quota-type sample of 604 manual workers or their dependants in six large urban English constituencies, found that '83 per cent . . . favoured government action to restrict coloured immigration; Labour and Conservative voters supported this view with almost exactly the same frequency.'[52] In May 1961, the Gallup poll carried out an exhaustive survey of English attitudes towards Third World immigrants which included the question, 'Do you think that coloured people from the Commonwealth should have the right of completely free entry into Britain, should there be restrictions on entry, or should they be kept out completely.' Only 21 per cent favoured free entry, 67 per cent advocated restrictions, 6 per cent wanted blacks completely excluded, and 6 per cent were undecided.[53] The electorate had rejected the bi-partisan front bench solution, and instead opted for the solution of those who had aroused their endemic xenophobic and racial prejudices.

In theory, the civil service is apolitical; its role is to advise and administer. Yet, as Richard Crossman has noted, 'the powers of the Cabinet have been eroded by the growing ascendency of Whitehall'.[54] In evidence presented to the Fulton committee on civil service reform, Dudley Seers similarly argued 'that the Civil Service does really possess political power . . . a minister has to rely heavily on the advice he receives from his senior officials, especially his Permanent Secretary'. Thus civil servants are part politician, and 'being politicians, civil servants have also to assess, to the best of their ability, the political forces at work, if they are to avoid trouble for their department'. Here, Seers maintains, 'intuition

---

[50] *Evening News* (17 March 1955).

[51] At the Brighton conference in October, of the 536 motions submitted on the agenda, thirty-nine concerned restrictions on Commonwealth immigration, ten dealt with colonial affairs, twenty with education, forty with the Common Market, and sixty-six with crime and punishment; *Guardian* (27 September 1961).

[52] Robert McKenzie and Allan Silver, *Angels in Marble: Working Class Conservatives in Urban England* (London, 1968), p. 152.

[53] Supplement to The Institute of Race Relations *Newsletter* (August 1961), p. 1.

[54] Richard Crossman, 'Introduction', to Walter Bagehot, *The English Constitution* (London, 1963), p. 47.

K

is particularly dangerous. The files are full of references to "public opinion" but this is rarely analysed any further.'[55]

Though the views of civil servants are particularly inscrutable, there is evidence indicating that after the summer of 1958 a significant number of civil servants were convinced that immigration curbs were necessary. 'It is no secret', an *Economist* leader-writer asserted in November 1958,

that some departments, looking at the way the situation may develop are considering how reciprocity might be introduced in the treatment of migrants from Commonwealth countries. . . . They think the liberal line—uncontrolled immigration—can be held for a few more years, but not indefinitely. Far from thinking that the British people will get used to colour, as they are reconciled to Poles, Irish or Middle Europeans, this school of opinion in Whitehall and beyond feels that when the tide of colour rises to a certain, as yet unspecified, point, the mass of British voters will demand that some check be imposed.[56]

This analysis has been substantiated by R. A. Butler who has noted that the dominant reaction in Whitehall to the Commonwealth Immigrants Bill was that it was not strong or tough enough, a view he found 'really extraordinary'.[57]

There is little doubt that the Government brought in controls with great reluctance. Butler, who supervised the drafting of the legislation and its passage has said that this task was the 'most unpleasant thing I have ever had to do in my public career'.[58] Constituency and public opinion, backbench pressures, Whitehall advice, and of most immediate importance, the sharply rising immigration figures convinced the Government to abandon its support of unrestricted Commonwealth entry.

In February 1961, Butler indicated to Harold Gurden, a leading control advocate, that he was now prepared to consider controls.[59] That month, Butler raised the matter in the Cabinet and indicated that legislation might be necessary. The Minister of Education, Sir Edward Boyle, and the Colonial Secretary, Iain Macleod, voiced strong opposition, and in the spring took their case to the country. In April, Boyle, after touring the Birmingham 'twilight' area of Handsworth, told the officers of the Birmingham Immigration Control Association that the Government would not bring in immigration legislation.[60] A month later, Macleod remarked that it would be 'extremely distasteful if it had to come to imposing legislation which would run counter to the long-established

[55] Dudley Seers, 'The Structure of Power', in Thomas Balogh, Roger Opie, Dudley Seers, and Hugh Thomas, *Crisis in the Civil Service* (London, 1968), pp. 87-8, 95-6.

[56] 'Keeping the Door Open', *The Economist* (29 November 1958).

[57] Butler interview.

[58] Ibid. See also Kenneth Harris, 'Lord Butler Looks Back', *The Listener* (Vol. 38, 28 July 1966).

[59] Gurden interview.

[60] *Birmingham Mail* (10 April 1961).

position of Britain as the head of the Commonwealth'.[61] Later that month, 'a number of London political correspondents referred to a "top secret" warning issued by the Cabinet to Conservative backbenchers that the Cabinet will not act to impose legal curbs for at least a year, until the Federation of the West Indies comes into being.'[62]

As late as June, according to Butler, the issue was not yet decided; 'legislation seemed so drastic'.[63] The Government, however, began to prepare the public for its prospective *volte-face*. In June Butler replied to a question on the integration of black children in primary schools at the annual conference of the Conservative and Unionist Teachers Association:

The Government will have to give consideration to the question of how much this inflow can be assimilated into our society at the present time. If you give the Government a little longer, we should try to find a solution as friendly to these people as we can, and not based on colour prejudice alone.[64]

By the early autumn, as the numbers of immigrants rose, party, and public, and Whitehall pressures intensified, the Cabinet was ready to give its assent; the exact date of this approval is difficult to determine, but it could not have been too long before the Bill was announced in the Queen's Speech, for as Butler admits, 'There was a terrible rush to get the Bill ready. We had great difficulty in drafting the Bill, and brought it forward in an atmosphere of urgency.'[65]

V

The reaction of the Labour party to the politicization of race took place in the context of internecine party quarrels between rival leadership groups, each with substantial constituency support.

Before the general election of 1959, the party had managed to paper over its ideological cracks to fight the election apparently united. But with the party's crushing defeat (the Labour party polled almost 1,750,000 fewer votes than it had in 1952, and 200,000 less than in 1955), its synthetic unity was shattered. Miliband has acutely noted that:

. . . the battles which broke out in the Labour party after the General Election of 1959 were not only about nationalization or nuclear strategy. They were the specific expressions of a more basic question, namely whether the Labour party is to be concerned with attempts at a more efficient and humane administration of a capitalist society; or whether it is to adapt itself to the task of creating a socialist one.[66]

[61] The Institute of Race Relations *Newsletter* (June 1961), p. 5. Macleod remarks of 4 May 1961.
[62] See the Institute of Race Relations *Newsletter* (July 1961), p. 5.
[63] Butler interview.
[64] *The Times* (19 June 1961).
[65] Butler interview.
[66] Ralph Miliband, *Parliamentary Socialism* (London, 1964), p. 344.

Gaitskell, who supported the first option, and who attributed the party's defeat to its lack of appeal to marginal middle-class voters who were repelled by the ideological baggage of nationalization and unilateralism, urged the party at the post-election November 1959 Conference, to abandon Clause Four, the socialist core of the 1918 constitution.[67] Largely because of trade union opposition, Gaitskell did not get his way and was compelled to accept a compromise draft of principles which were appended to Clause Four. This explanatory declaration, drafted by the National Executive in March 1960 and approved by the 1960 Party Conference, began unambiguously:

The British Labour Party is a democratic socialist party. Its central ideal is the brotherhood of man. Its purpose is to make this ideal a reality everywhere. Accordingly—
1. It rejects discrimination on the grounds of race, colour or creed and holds that men should accord to one another equal consideration and status in recognition of the fundamental dignity of Man.[68]

When the Government introduced the Commonwealth Immigrants Bill in late October 1961, the Blackpool party conference had just voted to reverse the party's 1960 decision taken at Scarborough in opposition to the leadership to support the unilateral renunciation of nuclear weapons. The Clause Four and nuclear weapons disputes had left deep wounds which had to be healed if the party were to regain popular esteem. The party needed an issue on which it could enthusiastically unite, and unite on principle. Immigration control was such an issue.

Gaitskell, who was more of an egalitarian liberal than a socialist, rose in the House on 16 November 1961 to oppose the second reading of the control bill. In what many have called the finest speech of his political life, the Labour leader described the occasion as 'tragic', and denounced 'this miserable, shameful, shabby bill', calling it, 'an appalling confession of failure by the Government. . . . It means in effect that Great Britain cannot absorb or integrate with our community more than 1 per cent of the population. We had better stop throwing stones at the Southern States.'[69]

The government front bench, according to David Renton, 'were utterly shocked by Gaitskell's speech, by his indignation, by the force of his opposition'.[70] 'He had great effect'; Butler recalls, 'he united his party, and we were awfully hard-pressed.'[71]

The second reading debate was particularly caustic. The Government,

---

[67] The conference was held on 28 and 29 November 1959.
[68] The declaration was released on 16 March 1960. For discussions, see Harold Wilson, *The Relevance of British Socialism* (London, 1964), pp. 6–7, and Henry Pelling, *A Short History of the Labour Party* (London, 1968), pp. 120–1.
[69] *Hansard*, H. of C. (16 November 1961), Vol. 649, col. 792–803.
[70] Interview with Sir David Renton, M.P., at the House of Commons (6 March 1969).
[71] Butler interview.

according to John Hare, the Minister of Labour, 'felt they have to take action because of the rise in the number of immigrants during the last three years.'[72] Butler paid tribute to the immigrants already here, but argued 'that the drive for improved conditions will be defeated by the sheer weight of numbers and the immigrants will be among those to benefit most if the powers in fact prove, as we hope, to be effective.'[73] Central to the Government's case were the related notions that the number of dark faces in Britain would determine the reception they received, and that coloured immigration strained the country's overburdened social resources.

The Labour party rejected this assessment, contending that it placed the cart before the horse. Coloured immigration, they maintained, made visible existing social deficiencies but did not cause them. Thus George Brown, for example, asserted that the Bill was inadequate and misleading because it made,

. . . no attempt to deal with the real problems that lie behind this; no ability to recognise that they are social problems and welfare problems; that these are community problems that we provide for communally, and that that is exactly the field in which Her Majesty's Government have chosen to make their most vicious cuts and most vicious attacks on housing expenditure and provision.[74]

Gaitskell's rhetoric, already cited, was unusually acerbic. Gordon Walker too spoke in an uncharacteristically heated tone, labelling the Bill an example of 'bare-faced open race discrimination'.[75]

Though a small number of Labour M.P.s were dissatisfied with this position, the party was finally united, on principle, behind its leader. In particular, Gaitskell's adversaries on the left were jubilant. In an article which summarized their view headlined 'The Way to Beat the Tories', Michael Foot wrote in the *Tribune*:

Suddenly the place came alive. Certainly the House of Commons had witnessed nothing like it for months. Labour's Front Bench went into action, wielding every weapon, conventional or otherwise. And the enemy this time was the Tories.

No praise is too high for the manner in which it was done. Hugh Gaitskell in particular debated with a devastating passion which spread terror and shame along the Government benches. . . . The spectacle of the Labour party asserting its principles in the face of what is supposed to be the popular need of the moment and resolving to withstand all the pressures of expeciency is something fresh and exciting, a new element on the political scene. . . . The Party is united, and not merely united but exhilarated.[76]

[72] *Hansard*, H. of C. (16 November 1961), Vol. 649, col. 810.
[73] Ibid., cols. 687–95.
[74] *Hansard*, H. of C. (1 November 1961), Vol. 648, cols. 167–9.
[75] *Hansard*, H. of C. (16 November 1961), Vol. 649, col. 706.
[76] Michael Foot, 'The Way to Beat the Tories', *Tribune* (24 November 1961), p. 5.

The search for coherent racial policies within the parties had destroyed the pre-political consensus and had produced, for the first and last time within Parliament, a debate which found the parties divided fundamentally on the issues of race. Though some members of the national political elite welcomed this division, most felt menaced by the disruption of the pre-political accord that had kept race off the political agenda. Once again, for them, the politics of race were in search of coherence.

Chapter Nine

The Institutionalization of Political Consensus

To borrow a metaphor from Robert Paul Wolff, the territory of liberal group politics is like a plateau that drops sharply on all sides to a deep valley below. Legitimate, 'rational' interests, ideas, and groups are placed on the plateau itself, and are tolerated and conciliated. But those ideas, interests, and groups in the valley are excluded from the political process of discourse, compromise, and accommodation.[1] In the 1950s, by bi-partisan consent, the unstructured, incoherent politics of race was kept in the valley. But as a result of the factors discussed above, the Conservative party placed immigration controls on the political plateau; by virtue of this new (legitimate) position, the advocates of controls now had to be bargained with and conciliated. They were included in the broad embrace of liberal tolerance.

The pre-political consensus, paradoxically, had managed to structure the politics of race by the agreement to leave the issues unstructured. With the Commonwealth Immigrants Act, however, the politics of race, by being partially structured, became incoherent. Not surprisingly, therefore, the parties moved between 1962 and 1965, haphazardly, obliquely, but unmistakably, towards a new consensus, politically arrived at, which, it was hoped, would be capable of relegating race from the political plateau to the valley below. The definition and institutionalization of the political consensus which this chapter explores was made without Third World immigrant participation or access to positions of political control. There were, in this period, and to date, no black M.P.s, and, with the exception of the Campaign Against Racial Discrimination (C.A.R.D.) which was founded in December 1964, whose principal concerns were anti-discrimination legislation, and whose interracial, intellectual, middle-class membership was hardly representative of the Third World community, there were no organized groups with access to national decision-makers who could articulate and transmit the views and

[1] Robert Paul Wolff, 'Beyond Tolerance', in Robert Paul Wolff, Barrington Moore, Jr., Herbert Marcuse, *A Critique of Pure Tolerance* (Boston, 1965), pp. 45ff.

demands of the immigrants. Thus the Third World migrants were the objects, not the subject participants, of the political consensus.

I

On 23 March 1965, Peter Thorneycroft, the Conservative Shadow Cabinet spokesman on race and immigration initiated a Commons debate which acknowledged the development of a bi-partisan political consensus. Though Thorneycroft began by asserting that immigration 'is a political topic', and that 'it is right in the centre of political subjects', the debate's self-congratulatory tone, perhaps as much as its substance, revealed a longing to depoliticize the issues of race.

Thorneycroft proposed 'a drastic reduction in the inflow of male immigrants . . . through the granting or not granting of vouchers; and, of course, also in tightening up provisions against evasion'. On the positive side, he advocated devoting 'our utmost energy to promoting the absorption of these communities within the fabric of the civilisation of which we in these islands are so proud.' Controls and integration measures, he stated, are 'two sides of the same medal'. He concluded by commending the work of local race relations committees and the National Committee for Commonwealth Immigrants which had been set up in April 1964 on the recommendation of the Commonwealth Immigrants Advisory Council.[2]

Speaking for the Labour Government, Herbert Bowden, the Lord President of the Council, noted that the 'voucher problem' and evasions were under review and would be dealt with. He reminded the House that on 9 March Mr. Wilson had announced that a mission headed by Lord Mountbatten would shortly be dispatched to consult with the countries of the Commonwealth 'to see what measures might be adopted particularly in the country of origin . . . to regulate the flow of immigrants to the United Kingdom, including the need to prevent evasion of control.'[3] The days of fundamental debate were over.

Members on both sides of the House welcomed this development. Sir John Vaughan Morgan (Conservative, Reigate) contrasted this debate to those of late 1961 and early 1962:

I have just been reading the debates of the Second and Third readings of the Commonwealth Immigrants Bill and they do not make very attractive reading.... I am not trying to be provocative or in any way raise the temperature when I say how pleased we all are at the change in tone compared with some previous debates on this subject.[4]

Brigadier Sir John Smyth (Conservative, Norwood) similarly declared,

[2] *Hansard*, H. of C. (23 March 1965), Vol. 709, cols. 334–45.
[3] Ibid., cols. 352–3.
[4] Ibid., col. 357.

It is high time that the two sides of the House got together, as they are doing today, on this most difficult and important problem . . . with the passing of only a few years the two sides are meeting one another *in the middle*. It is extraordinary how much movement together has taken place.[5]

'On both sides of the House', noted Sir George Sinclair (Conservative, Dorking), 'we are coming together on perhaps two aspects . . . to have a balanced policy towards immigration and immigrant communities in our midst—control and adjustment.'[6]

The new party amity was not exulted merely on the Tory right and centre. Norman St. John-Stevas, a leading party liberal, welcomed 'the broad area of agreement on this question. . . . We are all agreed on the need for control'. Nigel Fisher (Conservative, Surbiton), who had opposed the 1962 Act, now recanted, 'I have no doubt in retrospect that I was wrong to do so', adding, 'I myself am a believer in the bi-partisan approach to the problem. I think that as far as possible it should be taken out of party politics.'[7]

To a man, the Labour M.P.s who spoke concurred with these views. Donald Chapman (Birmingham, Northfield) was 'glad that this issue is being raised today out of the bickering and the name calling of earlier years to a higher level of . . . a Council of State.'[8] David Ennals (Dover), later appointed in January 1967 as Under-Secretary at the Home Office with special responsibilities for immigration and race relations, endorsed the view that we must try 'to take a bi-partisan approach', and search 'to see how far we can speak as a House of Commons rather than as parties.'[9] Roy Hattersley (Birmingham, Sparkbrook) summarized the new consensus:

We are all in favour of some sort of limitation. We all wholeheartedly oppose any sort of discrimination. We all wholeheartedly agree that there should be assimilation or adjustment, whichever word one prefers to use. Those three points of view characterise the view and principles of both major parties.[10]

Sir Frank Soskice, the Home Secretary, ended the debate by noting with satisfaction and relief that:

. . . there has been disclosed in the course of the debate a very great degree of unanimity on the broad aspects of the problem with which we are faced. . . . The Government accept that there must be—simply because of the scale of possible immigration—effective control of numbers.[11]

These remarks could have come from either side of the House.

The remarkable accord revealed in this debate was codified and given systemic expression fourteen weeks later in the Labour Government's White Paper, 'Immigration from the Commonwealth', published on

---

[5] Ibid., col. 378. (Italics added.)   [6] Ibid., col. 434.
[7] Ibid., col. 385.   [8] Ibid., col. 369.   [9] Ibid., col. 391.
[10] Ibid., cols. 378-9.   [11] Ibid., col. 443.

2 August which set out 'the Government's future policy on immigration to Britain from other parts of the Commonwealth and on the problems which it has given rise.' This policy had,

... two aspects: one relating to control on the entry of immigrants so that it does not outrun Britain's capacity to absorb them; the other relating to positive measures designed to secure for the immigrants and their children their rightful place in our society and to assist local authorities and other bodies in areas of high immigration in dealing with certain problems which have arisen.[12]

The retreat from the Gaitskell line on immigration of four years earlier was complete. The Government argued now much as the Conservatives had in 1961 that the number of coloured immigrants (not immigrants collectively) was the crucial factor in determining the state of British race relations;[13] the White Paper spoke of 'the need to control the entry of immigrants to our small and overcrowded country', and announced that the annual rate of issue of labour vouchers would be cut drastically to 8,500, of which 1,000 would be allocated to Malta. Moreover, category C vouchers, for those who did not have a specific job to come to and/or lacked special qualifications and skills, would be discontinued permanently.[14]

The limitations on voluntary immigration were linked in the White Paper to the establishment of new institutional mechanisms, officially sponsored yet largely voluntary, to link the immigrants to the local and national political systems. The document announced a new National Committee for Commonwealth Immigrants which would:

... co-ordinate on a national basis efforts directed towards the integration of Commonwealth immigrants into the community. In particular, the Committee shall be required to:
(a) Promote and co-ordinate the activities of voluntary liaison committees and advise them on their work;
(b) Where necessary, assist in the recruitment and training of suitable men and women to serve these committees as full-time officials;

[12] 'Immigration from the Commonwealth', Government White Paper, Cmnd. 2739 (London, 1965), p. 2.
[13] Ibid., pp. 6–9. The White Paper significantly began by giving separate figures for white and Third World Commonwealth countries.
[14] According to Gerald Kaufman, Mountbatten recommended that voucher issues be cut to 10,000 per year. At meetings of a cabinet committee chaired by Herbert Bowden, Soskice argued for a much more drastic cut, and was opposed by Barbara Castle and Arthur Greenwood who sought to preserve Mountbatten's recommendation of 10,000 as a minimum figure. Thus the decision to issue 7,500 vouchers annually to Third World immigrants, plus 1,000 to Malta citizens, was a political decision balancing cabinet views rather than a well-thought-out number related to Britain's absorptive capacity and need for labour. Gerald Kaufman, 'Dutch Auction on Immigrants', *New Statesman* (Vol. 35, 9 July 1965). See also, Robert Moore, 'Labour and Colour—1965–1968', Institute of Race Relations *Newsletter* (October 1968), p. 383.

(c) Provide a central information service;

(d) Organise conferences, arrange training courses and stimulate research;

(e) Advise on those questions which are referred to them by Government or which they consider should be brought to the attention of Government.[15]

The National Committee's personnel was to consist of a Chairman, Deputy Chairman, and eighteen other members, all voluntary, part-time, and unpaid. The Government's unsuccessful attempt to persuade Lord Butler (who as Home Secretary had introduced controls on Commonwealth immigration in 1962) to accept the Chairmanship of the National Committee (N.C.C.I.),[16] and the subsequent appointment of the Archbishop of Canterbury to the post graphically symbolized the Government's attempt to eliminate race as a public political issue dividing the parties. What considerations and events produced the shift from fundamental debate to the institutionalized elite political consensus of 1965?

II

At the second reading debate on the Commonwealth Immigrants Act in November 1961, the Labour party had elevated the principle of the open door to the level of ideological commitment, but by the third reading in February, Labour had subtly, but significantly shifted its ground. Speaking for his front bench, Denis Healey discussed what Labour's attitude towards the Bill would be when it next won power:

If the information collected by a serious survey of the whole problem revealed that immigration control was necessary, we should regard it as essential to consult other Commonwealth Governments to see how this could be achieved with minimum damage to their interests and to their confidence in our loyalty and good will.[17]

The parties no longer divided over the *principle* of controls, but over consultations and timing, both pragmatic issues: 'We can see no ground whatsoever', Healey stated, *'at the present time* for such a Bill'.[18] Butler detected the shift, noticing 'a greater calm than when the Bill was introduced before Christmas'.[19]

In complementary fashion to the changes in Labour's rationale, the Government had modified the Bill at the committee stage: it would expire in eighteen months instead of five years; it recognized common-law marriages and illegitimate children for the purpose of defining wives and dependants; it now made explicit provisions for Commonwealth students,

---

[15] National Committee for Commonwealth Immigrants, *Report for 1966* (London, no date), p. 24.

[16] Interview with Lord Butler, Trinity College, Cambridge, 2 March 1968.

[17] *Hansard*, H. of C. (27 February 1962), Vol. 654, col. 1271.

[18] Ibid. Italics added.

[19] Ibid., col. 1189.

and set up a system of entry certificates; and, perhaps most importantly, the Home Secretary announced that he would appoint a Commonwealth Immigrants Advisory Council to advise him and co-ordinate positive government measures to promote integration. Thus by the third reading, immigration controls were firmly entrenched on the political plateau, while the idea of institutional government mechanisms to promote integration were ascending the steep cliffs. The outlines of a new political consensus, in spite of the party division at the February vote, could dimly, but surely, be perceived.

Hugh Gaitskell, whose absolute opposition to immigration controls had united the Labour party on principle when it had needed above all to heal the wounds of its internecine quarrels, died in January 1963. With the accession of Harold Wilson to the leadership, party unity, at least in the short run, was assured, for as Perry Anderson has commented, 'Wilson above all offered a strategy to the Labour Party—it is this that has enabled him to temporarily cancel the divisions within it and dominate the party.'[20]

Wilson's Bevanite past, tenous though it was, and his unsuccessful contests for the leadership in 1960 and the deputy leadership in 1962, secured for him the support of the Labour left. At a moment of theoretical impasse, he was the unity leader who offered the intoxicating vision of power to those long deprived of it. The old divisive issues were replaced by the new theme of a modernized Britain based on technological advance, a programme aptly described by Foot as 'a blueprint for revolution to the rank and file and a safe but efficient panacea to the floating voter'.[21] Within a week of winning the leadership to the 1964 general election, Wilson's severest critics muted their voices. With the party's cracks papered over, the Shadow Cabinet sought to balance fundamental principles of racial equality and socialist brotherhood with perceived pragmatic electoral imperatives.

The tension between principles and pragmatism is one of the basic dilemmas of parliamentary socialism.[22] Much as the Labour party, whose stated aims are socialist, has accepted the values and structure of the society it wishes to transform, so in the politics of race, the dialectic of fundamental beliefs and the demands of the liberal political process produced a policy which, though seemingly a compromise, conceded the legitimacy of the control advocates' position by accepting the place of racially-based controls on the political plateau.

The Commonwealth Immigrants Act expired in November 1963. Many Labour M.P.s, and the leaders of the party organization at Trans-

[20] Perry Anderson, 'Problems of Socialist Strategy', *Towards Socialism* (London, 1965), p. 221.

[21] Paul Foot, *The Politics of Harold Wilson* (London, 1968), p. 148.

[22] For discussions, see ibid., Chapter 10, and Ralph Miliband, *Parliamentary Socialism* (London, 1964), Chapter 10.

port House wanted to extricate Labour from its identification with Third World immigrants before the next general election.[23] The voice of *realpolitik* began to be heard around the Shadow Cabinet table as well. 'My position in 1963', Frank Soskice (now Lord Stow Hill), then Shadow Home Secretary, has stated, 'was simply that we had to allay the public's fears. I argued, therefore, that we should not challenge the continuation of controls.'[24] Soskice, joined by Patrick Gordon Walker, tried to convince their colleagues, but they were resisted, according to Ray Gunter, by George Brown who opposed any modification of Gaitskell's position. Though Paul Foot and some press accounts have reported that Wilson sided with Brown, Gunter remembers that Wilson tried to play a conciliatory role: 'We really did not know where Harold stood on this.'[25]

A drafting committee of four (Wilson, Brown, Soskice, and Gordon Walker) was appointed in September with the task of reaching a compromise. The final draft, written by Wilson, was accepted by the Shadow Cabinet and the P.L.P. by a vote of eighty-five to eight.[26]

On 27 November, Wilson informed the Commons of the party decision. As a gesture to Gaitskell's position, party principles, and the Labour left, he stressed measures 'needed to deal with the problem of assimilation', including a race relations bill (Brockway's proposals), aid to localities with large numbers of immigrants, and support of voluntary groups. The Labour party, he noted had opposed the Commonwealth Immigrants Act because it was 'based on race and colour discrimination', it 'discriminated against the Commonwealth', and it was 'not based on consultation, still less agreement, with Commonwealth countries'. These three features of the Act, he added, 'which were the ground of our opposition to the Bill are just as true today as they were then'. With unintended irony, he then pointed out that 'there are loopholes in the Act', and called for more effective health checks and a tightening of the deportation provisions.

Having stated his opposition to the Act and his determination to strengthen it, Wilson offered to vote for its continuation if the Government were willing to initiate a round of Commonwealth consultations. The reasoning was tortuous:

[23] In July 1963, a straw poll conducted by Labour whips 'confirmed the worst forebodings in the shadow cabinet that opinion on the issue had shifted alarmingly since two years ago Hugh Gaitskell bitterly attacked the Government for its introduction of discriminatory legislation.' Anthony Howard, 'The Skin Game', *New Statesman* (Vol. 33, 22 November 1963), p. 726.

'Results of local government elections in 1963 in a number of areas of immigration further convinced Transport House that it could not afford to be too closely identified in the public eye with coloured immigration.' A. Sherman, 'Deptford', in Nicholas Deakin, ed., *Colour and the British Electorate 1964* (London, 1965), p. 112.

[24] Interview with Lord Stow Hall, formerly Sir Frank Soskice, at the House of Commons (19 March 1969).

[25] Interview with Ray Gunter, M.P., at the House of Commons (21 January 1969).

[26] Howard, 'The Skin Game', op. cit., p. 726.

We do not contest the need for control of immigration into this country. . . . What we suggest should happen and what the Labour party would do if we were in power, is that we should enter into negotiations with the Commonwealth countries for the purpose of working out agreed quotas and arrangements for their implementation by effective control over the numbers leaving each country. Pending these negotiations, we recognise . . . that a hiatus between the ending of British national control as covered by this part of the Act and the coming into force of the revised arrangements which would result from consultations would be likely to lead to an artificial stimulus to immigration through large numbers jumping the gun.[27]

This 'compromise' formed the basis of Labour policy for the following two years.

For their part, the Conservative party, in Butler's words, 'mistook the effort of 1962 for a solution. We were too complacent.' Macmillan's government were convinced that immigration controls and the appointment of an advisory council would adequately depoliticize the politics of race and provide for harmonious race relations.[28]

At the 1964 General Election, the Conservative position was ambivalent. Though few candidates exploited colour for electoral gain (only eight Conservative, fourteen Labour, and three Liberal candidates discussed immigration and race relations in their campaign addresses),[29] and though most candidates were aware that their party's central organization 'would disapprove of any obvious exploitation of local problems and that to use the issue and fail with it would seriously damage any chance of obtaining another seat,'[30] not only did Peter Griffiths conduct his notorious Smethwick campaign, but on 6 October at Bradford and again two days later at Birmingham the Prime Minister argued that the Conservative party should be rewarded at the polls for preventing a flood of coloured immigrants.[31] The Smethwick result did embarrass the party, yet after the election Peter Griffiths was able to reflect accurately, 'At no point did I receive any criticism from Tory leaders though the attitude of Central Office was for some weeks one of studied politeness.'[32]

The traumatic shock of Gordon Walker's defeat at Smethwick reinforced the position of the 'realists' in the Labour party. The new Prime Minister might label Griffiths a parliamentary leper, but controls would now be tightened, not merely continued: 'We must reshape our control', Soskice stated in his first Commons speech as Home Secretary,

For the present, we are merely asking for the control to be continued for a year. I close with this remark so that there should be no doubt abut the Govern-

---

[27] *Hansard*, H. of C. (27 November 1963), Vol. 685, cols. 365–73.
[28] Butler interview.
[29] David Butler and Anthony King, *The British General Election of 1964* (London, 1965), p. 153.
[30] Deakin, *Colour and the British Electorate 1964*, p. 160.
[31] Butler and King, op. cit., pp. 119–20.
[32] Peter Griffiths, *A Question of Colour* (London, 1966), p. 181.

ment's views. The Government are firmly convinced that an effective control is indispensable. That we accept and have always accepted, although we couple it with the feeling that the Commonwealth must be brought in. We must have an effective control whatever else we have.[33]

At least one Conservative M.P. has alleged that this speech amounted 'to telling lies in the House'.[34]

In January, Gordon Walker was defeated again, this time at Leyton, with a swing of 8 per cent against Labour. Surveys conducted by Research Services and National Opinion Polls both found that race was the most significant factor in the result.[35] Labour politicians, anticipating a general election in the near future, wanted urgently to depoliticize race. Both parties toughened their positions on immigration control in early 1965 so that by the end of March they were, as we noted above, in substantial agreement. At Hampstead on 3 February, Sir Alec Douglas Home advocated repatriation of illegal immigrants, assistance to those who were prepared voluntarily to be repatriated, a cut in the number of vouchers issued, and urged that dependents be included in the overall limit.[36]

The following day, the Home Secretary told the House that because 'there is evidence that under the existing control evasion on a considerable scale is taking place . . . it is necessary to make stricter use of the existing powers of control.' Accordingly, he announced a reinforcement of overseas immigration staff, a review of the practice of admitting children under 16 to join those who are not their parents; he pledged to enforce deportation provisions to combat evasion and to scrutinize more closely at the port of entry the documents of those claiming to be students and dependents.[37]

The control advocates were not yet appeased. Immediately following Soskice's statement, eight Conservative M.P.s, including Cyril Osborne and Patrick Wall, signed a motion that welcomed Labour's conversion to the need for tight restrictions but regretted 'that Her Majesty's Government does not yet show a sufficiently realistic approach to the curtailment of mass immigration, irrespective of race, colour or creed.'[38] Later in the month, Peter Thorneycroft replaced Sir Edward Boyle as

---

[33] *Hansard*, H. of C. (17 November 1964), Vol. 702, cols. 289–90. Italics added.

[34] Interview with Sir David Renton, M.P., at the House of Commons (6 March 1969).

[35] Lionel A. Teear, 'Colour and Immigration in British Politics, with Particular Reference to Selected Groups', unpublished M.A. thesis, University of Sussex, 1966, p. 36.

[36] *The Times* (4 February 1965); the Institute of Race Relations *Newsletter* (March 1965), p. 3.

[37] *Hansard*, H. of C. (4 February 1965), Vol. 705, cols. 1284–5. For a critical discussion, see Peter Norman, 'Who is Guilty of Evasion?', the Institute of Race Relations *Newsletter* (November 1965), pp. 10–13.

[38] *Guardian* (5 February 1965).

Conservative spokesman on race and immigration; Boyle, according to David Renton, 'could not unite the party on this issue.'[39] Boyle, Patrick Wall has stated, 'though a man of considerable qualities was too left-wing on immigration'.[40]

It was reported on 5 February that Cyril Osborne would seek leave to introduce a bill on 24 February 'to prohibit all immigration into the United Kingdom, except for those whose parents or grandparents were born there, until local authorities have dealt with the urgent problems arising from previous immigration.' On Thorneycroft's advice, Osborne modified the bill to call instead for precise limits to be announced regularly. The division on 2 March was a free vote, yet the House divided roughly along party lines as Home and Heath, as well as most of the Shadow Cabinet, led their party by voting in the affirmative. Though 128 Conservative M.P.s (including Boyle, Hogg, Macleod, and Maudling) and sixty-six Labour M.P.s (including Gunter, Healey, Shinwell, and Wigg) took no part in the division, of the 261 votes against the bill only seven were Conservative and seven Liberal. Cyril Osborne, the *Economist* asserted, was now the voice of his party.[41]

This impression was reinforced at a conference of the Conservative Party Central Council on 6 March. Thorneycroft called for a sharp reduction in immigration vouchers, the deportation of illegal immigrants and criminals, better health checks, a voluntary repatriation scheme, and financial assistance to aid immigrant adjustment in the United Kingdom. In supporting Thorneycroft's motion, Patrick Wall stated bluntly: 'We must reject the "multi-racial state" not because we are superior to "our Commonwealth Partners", but because we want to maintain the kind of Britain we know and love.' Home closed the meeting by stressing the dual aspect of Tory policy: stricter control for those who want to come, and the right to equal treatment for those immigrants already here.[42]

Wilson moved quickly to close the gap between the parties by announcing a programme that accepted the two-pronged approach. A mission led by Lord Mountbatten would shortly be dispatched on a Commonwealth consultative mission to discuss more effective control measures. To promote and co-ordinate government and voluntary integrative action, Maurice Foley was appointed Parliamentary Under-Secretary at the Department of Economic Affairs.[43] And in fulfilment of his party's long-

[39] Renton interview.

[40] Interview with Patrick Wall, M.P., at the House of Commons (26 February 1969).

[41] *The Economist* (6 March 1965), p. 3. The revised Osborne bill read: 'A Bill to make provision for the fixing of periodic and precise limits on immigration into the United Kingdom (until local authorities have dealt with the urgent problems arising from previous immigration); and to stop the widespread avoidance of existing regulations . . .'. See the Institute of Race Relations *Newsletter* (April 1965), pp. 2–3.

[42] *Guardian* (6 March 1965).

[43] The selection of the D.E.A. was a curious choice, probably made because of George Brown's interest in race relations and the relationship of immigration rates, demand for labour, and the National Plan.

standing pledge, he stated that the Government would introduce shortly a Race Relations Bill to deal with discrimination. Home found Wilson's statement to be 'sensible and very fair'.[44] The debate of 23 March, cited above, followed, acknowledging the development of the bi-partisan racial accord.

The details of the consensus were sketched in by August. The Race Relations Bill which was published on 7 April made discrimination in public accommodations and incitement to race hatred criminal offences punishable by penalties of £100, and £1,000 or two years in prison respectively. Largely as a result of intensive lobbying by the Campaign Against Racial Discrimination (C.A.R.D.) and Conservative opinion, the Government substituted conciliation procedures for criminal prosecution for discriminatory acts by amendments at the committee stage which established a national Race Relations Board and local conciliation committees to consider complaints about alleged discrimination. The scope of the Act was limited to specifically mentioned public places; housing and employment were excluded. In fact, only the votes of Conservative right-wingers, including Peter Griffiths and Harold Gurden, at the committee divisions had prevented the strengthening of the Act. The alliance of Griffiths, the parliamentary leper, and the Labour government, was graphically symbolic of the developing consensus. The Act, which was acceptable to the vast majority of M.P.s in all three parties, was primarily declaratory.[45]

As the Race Relations Bill progressed through the House, Maurice Foley established a small bureau of civil servants in the Department of Economic Affairs to work exclusively on the problems of race relations which developed the outlines of an integration programme. Local liaison committees would be encouraged; dispersal in housing and education would be promoted; and trade unions would be urged to help overcome their membership's objections to admitting coloured workers to skilled trades and supervisory positions.[46]

III

'The most important battle waged by any group in . . . politics', Wolff has written, 'is the struggle to climb onto the plateau. Once there, it can count on some measure of what it seeks. No group ever gets all of what

[44] *The Times* (10 March 1965).

[45] Keith Hindell, 'The Genesis of the Race Relations Bill', in Richard Rose, ed., *Policy-Making in Britain* (London, 1969), pp. 188–91, especially pp. 194, 197.

[46] *Hansard*, H. of C. (4 June 1965), Vol. 713, col. 2172; the Institute of Race Relations *Newsletter* (May–June 1965), p. 2. In mid-June, Anthony Crosland, the Minister of Education, issued a circular calling for an approximate limit of one coloured child in three in any school, special English classes and adult education programmes for immigrants, and extra staff, including social workers, for schools with a large proportion of coloured pupils. See the Institute of Race Relations *Newsletter* (July 1965), p. 9.

L

it wants, and no *legitimate* group is completely frustrated in its efforts.'[47] Seen in this light, the institutionalized consensus of the White Paper was the outcome of the liberal political process of bargaining between legitimate groups, between the advocates of immigration controls and integration measures. Thus the distinction made by Deakin and Kramer among others between the regressive and constructive features of the White Paper misses the point. In policy terms, the document is inconsistent; on the one hand, the integration measures implied that colour was irrelevant while on the other hand, colour distinctions were at the root of immigration control. Yet in *political* terms, from the perspective of the British political elite, the document and its policies are coherent; immigration controls and the local and national liaison committee structure were two sides of the same coin of depoliticization.[48]

The structural–behavioural distinction discussed in Part I provides the basis for distinguishing critical from routine periods and decisions. Thus, critical decisions are structural decisions that not only limit but shape the direction of choice; critical periods are the 'social time' periods when critical structural decisions are made.[49] In the critical period of migration of Third World people to Britain, the most critical structural decision made was the establishment of national and local institutions outside of the traditional political arenas to deal with the issues of race. The structural arrangements announced by the political consensus White Paper did not integrate the Third World immigrants into the politics of institutionalized class conflict that characterize the liberal collectivist age, but rather set up alternative political structures to deflect the politics of race from Westminster to the National Committee for Commonwealth Immigrants, and from local political arenas to voluntary liaison committees.

As a result, the Third World population has been structurally linked to the polity indirectly through buffer institutions. This mediating, buffering role[50] has been acknowledged explicitly by N.C.C.I. 'The National Committee and the voluntary liaison committees', N.C.C.I.'s 1967 report asserts, 'have to steer the most difficult course of all. The concept "liaison" indicates the tightrope on which they must walk. . . . Success depends on retaining the confidence of the authorities in order that one's views will be heeded when it comes to policy-making. No less important is the confidence of the immigrants.'[51]

The nature, goals, power relationships, and impact of the political

---

[47] Wolff, op. cit., pp. 45–6.

[48] Nicholas Deakin, 'The Politics of Integration: Policies and Practice', unpublished paper, 1969, p. 6; Daniel Kramer, 'White versus Colored in Britain: An Explosive Confrontation?' *Social Research* (Vol. 36, Winter 1969).

[49] See Chapter 2, Section III.

[50] For a discussion of buffering, see Chapter 2, section III.

[51] National Committee for Commonwealth Immigrants, *Report for 1967* (London, 1968), p. 14.

consensus buffer institutions can be examined best by looking in detail at a concrete case at the local level. To that end, let us turn, in the next chapter, to an examination of the terms of Third World immigrant political participation made possible by the White Paper arrangements in Nottingham, whose developed race relations institutions both predated and informed the White Paper.

Chapter Ten

Local Structures: Nottingham as a Limiting Case

I

THE significance of the local response to Third World immigration in Britain cannot be overstated, for if the shape of the cloth of British race relations has largely been determined by the outputs of the national political process, its specific patterns and texture have been woven in the cities. It is at the local level that the newcomers, individually and collectively, have attempted to fashion new economic, social, and political relationships that affect their lives directly. For this reason, Professor R. M. Jackson was right when he asserted that solutions to the often divisive issues of race 'may best begin at the local level. A local authority, truly representative of its population, may do more by its works than a whole series of conference resolutions.'[1] This chapter examines the politics of race in one urban community, Nottingham, which uniquely combines a reputation for racial harmony, progress, and enlightenment with features typical of the country's areas of black settlement. It was selected for detailed study since the institutions developed there became the model for the White Paper network of organizations, and because, in Nottingham, buffering institutional arrangements are most developed.

'The situation in Nottingham', the West Indian High Commissioner declared in 1961, 'seems to be as good as any other provincial city in the country.' Three years later, his successor similarly observed 'that Nottingham is one of the best examples of integration of its kind'. After surveying local authority activity, R. B. Davison concluded that Nottingham 'is probably the most active of all the provincial centres in developing a positive approach to race relations'.[2] Not surprisingly, given its developed race relations structures, Nottingham has been singled out for praise by the National Committee for Commonwealth Immigrants:

[1] R. M. Jackson, *The Machinery of Local Government* (London, 1965), pp. 364–5.
[2] Nottingham *Guardian-Journal* (19 September 1961); Nottingham *Evening Post* (8 August 1964); R. B. Davison, *Commonwealth Immigrants* (London, 1964), p. 53.

The Nottingham Citizens Consultative Committee, one of the oldest in the country, continues to be among the leading groups. Because of its early start it was able to anticipate and minimise many of the difficulties such as housing shortage, discrimination in employment, problems of immigrant relations, and youth problems. After so many years of solid work and pioneering activity, the Nottingham committee . . . may well set an example in this field from which many of the newer committees will benefit.[3]

Thus, Nottingham provides a critical locale for the assessment of the linkages fashioned between the Third World immigrants and the polity. It will be argued below that the city's reputation is only partially deserved. Though Nottingham has in fact done more institutionally than most British cities, the officially sponsored integration mechanisms are seriously flawed. By discussing these structures and their shortcomings in Nottingham—the limiting case—it is possible to illuminate indirectly the politics of race in other British cities, an objective made possible because Nottingham's economic characteristics and patterns of immigrant settlement are so typical.

On the basis of the distribution of internal migration and the demand for labour, Peach has defined three types of economic regions in Britain:

First there are regions of negative demand and net outward migration balance. Secondly, there are regions of high demand for labour with high net inward migration balances. Thirdly, there are regions of demand which have either failed to attract much migration or have a net outward migration balance.[4]

On the whole, the Third World immigrants have settled in the third kind of region: 'in spite of the shortcomings of the available statistics, it seems clear that West Indians have acted as a replacement population in this country. . . . They have gone to the decreasing urban cores of expanding industrial regions'.[5]

In the last two decades, the East Midlands, whose largest city is Nottingham, has had a chronic labour shortage caused by an inability to attract a sufficient number of workers. 'The number of jobs to be filled', according to the region's Economic Planning Council, 'increased faster than the number of people to fill them. . . . The labour problem of the East Midlands is one of too many jobs looking for too few people to fill them.'[6] Nottingham in particular has not attracted mobile workers from other areas of Britain primarily because of the city's lower than average proportion of managerial and high-paid jobs, the consequence of having a 'smaller proportion of employees in expanding industries and a far bigger

[3] National Committee for Commonwealth Immigrants, *Report for 1967* (London, 1968), p. 21.
[4] Ceri Peach, *West Indian Migration to Britain* (London, 1968), p. 82.
[5] Ibid., p. 82.
[6] Department of Economic Affairs, East Midlands Economic Planning Council, *The East Midlands Study* (London, 1966), pp. 29, 21–2.

one in contracting industries . . . than throughout the country as a whole.'[7]

It is in this sense, then, that Nottingham's black population of approximately 22,000 (about two-thirds West Indian and 6 per cent of the city total) is a replacement population, an observation that is confirmed by their settlement in the nineteenth century proletarian central city neighbourhoods of the Meadows, the Arboretum, and St. Ann's.

II

The response of Nottingham's political community to black immigration cannot be understood without some preliminary observations concerning the nature of the city's politics, the racial attitudes and goals of its politicians, and the fragmented nature of the immigrant communities.

Though the city's politics are based formally on Labour–Conservative party conflict, the cozy atmosphere of Nottingham's council politics makes the party division often misleading and largely irrelevant. Close bipartisan consultation, an ex-Lord Mayors' club, and, above all, the policy of allocating a high proportion of council committee chairmanships to the minority party dampen issue partisanship. Because the processes of boundary management and direct bargaining are conducted, more often than not, away from the glare of publicity, public political controversy, even with regard to the relatively coherent issues of class, is muted. When dealing with the potentially disruptive issues of race, the political community's usual unity has been especially pronounced; unlike their national counterparts, Nottingham's politicians have never divided fundamentally on these issues along party lines.

Indeed, the racial attitudes and goals of Nottingham's politicians exhibit striking uniformities across party lines. In February 1968, I posted a questionnaire to Nottingham's fifty-one councillors (thirty-four Conservative and seventeen Labour), and received twenty-eight completed replies (fourteen Conservative and fourteen Labour).[8] The survey will be dealt with more completely below, but what is significant here is the definition the councillors gave, by implication (they were not asked for one directly), to the goal of 'integration'. Their implied definitions were revealed principally in reply to the two questions: (a) What actions can local authorities take to successfully integrate coloured immigrants within the community? and (b) Can leading members of the coloured immigrant communities help? If yes, how; if no, why not?

None of the councillors rejected the term integration, though many of the replies were vague. Yet a sizable majority in both parties saw the process of integration in terms of a movement towards conformity, towards some indefinable 'British way of life'. Eight Labour and nine

[7] Ibid., pp. 25, 49.

[8] I am indebted to Councillor O. W. Watkinson who nagged and cajoled his fellow councillors to return their completed questionnaires; without his assistance, the response rate would have been much lower, and the survey less representative.

Conservative replies unmistakably identified integration with a flattening cultural process. Thus the Conservative deputy leader wanted immigrant leaders 'to encourage their colleagues to integrate at all levels and in all city activities', but added that his goal was 'standardization and conformity to traditional British attitudes and practices'. For him, integration was a one-way process: 'I see no reason to embrace the immigrants and their customs. We have not been waiting for them for generations; shall I tell them we've just been waiting around for them to come?' Another Conservative councillor called for 'sympathetic and realistic educational and social welfare attitudes'. He thought 'articulate coloured immigrants can help by educating their nationals in the British way of life—habits, customs, etc.' A Labour councillor too thought their task was that of 'talking to their own people about ways of living and fitting into an established community'. A party colleague concurred: 'Immigrant leaders should teach the immigrants to conform to the community way of life as practiced by the nationals.' Only two councillors, both members of the Labour party, substantively differed, stating that the local authority should be responsible for 'making sure that immigrants know their rights', and for 'trying to eliminate discrimination in housing and employment'.

Existing evidence indicates that the attitudes of Nottingham's political community are widely held in Britain. Graham Thomas concluded after analysing the examination papers of eighty local government officers who came from all parts of the country and who were asked about local authority activity to aid integration that:

. . . perhaps the most significant and interesting thing to emerge from the sample analysed was the respondents interpretation of the term 'integration' in the question. 'Integrate' was used as a synonym for 'assimilate'. Practically everyone assumed that immigrants must become as similar to the British people as possible. . . . There was practically no consideration of the desirability of allowing immigrants to retain their own identities and characteristics.

Thomas found too that most of these officers wished 'to do things *for* the immigrants; they have a rather paternal attitude and show little sign of thinking it desirable to get the active co-operation of immigrant bodies.'[9] Though Nottingham's political response, we will note below, has been in keeping with these paternal sentiments, the city's formalized integration mechanisms do make use of existing immigrant organizations.

But by contrast to the situation that obtained in the Northern United

[9] Graham Thomas, 'The Integration of Immigrants: A Note on the View of Some Local Government Officials', *Race* (Vol. IX, October 1967), pp. 240, 244. E. Avison, to cite another example, who was Bedford's chief public health inspector, writing about his city's coloured population, argued, 'If they would only accept conditions as they find them, and not prejudge every case they encounter, I feel sure they would soon be accepted in this area as useful citizens . . . as the children become educated and adopt our customs, the transformation will be complete.' E. Avison, 'Immigrants in a Small Borough', the Institute of Race Relations *Newsletter* (October 1965), pp. 14–15.

States, 1900–30, many of the factors that promoted black political activity are absent in Britain. Unlike the Southern migrants to the North, the Third World immigrants to Britain come from societies where they were permitted to participate politically, yet, for them, political participation made little difference. English politics pre-eminently are the politics of class, a fact that makes ethnic or racial political organization difficult (though not impossible). As a result of these factors, and others including national and class divisions among the immigrants themselves, with few exceptions the immigrants tended (at least until 1968) to be politically inactive and organizationally fragmented. Of Nottingham's twenty leading black organizations, only three—the Afro-Asian–West Indian Union, the Indian Workers Association, and the Pakistan Friends League—were overtly concerned with politics. The Afro-Asian–West Indian Union, whose thirty odd members were predominantly West Indian, was, at least to 1969, very much a fringe group. Its leaders, one of whom was a councillor at Long Eaton, who favoured radical change and rejected co-operation with both major parties, admitted that 'political consciousness in the West Indian community is very low. We have not had much success.'[10] The Indian Workers Association like the Afro-Asian–West Indian Union, has a socialist outlook, but unlike the West Indian organization has a large, well-organized membership of about 750 and co-operates with the local Labour party. The I.W.A.'s effectiveness has been limited, however, by its continuing competition with the moderate, largely middle-class Indian Association and the Indian Welfare Association whose membership includes both workers and members of the middle class. Though the Pakistan Friends League, which has about 400 members, is, according to its president, 'very much a political pressure group', it eschews direct political action and organization and works instead through the officially sanctioned voluntary liaison committee; 'we are not strong or effective enough to act directly apart from other immigrant groups'.[11] The organization's secretary, however, has disparaged the I.W.A., arguing that immigrant political action would only alienate white Englishmen, stating, 'We are not politically minded. I oppose playing a power game, and I am very sceptical about immigrant unity.'[12] These objective circumstances, in short, acted to inhibit immigrant political activity. West Indians especially, David Pitt has observed 'feel that the politics of this country do not concern them and to use the words that were used to me, "this is Red Man's business, not mine!"'[13]

[10] Interview with O. G. Powe, H. McLean, and other members of the Afro-Asian–West Indian Union (9 November 1968).

[11] Interview with D. Ajeeb, president of the Pakistan Friends League (18 January 1968).

[12] Interview with M. Aslam, secretary of the Pakistan Friends League (18 January 1968).

[13] Cited in Nicholas Deakin, ed., *Colour and the British Electorate 1964* (London 1965), pp. 6–7.

III

These factors inhibiting first-generation immigrant participation underscore the extent to which the critical structural decisions made in the period of migration have been almost exclusively decisions made by white political elites. Like their national counterparts, before 1958 Nottingham's political community dealt with the issues of race by denying them political recognition. Yet the pre-political period of race relations in Nottingham is of considerable interest. During the middle 1950s, quasi-political mechanisms to deal with race relations were established which, after the violence of 1958 which politicized race, provided the city's political community with the means to institutionalize and manage the new politics of race with a minimum of disruption, and, as we shall see, with a minimum of change.

In May 1954, when the city's predominantly Jamaican coloured Commonwealth citizens numbered between 700 and 1,000,[14] the Council of Social Service (C.S.S.) and the Council of Churches decided to found the Nottingham Consultative Committee for the Welfare of Coloured People 'to help the local coloured community settle down as happily and as easily as possible'.[15] No blacks were present at the founding meeting. A second planning meeting was called for 27 September 'to hear from the colonial peoples themselves what they felt they needed'. Accordingly, three members of the non-political Colonial Social and Cricket Club (later called the Colonial Social and Sports Club), including the organization's secretary Eric Irons, were invited to represent the city's West Indians. They assented to the plans to found a committee, and agreed to serve on it.

Thus of the twenty-nine individuals who attended the first official meeting of the Consultative Committee for the Welfare of Coloured People in February 1955, only six were West Indian, and they were all members of the Colonial Club. The other participants were delegates appointed by the city's leading voluntary organizations including the Rotary Club, the Trades Council, the Y.M.C.A., the City Business Club and the Salvation Army. The formal political community was not invited to participate.

The new committee was meant to link West Indian and local community leaders, but the attempt suffered from serious shortcomings. With the exception of a hard-core of interested whites, notably the committee's part-time secretary Dorothy Wood, who also led the C.S.S., and A. F. Laird the committee's chairman who was the head of the Welfare

---

[14] Nottingham Consultative Committee for the Welfare of Coloured People, 'Minutes' (19 May 1954)—estimate of 700; Nottingham *Evening Post* (3 October 1955)—estimate of 1,000.

[15] Interview with Miss D. M. Wood, founding secretary of the Consultative Committee (24 April 1968).

Committee of the C.S.S., the representatives of the voluntary agencies contributed very little. Most attended very few of the monthly meetings; the committee's minutes in this period abound with references to disappointing attendance.

More significant from the perspective of the Third World immigrants was the dual (socially descriptive) non-representative character of the committee. Not only were there few West Indians on the committee, but they were hardly typical members of their community. Most of the Colonial Club's approximately twenty-five members were 'old settlers' who had served with the R.A.F., married white wives, settled in Nottingham after the Second World War, and had middle-class occupations. They were on the whole uninterested in politics.

The Colonial Club delegates provided a useful inter-racial gloss to the Consultative Committee's work. 'We depended on the Colonial Club's leaders', Miss Wood recalls. 'They were moderate, reasonable men.'[16] A. F. Laird remembers that 'in the old days, the immigrant leaders were easily recognizable and could be depended on'.[17] Eric Irons and his colleagues, it is true, were at least part of the visible immigrant elite, but they were leaders in the main only in the sense of visibility. They failed to act successfully as a communications linch-pin linking West Indians to the existing social structure, and they failed to involve the people they claimed to represent. 'It was felt', the secretary recorded in 1957, 'that the number of coloured people in the district who knew about the facilities available for their help was only a small fraction of the total; the difficulty of getting in touch with them was a very real problem.'[18]

The committee did try to be responsive, however, but was not very effective. The 'non-sectarian, non-political' Coloured People's Housing Association which it founded in early 1956 to purchase small houses to let on a temporary basis to families with acute housing needs did not buy its first house until June 1957, and as late as the summer of 1958 only eleven families had been assisted in any way. A 1957 course in basic English and the 'English way of life' which had twenty openings averaged three pupils in attendance at each of its twelve class meetings. Only twelve immigrants came to the first twenty-eight weekly advice sessions. The number of inquiries rose substantially during the 1957–8 recession to almost eighty a month, most concerning employment. The committee, however, found itself 'unable to be constructive in most cases'.[19]

The committee on occasion did useful, peripheral welfare work: relatives were put in touch, a depressed, lonely woman was directed to a neighbourhood Jamaican women's group, a student was helped secure

---

[16] Wood Interview.

[17] Interview with A. F. Laird, founding chairman of the Consultative Committee and chairman of the Council of Social Service (24 April 1968).

[18] Consultative Committee, 'Minutes' (14 February 1957).

[19] Consultative Committee, Employment Sub-Committee, 'Minutes' (14 July 1958).

temporary work pending his National Service call-up.[20] But this limited activity made little impression on the basic needs of the majority of immigrants. Thus the pre-1958 Consultative Committee closely resembled the 'ideal-type' we called ineffectual paternalism.[21]

If with John Rex and Robert Moore 'we understand urban society as structure of social interaction and conflict',[22] and if we view competition for the allocation of scarce resources as a political process involving political decisions, then it is clear that the immigrants, who comprised an identifiable group competing for an equitable allocation of homes and jobs, needed access to positions of political control. Yet the most obvious access point, the Consultative Committee, was officially non-political and avoided political controversy. When the Trades Council, for example proposed that an open forum on discrimination be conducted, the proposal was rejected because 'it might lend unhealthy significance to the problem which could best be solved by more quiet and constructive steps'.[23]

In fact, the committee's official non-political position had political ramifications, for it helped isolate the political community from potential immigrant political demands. Thus the council could avoid taking the political risks of a programme designed to assure a fair allocation of resources to the newcomers. Immigrants who sought the assistance of their councillors and those who complained of discrimination were often directed to the politically impotent Consultative Committee.[24] When the committee made its only implicitly political requests before 1958 for the appointment of a special welfare worker and for permission to use the city's information centre for weekly advice sessions, the council refused. The Town Clerk explained:

Full consideration was given to the resolution passed by the Consultative Committee and to your comments, but my committee came to the conclusion that it would not be proper to appoint a Welfare Officer for one small group, nor would it be proper to provide any services above those available for citizens as a whole.[25]

[20] Consultative Committee, 'Minutes' (19 July 1956).

[21] See below, Chapter 2, pp. 49–51. It should be noted that the welfare–social work approach of the committee indicated that the committee assumed implicitly that it was dealing with 'people who have psycho-social problems, that is to say, people who have problems of adjustment between themselves and their environment'. It was assumed, therefore, that the immigrants, not the environment, needed adjustment; hence integration was viewed as a one-way process. The quote is from a Cambridgeshire and Isle of Ely County Council pamphlet entitled 'The Principles of Social Casework', based on Felix P. Biestek's standard textbook, *The Casework Relationship* (London, 1967).

[22] John Rex and Robert Moore, *Race, Community, and Conflict* (London, 1967), p. 13. The authors explain their theoretical perspective in their Introduction, pp. 1–18.

[23] Consultative Committee, 'Minutes' (16 February 1955).

[24] Wood interview.

[25] Consultative Committee, 'Minutes' (13 April 1955).

IV

The violence of the summer of 1958 compelled the political community to reassess its 'colour-blind' policy. The issues of colour which, with the assistance of the Consultative Committee, had been kept off the local political agenda, now had to be dealt with politically, at least in the sense of trying to make them coherent and manageable.

Members of the political community publicly dismissed the importance of the violence that had shattered the city's façade of harmonious race relations. It was 'just a pub brawl', according to Alderman Foster, who was the acting leader of the majority Labour party during the disturbances, 'it was just a bit of trouble we had in St. Ann's Well Road that did not involve the man in the street.'[26] At the request of the council, the quasi-political Consultative Committee at an emergency meeting issued a statement that expressed—

... deep concern about the incidents which took place on Saturday and especially deplore the use of weapons which is a serious breach of law. They are satisfied that they arose from the actions of irresponsible individuals, white and coloured. This small minority by taking the law into their own hands have done unmeasurable harm to the good relations which have always existed between all races in the city. . . . They are determined that their work shall continue and grow and that one unfortunate incident shall not be exaggerated or allowed to undo the good work of the past.[27]

Members of the political community were more candid in private. The disturbances were given over-sensational treatment by the press; nevertheless, a total of approximately 4,500 people were involved as participants and spectators on 23 and 30 August.[28] 'The violence made us realize', Miss Wood recalls, 'that something had been lurking about that we knew nothing about.'[29] William Taylor who came to Nottingham in 1966 to serve as the Consultative Committee's first full-time secretary was surprised to find the political community still obsessed by the 1958 events:

The city's politicians now say that it was all exaggerated by the press. Perhaps they are correct, but they still go on about it. The politicians minimise the effect of the violence, but the effect has been considerable . . . they are afraid it will happen again.[30]

Dahrendorf has usefully distinguished between questions and problems: 'To answer a question or not is our free decision; if we like we can

---

[26] Interview with Alderman E. Foster, Leader of the Labour Party (19 March 1968).
[27] Consultative Committee, 'Minutes' (26 August 1958).
[28] For an account see James Wickenden, *Colour in Britain* (London, 1958), pp. 23–35.
[29] Wood interview.
[30] Interview with William Taylor, Secretary of the Consultative Committee (25 January 1968).

postpone a question or forget it. . . . By contrast, it is a condition that we solve problems; we can neither postpone a problem nor forget it, for unlike the failure to answer a question, the failure to solve a problem is itself a resolution.'[31] For Nottingham's political community, the events of August 1958 transformed race relations from a political question to a political problem. In keeping with the city's tradition of amicable council politics, the parties did not divide over the issues of race, but acted in concert to resolve their common problem by attempting to structure race relations and domesticate racial conflicts.

In February 1960, the Council appointed Eric Irons, the leader of the Colonial Club West Indians who served on the Consultative Committee, to the specially created post of organiser for educational work amongst the coloured communities. Irons, who was a clerk at the time at a local ordnance depot, was appointed to fill a position which was intended to be political primarily and educational only secondarily. As Miss Wood put it, 'The city's tarnished image had to be restored . . . Mr. Irons was principally appointed because of the fracas of 1958.'[32]

Irons's appointment was complemented by official recognition of the Consultative Committee as a quasi-political institution. The committee which had been financed by Pilgrim and Cadbury Trust grants, was now awarded a £500 annual grant from the council.[33] Thus within a year of the disturbances, the political community had established officially sanctioned access points, both within and outside of the local authority, for the immigrant population. Neither access point provided for direct access to the political community, but acted instead, under the conceptual heading of liaison, as political buffers. Immigrant needs and demands were filtered through them: Irons's office dealt with individuals, the Consultative Committee with organized immigrant groups. These structural mechanisms, established when the city's black population numbered just over 3,000,[34] remained virtually unchanged through the 1960s.

'In one sense', Eric Irons wrote in his 1961-2 report to the Council, 'the organiser looks upon his functions as being that of an "interpreter" between the new and the established communities, in that he is in direct, personal contact with the coloured communities and his advice and help are often sought by statutory and voluntary bodies in their approach to these sections of the population.'[35] In this role, Irons has acted much like the black political leaders of New York's United Colored Democracy and of Chicago's Carey–Wright–De Priest South Side machine. The American

[31] Ralf Dahrendorf, *Essays in the Theory of Society* (London, 1968), p. 257.
[32] Wood interview.
[33] The grant was formally approved in August 1959. In March 1959, the council offered the Coloured People's Housing Association a loan of £500 to help with the purchase of four additional houses.
[34] Wickenden, op. cit., p. 23.
[35] City of Nottingham Education Committee, 'Report of the Organiser for Educational Work Among the Coloured Communities, February 1961 to March 1962', p. 2.

blacks offered their communities patronage, in limited amounts, without political control. Irons offered the knowledge and access which are essential in securing benefits made available by the welfare state: 'It is not the task of the Organiser to deal himself', he told the council in 1965, 'with the welfare needs of the immigrant, but he is able to clarify for them just exactly what they want and then put them in touch with the appropriate agency.' Though he worked out of the education department, 'it is difficult to discriminate between educational and general social needs'.[36] Irons's position as an 'interpreter' has been buttressed by the political community which conferred on him the prestige of being appointed England's first black J.P. in 1962 and which channelled blacks with problems to him.[37] Blacks who would have been referred to the Consultative Committee in the 1950s were in the 1960s referred to Irons. By virtue of his institutionalized political position, Irons became the officially sanctioned leader of the city's coloured immigrants.

Like his black American counterparts, Irons made few demands on the political community; 'I deal with people, not political issues.'[38] Despite this disavowal of political activity, Irons's structural role was a political one—that of providing his patrons with a buffer service.

Although the needs of the Third World immigrants he claimed to represent were political in the sense that they comprised a distinct group competing for scarce resources, Irons assisted the political community by defining his people's needs in non-political terms. In his first report to the council after the 1958 violence when, presumably, the city's politicians were most receptive to immigrant requests, Irons wrote: 'The needs of the racial groups require specific consideration, but for brevity they can be grouped under the following headings: Education, Advice and Information, Assimilation.' This definition, which avoided the prickly issue of discrimination in housing and employment, neatly coincided with the political community's dominant view that the process of integration should be one of immigrant adjustment, of a movement towards conformity with the 'British way of life'. Conveniently too, Irons concluded that 'education in its broadest sense is the most pressing need of all sections of the coloured communities'.[39]

In his reports to the council, Irons consistently maintained that progress towards assimilation was being made, a claim related no doubt to the maintenance needs of his office. By his third report in 1961, he was 'encouraged', by the fourth, a year later, there was 'every indication that

[36] City of Nottingham Education Committee, 'Report of the Organiser for Work with Coloured People', p. 1.

[37] Irons was appointed to the bench in May 1962, and began to serve in court in July. A second coloured J.P., Mr. M. Aslam, was appointed in 1967.

[38] Interview with E. Irons, organiser for work with coloured people (11 December 1967).

[39] City of Nottingham Education Committee, 'Report of the Organiser for Work among Coloured People' (July 1960), p. 1.

more tact and tolerance are being exercised by both the immigrants and the local people'.[40] In all his annual reports through to 1969, there was only one mention of discrimination, and even this reference was as innocuous as possible:

The employment figures amongst coloured adults and young people are encouraging and have a stabilising effect on community relations. . . . There is no doubt that there are some kinds of employment which the coloured school leavers find difficult to obtain. On the other hand, there is also a failure on the part of some immigrant parents to understand that minimum educational qualifications are necessary for apprenticeships and other skilled occupations.[41]

Irons's November 1965 report is perhaps most revealing of all, for in it he candidly, if indirectly, made clear his political role. The Labour government had published its White Paper on immigration in August. Many of Nottingham's immigrants felt betrayed, and there were fears that dependents might be excluded. As a result, a number of immigrant organizations, principally the Indian Workers Association and the Afro-Asian–West Indian Union, met an unusually favourable response from their normally politically quiescent communities. Much like the effect Enoch Powell's speeches were to have three years later, the insecurity caused by the White Paper promoted immigrant political consciousness.[42] It was in this context that Irons reported in November:

The past year has been a difficult one for the immigrant communities, that is Indian, Pakistani and West Indian nationals. They have been under considerable social pressures, *particularly from within their respective racial groups*. These pressures have tended to undermine the confidence of the immigrants and have been, therefore, a real test of the effectiveness of the work that has been carried out in the City over the years.

The difficulties were surmounted largely because of the intelligent and responsible manner in which the majority of the coloured community reacted to the situation; the increasing knowledge of the social needs and background of the coloured people; and the splendid liaison work and very flexible policies adopted by Local Authority departments and other statutory bodies, the Trade Unions and the many other organisations that are directly or indirectly concerned with the assimilation of the immigrants into the communal and industrial life of the City. Nevertheless, the strain experienced has underlined the *need for a much stronger stabilising influence amongst the immigrants*. In this respect credit must be paid to the Nottingham Standing Conference of Commonwealth Citizens, the Nottingham Indian Association, the Pakistani Welfare

40 'Reports', 1961, 1962.
41 'Report' (November 1966), p. 1.
42 'There is however one group of coloured immigrants in Nottingham who see promise and opportunity in Powellism: the activist groups. To them Powell has proved the best educator of black people in the country.' John Heilpern and Dilip Hiro, 'The Town We were told was Tolerant', *The Observer* (1 December 1968), p. 11.

Association, the Commonwealth Citizens Association and the Pakistani Friends League for their work during these difficult months.[43]

In interpreting the immigrant community to his employer, Irons identified intelligence, responsibility, and stability with immigrant political quiescence. The I.W.A. and the Afro-Asian–West Indian Union are notable for their absence from the list of helpful immigrant organizations. Indeed the groups cited that had West Indian members (just over two-thirds of Nottingham's blacks are West Indian), were both led by Irons. The Commonwealth Citizens Association, the successor organization to the Colonial Social and Sports Club, was a West Indian club whose membership was confined to its 'old settler' founders, while the Standing Conference of Commonwealth Citizens, which was founded by Irons in 1959 as a loose federation of women's social groups and was later expanded as West Indian men were invited to join, was sponsored by the adult education office and saw as its principal function 'considering ways in which helpful information could be circularised to immigrants'.[44] Irons, then, not only sought to link the immigrant and political communities, but also created and promoted an organizational structure within the immigrant communities that expressed views he considered moderate and responsible which he then could interpret to the political community.

V

Irons and the organizations he sanctioned represented the city's blacks on the Consultative Committee, whose change of name in 1960 to the Commonwealth Citizens Consultative Committee recognized the new division of labour: welfare and individual liaison were now dealt with by Irons, organizational group liaison by the committee.

Liaison is a vague operational concept. Since 1959, the committee has sought to give content to the concept and define its purpose. This effort has passed through three discrete phases. During the first, roughly from 1959 to mid-1963, fundamental questions of representativeness and responsiveness were debated. In an effort to bring all the existing immigrant organizations within the structural machinery of the committee, the I.W.A. and the Afro-Asian–West Indian Unions were invited to affiliate after the 1958 disturbances. The West Indian group, in particular, attempted to politicize the committee and arrange for direct immigrant participation in its affairs; these efforts were coupled with a 'campaign to abolish Special Officers for coloured people', directed at Irons's new office.

In September 1959, George Powe, the secretary of the Afro-Asian–West Indian Union, made clear in an organizational report their opposition to the city's new structural arrangements:

[43] City of Nottingham Education Committee, 'Report of the Organiser for Work with Coloured People' (November 1965), p. 1. Italics added.
[44] 'Report' (May 1962).

Since the racial disturbances in Nottingham last year the aim has been to change the composition of the committee. The people in charge are trying to replace some of the Europeans with colonial stooges. This does not change the basic character of the committee whose purpose is to confuse the coloured people and the British Labour Movement and to spread the illusion that something is really being done to solve the problems of immigrants from the West Indies. . . . They aim to make coloured people docile enough to accept paternalism as a solution to their problems.[45]

The differences between the Afro-Asian–West Indian Union and Irons's Standing Conference and Commonwealth Citizens Association were most pronounced at Consultative Committee meetings held to discuss immigration controls in 1961 and 1962. In April 1961, Powe argued that the committee should publicly oppose immigration controls. Irons demurred; he felt, the minutes record, 'that the Committee should concentrate on work in Nottingham and that the matter of restriction should be left to the politicians'.[46] A sub-committee on immigration restrictions was appointed, whose membership included Irons but not Powe, which reported in June advising that no action be taken: 'Mr. Irons preferred that the Committee should concentrate on local needs. From his experience he had found that local West Indian people preferred that nothing should be done—they are very reluctant to give information.'[47] The committee as a whole, however, decided to meet local M.P.s on a confidential basis.

After the introduction of the Commonwealth Immigrants Act, Powe's group appeared to gain the upper hand. In December, a letter opposing controls as discriminatory was sent to the Home Secretary, and in February the committee decided, with Irons voting in the negative, to issue a public statement deploring the bill.

Encouraged by the committee's decision to oppose immigration controls, Powe presented the committee with his organization's proposals for structural change in early 1962. He urged that committee meetings be opened to all interested coloured people who would be allowed to vote, and that 'individuals should no longer be spoken of as "leaders" of a particular section of the community'.[48] The committee decided in April that meetings would be opened, but resisted the transformation of the committee into an open forum by appending the conditions that notice of attendance be given in advance and that those who came could observe but not vote. Irons welcomed this decision, noting that 'the rejection of these proposals will permit us to press on without extraneous criticism'.[49]

[45] C. G. Powe, 'Report from Afro–Asian–West Indian Union' (Nottingham), *Information Bulletin* (September 1959), p. 5.
[46] Consultative Committee, 'Minutes' (10 April 1961).
[47] Consultative Committee, Sub-Committee on Restriction, 'Minutes' (5 June 1961).
[48] Consultative Committee, 'Minutes' (4 February 1962).
[49] Consultative Committee, 'Minutes' (2 April, 1962).

M

Shortly thereafter, Powe and his Afro-Asian–West Indian Union colleagues resigned their seats on the committee, as a result of a combination of pressure by the committee's white leadership and their own decision that they could be more effective in their efforts to build a politically conscious immigrant community if they disaffiliated from what they considered to be a tainted organization. 'We didn't find the militants very constructive', A. F. Laird has stated, 'They didn't think we were an effective body. They wanted to issue political statements and ban employers who discriminated. Unfortunately, they wanted to be more forceful than we thought tactful.'[50] Miss Wood recalls, 'We used to call that group "the rebels". They were all jealous of Irons; that was the top and bottom of it. They tried to put him in an unhappy light. Because we were not firm with them and did not muzzle them they caused bitterness at our meetings, they were unhappy meetings.' In 1963, she added, 'we felt we must do something. We drew up a new constitution that restricted participation to invited organizations. We never formally asked them to leave, but they did leave at that point and our aim was achieved.'[51] Powe doesn't dispute this account, but emphasizes that 'although some liberal whites on the committee wanted changes made, the committee's leadership and structure made that impossible. That's why we left.'[52]

With the departure of the members of the Afro-Asian–West Indian Union, the activities of the committee reflected the views of Irons, Laird, and Wood, whose position was consolidated. The shift in the committee's work to 'non-controversial liaison and integration work',[53] was made clear when the recommendations of the sub-committee on integration were unanimously approved in April 1963. The new programme included thirteen points, none the least bit controversial, the most important of which were: 'increased opportunities for social contacts, help to the Commonwealth Citizens Association to set up a clubroom, . . . the importance of personal friendships, . . . a schools 'Commonwealth Week', a Commonwealth children's dance group, and an effort to convince the public library to produce a reading list on race relations.'[54] Appropriately, Harry Pacey, Nottingham's welfare officer, served as the committee's chairman during this period of peripheral social activity, for in these years, mid-1963 to early 1966, the committee's outlook was very similar to its pre-1958 welfare, adjustment-oriented approach.

Eric Irons succeeded Pacey in January 1966. More significant, though, was the appointment of William Taylor, who had previously worked at

---

[50] Laird interview.

[51] Wood interview.

[52] Interview with O. G. Powe, Secretary of the Afro-Asian–West Indian Union (19 October 1968). Powe, of course, does dispute Miss Wood's assertion that his differences with Irons are personal.

[53] Wood interview.

[54] Consultative Committee, 'Minutes' (14 February 1963).

the national office of N.C.C.I., as the committee's first full-time secretary. Soon after his arrival, representatives of the local Labour, Conservative, Liberal, and Communist parties joined the committee.[55] Taylor, an admirer of Oxford's consultative committee which had functioned primarily as a pressure group, attempted to have the committee intervene discretely but directly in political matters. In July 1966 for example, the committee addressed its first request to the council since 1955. It requested that the council pass a resolution, similar to one approved by the Camden Borough Council in May, indicating that the council would require a non-discriminatory statement of intent from companies it contracted for goods and materials. The Town Clerk replied negatively a month later, stating that the suggestion had been discussed and rejected by the Finance and General Purposes Committee of the council because it was thought to be unenforceable.[56]

Other committee efforts to intervene in local authority matters that directly affected the city's Third World population in 1966–8 were equally unproductive. In particular, efforts to arrange special English classes for Indian and Pakistani teenage children and to promote the recruitment of black policemen were rebuffed.

Housing is the blacks' most pressing problem; according to the 1966 Sample Census, at least 75 per cent of the city's black population lives in sub-standard housing, a situation caused by the general unavailability of decent housing at reasonable rents, discrimination in the letting and sale of property, difficulty in securing mortgages, and a deliberate local authority policy of placing few blacks on council estates by encouraging them instead to take up offers of sub-standard council-managed properties.[57] The Consultative Committee's inability to influence local policy making is most glaring and significant in this area.

In January 1967, the newly created housing department, managed by M. C. Lee, assumed responsibility for approximately half of the land and 40 per cent of the houses in Nottingham, those owned by the corporation, and, in particular, for the extensive slum clearance and redevelopment scheme for St. Ann's, an area which then had a black population of

---

[55] The admission of political representatives was approved only after heated debate on 17 October 1966.

[56] Consultative Committee, 'Minutes' (17 October 1966).

[57] For an extended documented discussion, see Elizabeth Burney, *Housing on Trial* (London, 1967), Chapter 8, especially pp. 198–205. The city's housing manager confirms that most coloured council tenants live in sub-standard housing, but argues this is the result not of a conscious policy but of the fact that since blacks are desperate for accommodation, they opt for sub-standard housing with a one-year waiting list rather than wait the usual five years for a decent house. Interview with M. C. Lee (11 December 1967). Burney, however, found that 'coloured applicants are usually completely unaware that any other alternative exists; they are just handed the keys of a terraced house without any suggestion of choice. . . . As long as these are virtually the only houses offered to coloured people, it cannot be said that Nottingham's housing policy is free from discrimination' (p. 201).

about 3,000 (10 per cent)[58] and the scene of the 1958 disturbances.

At the committee's request, Lee met Taylor and the coloured members of the Consultative Committee in mid-February. Their discussion chiefly concerned the accommodation that would be offered those black residents in the St. Ann's district who had a statutory right to be re-housed by the council when their homes were demolished. According to the committee's minutes, Lee stressed that 'there are inspections by lady visitors who assess whether the families deserve new accommodation or if they should be sent to older properties owned by the Corporation. The main criterion was whether or not the family is 'dirty'.[59] When, later in the year, the committee inquired about the proportion of white and coloured people who were at that time and expected in the future to be housed in sub-standard corporation housing, Lee replied that 'no statistics were kept of the racial origin of tenants, and hence it was impossible to supply this information.'[60]

In fact, ethnic records are kept by the housing office. In December 1967, the housing department allocations officer showed me the applications for rehousing filed by twelve coloured families. In the right-hand corner of each, the initials 'W.I.', 'P.', and 'I.' were clearly pencilled in.[61] That these records are kept is not in itself significant (they could be used, for example, to facilitate a policy of dispersal on council estates). What is important is that this information was deliberately withheld from the Consultative Committee.

Moreover, there is reason to believe that blacks were not being rehoused in the St. Ann's scheme on the same basis as whites. In late 1967, before the first stage of redevelopment had been implemented, Lee stated, 'We are in business to help people, but we are also in business to protect the interests of the corporation. We shall have to be careful when we deal with St. Ann's because people on our estates are prejudiced and we must take their prejudice into account. It would be stupid to close our eyes to this.' He added that he had not yet decided what to do.[62] By late 1968, with a handful of exceptions, only whites in St. Ann's had been rehoused.[63]

[58] Heilpern and Hiro, p. 11.

[59] Consultative Committee, Housing Sub-Committee 'Minutes' (20 March 1967).

[60] Consultative Committee, Housing Sub-Committee, 'Minutes' (4 October 1967).

[61] Interview with Mr. D. Bexon, Housing Department Allocations Officer (11 December 1967).

[62] Lee interview.

[63] Heilpern and Hiro, p. 11. A Fair Housing Group was established in 1968 whose membership included representatives of the coloured people's organizations represented on the Consultative Committee, representatives of professional organizations concerned with housing, representatives of relevant voluntary agencies, and local authority representatives. The group began active operations in early 1969, falling outside the scope of this chapter. Its composition and non-statutory powerless status are similar to the situation of the Consultative Committee.

VI

Nottingham's quasi-political structural mechanisms to promote harmonious race relations clearly have been ineffectual. Irons's office and the Consultative Committee, despite Irons's claim that 'there is a depth to our work',[64] and despite sporadic attempts to be responsive to the needs of the black community, were not effective in improving the average immigrant's life chances, access to a decent home, and quality education for his children. This ineffectual record is directly related to the fact that the officially sanctioned race relations structures occupy an anomalous and essentially powerless position. They were created and supported by the white political community and the local authority. As a result, their independence was compromised; 'It has been awfully difficult for us to know', Miss Wood observed, 'how far we could go in supporting immigrant demands without alienating the council.'[65] In June 1967, the finance and general purposes sub-committee of the Consultative Committee reported at the monthly meeting that it felt 'that we had a long way to go in order to get our image across to the City Council and the public at large. In doing so, it was important not to upset the Town Clerk and Heads of Departments'.[66] Thus earlier in the year when the committee discussed the possibilities of pressuring the council to hire black policemen and appoint blacks to school management boards, no action was taken because of 'the dangers of arousing negative feelings by *pushing* immigrants on to these bodies'.[67]

The committee was meant to link immigrant organizations and the political community, but this liaison function was, in terms of power, a one-way process, for the committee's functions, powers, and legitimacy were defined from above while the predominantly non-political immigrant groups who served on the committee were essentially powerless. They depended on their association with the committee to promote their interests, yet the committee too was without power, sufficient finances, or adequate staff.[68]

Furthermore, by providing access to the immigrants' conspicuous, moderate, largely middle-class organizational elite, the committee was not only descriptively unrepresentative, but also muffled immigrant protest and divided the black population. Their politicization not only was not encouraged, but actively discouraged; stability and harmony were stressed at the expense of political organization. There was striking

[64] Irons interview.
[65] Wood interview.
[66] Consultative Committee, Finance and General Purposes Sub-Committee, 'Minutes' (30 June 1967).
[67] Consultative Committee, Integration Sub-Committee, 'Minutes' (10 January 1967). Italics added.
[68] (*Footnote overleaf.*)

agreement among the committee's supporters and detractors that, above all, the existence of the committee insulated the political community from pressures for change of the racial *status quo*. 'We have succeeded', Laird boasted, 'and this is our most important achievement, in acting as a safety valve. If the committee had not existed, or stopped functioning today, the immigrants would be at the mercy of left-wing coloured political agitators. We prevent trouble.'[69] Powe, one of the committee's most vocal critics, noted too that 'there is no doubt that the committee is deliberately used as a political safety valve. Whites are involved directly in politics; blacks are expected to be involved indirectly.'[70] William Taylor observed that 'our senior members tell me that it is important that we channel discontent, but I wonder sometimes if it perhaps were better that the committee did not exist. We have sometimes played the role of a lightning-rod. We are, as a result, hiding the problems.'[71]

The existence of structured integration mechanisms primarily benefits the political community and a small group of predominantly middle-class coloured 'leaders' who want recognition from the white political community and who will not jeopardize their prospects by making political demands and encouraging black political participation. They were not

[68] Taylor was the only full-time paid employee.

TABLE: CONSULTATIVE COMMITTEE BUDGET, YEAR ENDING
31 MARCH 1967

Income	£	s	d
Membership fees, affiliation fees, and subscriptions	46	17	1
Corporation grant	1,050	0	0
Special efforts efforts (jumble sales, etc.)	286	12	4
Students' fees	40	0	0
Sundry items	5	0	0
N.C.C.I.	1,500	0	0
Deficiency	188	11	6
Total	£3,117	0	11
Expenditure			
Salaries and national insurance	2,043	0	9
Children's Christmas party	24	13	9
Allocation for Welfare Committee	300	0	0
Allocation for general deficiency	749	6	5
Total	£3,117	0	11

SOURCE: Courtesy of William Taylor. The committee, it should be noted, had no money for publicity or field work of any kind.

[69] Laird interview.
[70] Power interview.
[71] Taylor interview.

given access to political control, but instead were granted a measure of paternal patronage in the form of seats on the committee, contacts with the local political and voluntary elites, the appointment of two black magistrates,[72] in addition to Irons's post at the education office. It is noteworthy, I think, that the only black council nominee to date has been A. S. Atwal, the secretary of the politically-minded Indian Workers Association.[73]

But most of all, the city's buffering racial linkages benefited the city's politicians, for these mechanisms permitted them to manage the politics of race with a minimum of dissensus while, simultaneously, they were able to assert that Nottingham had coped well with Third World immigration, citing Irons's office and the Consultative Committee as evidence. Thus the leader of the council's Conservative majority, Alderman Derbyshire, stated, 'I am proud of our bi-partisan approach to these matters. Nottingham has done very well. . . . I am sure,' he added, 'that we have no immediate problems to be dealt with in this area. We are very pleased with Mr. Irons's welfare work.'[74] His Labour counterpart, Alderman Foster, lauded Irons's and the Committee's efforts to 'help these strangers in a strange land', and praised their 'understanding that change must be acceptable to all', that 'there are no special rights for minority groups'. In Nottingham, he concluded, 'we have handled these problems more than reasonably well. . . . Coloured people like Mr. Irons who don't have a chip on their shoulder have helped us achieve real integration.'[75]

The council survey referred to earlier in the chapter highlights the functional role of the structural mechanisms and indicates the political community's attitudes towards black political participation and access to positions of control. All of the Conservative respondents (fourteen) and 57 per cent (eight) of the Labour councillors thought Nottingham had coped very well or reasonably well with coloured immigration; significantly, of this group, eight of the Conservatives and all of the Labour councillors mentioned the work of Eric Irons and/or the Consultative Committee, while none of the six Labour councillors who thought that Nottingham had not coped well cited Irons or the committee, and at least two of the dissenting Labour group indicated that they sympathized with the views of the Afro-Asian–West Indian Union (see Tables 10.1 and 10.2).

One 'advantage of local self-government', Birch has written, 'is that it provides a sphere of political activity which is open to almost everybody

[72] Nottingham in 1968 had 131 J.P.s, of whom eighteen were on the supplemental list. Thus 1·8 per cent of the city's magistrates were coloured.

[73] Atwal was nominated as the Labour candidate in St. Ann's ward, a safe Conservative district. He finished last with 515 votes. All three Conservative candidates were elected with the leading candidate receiving 2,205 votes. Nottingham *Guardian Journal* (10 May 1968).

[74] Interview with Alderman Derbyshire (19 March 1968).

[75] Foster interview.

TABLE 10.1: NOTTINGHAM COUNCILLORS: HOW WELL HAS NOTTINGHAM COPED WITH COLOURED IMMIGRATION?

	Labour ($N=14$)		Conservative ($N=14$)	
	No.	Per Cent	No.	Per Cent
Very well	2	14	4	29
Reasonably well	6	43	10	71
Not too well	4	29	0	0
Very badly	2	14	0	0
Total	14	100	14	100

SOURCE: Nottingham Council Survey (1968).

TABLE 10.2: NOTTINGHAM COUNCILLORS FAVOURABLY CITING THE CONSULTATIVE COMMITTEE AND/OR IRONS'S OFFICE, BY REPLIES IN TABLE 10.1

	Nottingham has coped:			
	Very well or reasonably well ($N=22$)		Not too well or very badly ($N=6$)	
	Mentioned	Did not	Mentioned	Did not
Labour	8	0	0	6
Conservative	8	6	0	0
Total	16 (73%)	6 (27%)	0 (0%)	6 (100%)

SOURCE: Nottingham Council Survey (1968).

who wants to take part . . . almost anybody could become a local councillor, both in the sense that it is easy to get elected and because the work need not disrupt a man's career.'[76] Yet only 29 per cent of the councillors surveyed thought that it would be a good idea for their party to nominate coloured candidates for council seats (see Table 10.3). On the other hand, 42 per cent of those who replied unambiguously favoured the co-option of immigrants to serve on important council committees (see Table 10.4), though the council rarely employed its powers of co-option in the past. The marked difference of support for council nominations and co-option is striking, and is to be accounted for, at least in part, by the fact that co-opted members are directly responsible to the political community, while councillors are ultimately accountable to the electorate. A Conservative councillor, asked if his party should nominate coloured candidates emphatically replied, 'No! Not unless he was exceptional and the ward mainly non-white', but favoured co-option stating, 'We could use all the expertise we can find.' Similarly, a Labour respondent who thought 'the time is not now' for coloured councillors thought co-option a good idea 'to

[76] A. H. Birch, *The British System of Government* (London, 1967), p. 245.

TABLE 10.3: NOTTINGHAM COUNCILLORS: WOULD IT BE A GOOD IDEA FOR YOUR PARTY TO NOMINATE COLOURED CANDIDATES TO CONTEST COUNCIL SEATS?

	Labour (N=14)	Conservative (N=14)	Total
Yes	5 (36%)	3 (21%)	8 (29%)
No	9 (64%)	11 (79%)	20 (71%)
	14 (100)	14 (100)	28 (100)

SOURCE: Nottingham Council Survey (1968).

TABLE 10.4: NOTTINGHAM COUNCILLORS: WOULD IT BE A GOOD IDEA TO CO-OPT COLOURED PEOPLE TO SERVE ON IMPORTANT COUNCIL COMMITTEES?

	Labour (N=14)	Conservative (N=14)	Total
Yes	6 (42%)	6 (42%)	12 (42%)
No	4 (29%)	4 (29%)	8 (29%)
Don't know or qualified answer	4 (29%)	4 (29%)	8 (29%)
	14 (100)	14 (100)	28 (100)

SOURCE: Nottingham Council Survey (1968).

prepare him or her for the time when the community as a whole is ready to accept them'. Thus instead of complete participation in the present, this councillor—and in this respect he was typical of the political community as a whole—was prepared to offer the substitute of token, powerless participation.

Most of the councillors showed a remarkable inconsistency regarding the relevance of colour as a political category. Blacks were urged not to develop group consciousness and to act as individuals: immigrant leaders 'should encourage assimilation by *discouraging* "coloured only" clubs and societies'; 'there is no difference between people of different colours. They must act and be treated alike'; 'it would be wrong to nominate someone for office because he was coloured'; 'to single minority groups out for special treatment would be wrong'; 'immigrants should participate *as individuals* in public and communal life, not as coloured people'. In short, colour should be irrelevant. Yet the same respondents argued implicitly in favour of differential treatment of whites and blacks: 'Coloured people should be nominated for office only in wards with a substantial immigrant population. In other wards such a nomination would be impolitic'; 'coloured nominees would be a good thing in some wards in the city where there are many immigrants'; 'party canvassing among coloured people should be done by coloured people'.

Thus it is clear that while the black population was expected to adopt a 'British way of life' and act as if colour were irrelevant, the political community viewed Third World immigrants as a group apart. Their participation, structured through the Consultative Committee and Irons's office, precluded direct access to the competition for positions of political power and control. Black patronage in this situation was meagre, doled out to a token, unrepresentative group of powerless leaders. Despite the city's elaborate structure of integration mechanisms, at the end of 1969 there were no black councillors, no black members of school management boards, no black policemen, no black people employed by the housing department. On the assumption that a system's output is in part a reflection of the process and structure of the system itself, Nottingham's integration mechanisms must be found wanting.

What then accounts for the city's enlightened, progressive reputation? Two factors, I think. While most local authorities have pursued a 'colour-blind' policy that evades *de facto* inequality, Nottingham, at least, has done *something*.[77] Moreover, what it has done conforms to the official prevailing wisdom of race relations 'experts'. The lesson of Nottingham's experience, however, indicates at a minimum that these recommended race relations structures, which have now been adopted in every British city with a Third World population of consequence, are seriously flawed.

Nottingham's reputation is to be accounted for, secondly, by the fact that the city's politicians have never divided fundamentally on the issues of race along party lines. The city's coherent, manageable, structured politics of race has kept colour off the local political agenda; indeed, it is a striking feature of the city's politics that no candidate to date for municipal office has attempted to exploit the racial prejudices and fears of the electorate. It is, in this sense, that Nottingham, from the perspective of local and national white political elites, has been a significant symbol; but from the perspective of the Third World immigrants (and, I will argue below, of future race relations) the price paid continues to be terribly high. The pre-1958 illusion of harmonious race relations has been restored, but in my view, it remains, unfortunately, merely an illusion.

[77] For a survey of local authority responses, see Dipak Nandy, 'An Illusion of Competence', in Anthony Lester and Nicholas Deakin, eds., *Policies for Racial Equality* (Fabian Research Series 262, July 1967).

Chapter Eleven

Racial Buffering: Colonial Relationships in the Mother Country

I

'How is it possible', Cobbett inquired in 1808, 'for us to justify our conduct upon any principle of morality? Conquests in India are not at all necessary to our safety or comfort.'[1] The imperialist response to this gnawing moral question was an affirmation of moral idealism—the backward races needed civilizing.[2] Exploitative racist and humanitarian impulses fused to produce an ennobling paternalist doctrine. The colonized were pictured as children, the offspring of the family of Empire, later the Commonwealth, headed by the benevolent matriarch Britain.[3]

[1] William Cobbett, in the *Political Register* (16 April 1808), in George Bennett, ed., *The Concept of Empire: Burke to Attlee* (London, 1953), p. 65.

[2] The Empire, W. E. H. Lecky argued in his inaugural lecture at Cambridge in 1893, had expanded because Englishmen 'have largely employed their redundant energies in exploring, conquering, civilising, and governing distant and half-savage lands', and spoke of 'an Empire planted amid the shifting sands of half-civilised and anarchical races'. Racism, Leon Epstein observed, 'seems an almost inevitable component of imperialism. In its crude form, as that the only good Indian is a dead Indian, it accompanied cruel and bloody conquests, and in its less ferocious form it went along with benevolent paternalism.' W. E. H. Lecky, *The Empire: Its Value and Growth* (London, 1893), pp. 22–3; Leon D. Epstein, *British Politics in the Suez Crisis* (London, 1964), p. 13.

[3] The ennobling theme of benevolent paternalism was adopted by socialist and Tory, imperialist and anti-imperialist alike. Thus while the Governor-General of Nigeria, in 1922, asserted that 'the standard which the white man must set before him when dealing with the uncivilised races must be a high one', the Labour party in 1926 declared as its official policy 'with regard to the native races' that 'the Empire should be, in the words of the Covenant, a Trustee for the well-being of the natives'. The death of Empire and the birth of the Commonwealth did not dim these sentiments. In 1953, for example, when the migration of West Indians to Britain was beginning to increase in numbers, Salisbury spoke of 'that portion of the Empire which is not yet grown up, which is not yet in a position to manage its own affairs, internal or external, without guidance from us. . . . We are dealing with people's of an infinite variety of races and colour and gradations of civilisation.' Similarly, the Conservative Commonwealth Council argued in 1955, 'A worthy colonial power has to perform the supreme and often thankless task of the old nobility and middle classes of the better kind: to keep civilisation alive and

Contemporary racial attitudes have been shaped by the colonial experience, forged in the crucible of imperialism. A nation's culture, both social and political, is the outcome of a unique historical process. Though not all learning is culture, all culture is learned, and Britain, in particular, is characterized by a hereditary culture.[4] As a consequence of the heritage of imperialism, British feelings of racial superiority became part of the country's cultural baggage, not always consciously felt, but always potentially operative. Most Englishmen alive today have grown up nurtured by a press, literature, and education that promoted the related notions of the civilizing mission and racial paternalism.[5]

Distinguishing between folk prejudice, politically relevant prejudice, and its structural–systemic expression, the history of the politics of race in Britain since 1948 is the paradoxical history of the politicization of prejudice and its national and local systemic expression in political consensus arrangements calculated to take race off the two-party political agenda. The operative phrase, nationally and locally, has been 'for immigrants', as the colonial ethos of racial paternalism found domestc rhetorical and institutional expression.

A key feature of classic colonial patterns of social control—indirect rule through a broker, native leadership—has been replicated in the mother

hand it over sound and safe to rising new bodies of men and women who previously were incapable of fending for themselves in the modern world.'
Bennett, op. cit., p. 395 (Sir Dealtry Lugard, later Lord Lugard, was the High Commissioner for Nigeria and later its Governor and Governor General. From 1922 to 1936 he was a member of the Permanent Mandates Commission of the League of Nations); Labour Party, 'Labour and the Empire: Africa' (London, 1926), p. 3; Lord Salisbury, 'Commonwealth and Empire', address to the Primrose League, 24 April 1953; Conservative Commonwealth Council, 'Colonial Rule: Enemies and Obligations' (London, March 1955), p. 4.

[4] For discussions, see Zevedi Barbu, *Problems of Historical Psychology* (London, 1960), especially pp. 6, 13, 42, 203, 212; Clyde Kluckhohn, 'The Study of Culture', in Lewis Coser and Bernard Rosenberg, eds., *Sociological Theory* (New York, 1966), pp. 40–53; and the comparative report on anti-semitism by Melvin Tumin entitled, 'Intergroup Attitudes of Youth and Adults in England, France, and Germany' (1953), based on a report prepared for a conference on the subject at Munich in October 1962.

[5] The ingrained stereotypes of backward races and white superiority have been perpetuated by British schools. Attlee recalled the great map at school 'with large portions coloured red, It was an intoxicating vision for a small boy, for, as we understood it, all these people were ruled for their own good by strong silent men, civil servants and soldiers as portrayed by Kipling. We believed in our great imperial mission.' The assumptions and language of racialism were incorporated into school histories. The widely used 1946, and sixth, edition of Robert Raynor's textbook *England in Modern Times*, for instance, discusses 'the peculiar qualities in the Englishman that make him so successful as a colonist and a ruler of backward races', and later states, 'The traditional policy of non-interference which had such happy results in the great self-governing dominions had not been so suitable for those colonies which, situated in the tropics and inhabited chiefly by backward races, were unfitted for democracy.' Clement Attlee, *Empire into Commonwealth* (London, 1960), p. 6; Robert Raynor, *England in Modern Times* (London, 1946), pp. 386, 395; for a brief discussion, see Robin Winks, ed., *British Imperialism* (New York, 1963), pp. 4–5.

country. Indirect rule, as Apter notes, is not a precise term; it refers, in an omnibus way, to a variety of colonial practices of governing in different areas. The essential feature of indirect rule is that native chiefs were an integral part of the colonial administration. As Lugard put it, 'There are not two sets of rulers—British and native—working either separately or in cooperation, but a single government in which the native chiefs have well defined duties. . . . They must be complementary to each other and the chief himself must understand that he has no right to place and power unless he renders his proper services to the state.'[6] Where traditional chiefs did not exist (for the Kikuyu or the Plateau Tonga of Northern Rhodesia, for example), they were invented.[7] 'The colonial administrator turned to them basically because he was faced with the problem of creating an administrative system where none existed;' to communicate and to control the colonized, the colonizers needed authority-figures who could provide 'a bridge of legitimation', and enable 'an administration to divide and rule: popular resentments and hatreds could be deflected on to the local officials while the ultimate authority could remain remote, unseen and "above the battle".'[8]

The arrangements of the 1965 White Paper institutionalized indirect rule with respect to the Third World immigrant population. 'In one sense', Eric Irons wrote in his 1961–2 report to the Nottingham Council, 'the organiser looks upon his functions as being that of an "interpreter" between the new and the established communities and his advice and help are often sought by statutory and voluntary bodies in their approach to these sections of the population.'[9] The national and local liaison committees were not meant to be spokesmen for the newcomers or organized pressure groups. Rather, their orientation was consensual. N.C.C.I.'s 1967 guidelines on the formation of local committees stressed that 'it should be emphasized at every stage that this is *not a committee to serve the interests of one section of the community but a committee to promote racial harmony. It is therefore beneficial to all*'.[10] Local representation, the guidelines urged, should include party representation, service organizations and clubs (Rotary, Chamber of Commerce, working men's clubs, etc.), voluntary and statutory service organizations (Council of Social Service, Family Welfare Association, probation office, the police, the welfare officer, etc), and *visible* immigrant leadership: 'There may already be immigrant associations in the area which can be approached for representation, but if not, the officers of appropriate High Commissions may be

---

[6] David Apter, *The Gold Coast in Transition* (Princeton, 1955), pp. 120–1.

[7] Peter Worsley, *The Third World* (London, 1967), p. 38.

[8] Ibid.

[9] City of Nottingham, Council Education Committee, 'Report of the Organiser for Work Amongst the Coloured Communities' (February 1961–March 1962), p. 2.

[10] National Committee for Commonwealth Immigrants, 'Notes for Guidance on the Formation of a Voluntary Liaison Committee', unpublished, April 1967. Italics in original.

able to supply some names, as also may the National Committee for Commonwealth Immigrants.'[11]

Seen in these terms, most of the literature on British race politics misses the significance of the critical structural decision to link the Third World population to the polity through buffer institutions, replicating key features of traditional colonial relationships. Thus, to cite only a few examples, Abbott has written, in the context of his critique of John Rex's work, 'It is probably not very important to decide whether or not the N.C.C.I. had a general "political" role'; and Kramer, Deakin, and Bourne distinguish between deleterious (political) immigration control features of the White Paper, and its (non-political) 'constructive' institutional arrangements.[12] Yet, as we have seen, the 1965 document was the outcome of the building of a *political* consensus, aimed at depoliticizing race.

In their attempt to create a stable, coherent, predictable politics (or non-politics) of race, British politicians had to deal with the immigrant–colonial amalgam. Hence it was necessary both severely to curtail immigration from the Third World Commonwealth and to create quasi-colonial institutional structures to deal with the issues of race outside of the traditional political arenas. As a result, the Third World population has been institutionally separated from the society-wide, largely class-based network of political institutions and associations, and has been unable to compete effectively for the scarce resource of political power.

From its founding, the instruments of indirect rule—N.C.C.I. and its local affiliate committees—were put in an impossibly ambiguous position: sponsored and financed by the Government, established by a document that gave systematic expression to cultural–folk prejudices, yet expected to somehow speak and act 'for immigrants'. Thus one N.C.C.I. development officer has complained, 'We have no policy', adding, 'We are caught in a bind. What can you expect from a government agency? We must be careful.'[13] The organization's general secretary accepted the politicians' non-political definition of N.C.C.I.'s role ('Politics is not my line').[14] As a consequence of its anomalous position, the organization, Dipak Nandy has observed, has generated 'an atmosphere of superficial liberalism and

---

[11] Ibid.

[12] Later in the essay, Abbott himself raises the important political issues. Simon Abbott, ed., *The Prevention of Racial Discrimination in Britain* (London, 1971), p. 318; Daniel C. Kramer, 'White versus Colored in Britain: An Explosive Confrontation?', *Social Research* (Vol. 36, Winter 1969); Nicholas Deakin and Jenny Bourne, 'Powell, Minorities, and the 1970 Election', *Political Quarterly* (Vol. 41, July 1970).

[13] Interview with Anne Evans, N.C.C.I. and CRC Development Officer for Northern England (21 January 1969).

[14] Cited in Ben W. Heineman, *The Politics of the Powerless: A Study of the Campaign against Racial Discrimination* (London, 1972).

of generalized good-will. . . . Its characteristic style is paralysis and non-statement.'[15]

A recent study of the work of ten local liaison officers revealed clearly the way in which the structural arrangements of the White Paper limited behavioural choices to a relatively meaningless set of alternatives. The liaison officers found that goodwill on their part could not be translated effectively into action; they felt constrained by the structural limitations they did not create. The officers uniformly found their financial dependence on the local authority led to embarrassment and ambiguity; most criticized the tri-partite obligation of liaison officers: they are paid by central government funds, and responsible both to the local authority and the executive committee of their organization.[16]

II

'Looking back upon the whole period from 1955 to the present day', the authors of *Colour and Citizenship* maintained, 'it is clear that it was too much to expect that "integration" could be decisively promoted or affected by the local voluntary committees unless they had more political backing.'[17] But the very origins and structure of the buffer institutions militated against this level of political support; the White Paper institutional network was created only incidentally to promote integration. Rather, it was meant to structure and deflect immigrant political participation into non-threatening activity.

At their best, buffer institutions can, despite their shortcomings, under certain circumstances, become significant arenas of inter-group accommodation in themselves which may be more accessible to new potential partisans than traditional established institutions. To assume this role, the buffers must have the capacity to affect the distribution and allocation of scarce resources. They must be descriptively representative in membership, responsive in policy, and efficient in policy-execution. To prevent the process of bargaining from becoming one of dictation, they must link groups that, in terms of power capacity, are relatively equal.

As we have seen, however, the race relations buffers established in Britain do not meet these standards. Though they have attempted at times to be responsive (substantively representative), their descriptively unrepresentative membership and their lack of efficacy have combined to resemble closely the ideal-type of ineffectual paternalism.[18] At their best, buffering institutions are an inadequate substitute for direct, bidirectional political participation. In Britain these structures, by rewarding

[15] Dipak Nandy, 'The National Committee for Commonwealth Immigrants: An Assessment', C.A.R.D. position paper (London 1967), p. 6.

[16] Margot Levy, 'The Work of Liaison Officers', unpublished paper, pp. 5, 8.

[17] E. J. B. Rose and associates, *Colour and Citizenship: A Report on British Race Relations* (London, 1969), p. 391.

[18] See below, chapter 2, section III.

complaisant 'leaders', by inhibiting the development of Third World political consciousness, and by permitting politicians to claim that integration is successfully being promoted,[19] have actually obstructed the development of more viable immigrant–polity relationships. The N.C.C.I. (and its successor the Community Relations Commission) and the committees it supervises have produced neither productive nor distributive justice.

The 1965 political consensus has taken race out of politics, then, in two respects. Immigrants' felt needs and demands are dealt with by quasi-political bodies like the Community Relations Commission and the Race Relations Board, which administer the country's anti-discrimination legislation, rather than by Parliament and the Government directly. In neither institution are Third World representatives selected primarily by the immigrant communities themselves.[20] Secondly, since 1965 the Front Benches of both parties have accepted the dual framework of very strict immigration controls coupled with anti-discrimination legislation and quasi-political buffering institutions. These institutions (there are now over eighty local committees) have pursued an elite, consensual strategy, leaving the mass of the Third World immigrants politically unanchored.[21]

Both aspects of the depoliticization of race have permitted the Government to avoid making political policy decisions in this field, some of which must be made if anti-discrimination legislation, which at present lacks adequate enforcement provisions, is to have any meaning at all. In the area of housing for example, the Race Relations Act of 1968, according to Moore 'will be rendered nugatory unless the Government takes a number of political decisions in an unambiguous manner (a major change in policy itself). . . . Local authorities must be prevented from discriminating in their housing allocation and planning policies, or by selective application of overcrowding regulations.'[22] Like the pre-political con-

[19] See, for instance, David Ennals, 'Labour's Race Relations Policy', the Institute of Race Relations Newsletter (November/December 1968), pp. 435–6.

[20] At a special general meeting of the Camden Committee for Community Relations on 4 April 1968, the Rev. Wilfred Wood, a West Indian, proposed that N.C.C.I. be replaced by a National Commission for Racial Equality with 25 per cent of its members to be nominated by the Government, 25 per cent elected by existing voluntary liaison committees, and 50 per cent elected by the Third World ethnic communities on the basis of registered membership. After some discussion in the national press, these proposals have been ignored by the media and by policy-makers.

[21] In preparing his forthcoming Ph.D. thesis, Daniel Lawrence found, in a random sample of 122 male coloured immigrants drawn from Nottingham's central parliamentary constituency that 75 per cent had not heard of the Consultative Committee; 19 per cent claimed to have knowledge of the organization, but in fact knew almost nothing about it; of the 6 per cent who knew something of the committee, two were members of immigrant organizations that had served on the committee. I am indebted to Mr. Lawrence for this information.

[22] Robert Moore, 'Labour and Colour—1965–68', the Institute of Race Relations Newsletter (October 1968), p. 390.

sensus of the 1950s, the political consensus of the late 1960s (and early 1970s) encourages elite deferment of policy questions of this kind.

Ironically, despite the broad area of bi-partisan agreement codified by the White Paper, race has only partially been depoliticized, for the effort to maintain the political consensus has entailed repeated concessions to those who have continued to appeal to the public's folk prejudices in demagogic fashion. The reaction to Enoch Powell's first major speeches on immigration in the spring and autumn of 1968 instructively illustrates the point.

In Birmingham on 20 April, Powell, then Shadow Minister of Defence, spoke in emotive terms about Third World immigration: 'It is like a nation busily engaged in heaping up its own funeral pyre.' He suggested not only that 'the total inflow for settlement should be reduced at once to negligible proportions', but also urged 'the encouragement of re-emigration. . . . In short, suspension of immigration and encouragement of re-emigration hang together, logically and humanely, as two aspects of the same approach.'[23] Edward Heath issued a statement the following day announcing that Powell had been dropped from the Shadow Cabinet:

I have told Mr. Powell that I consider the speech he made in Birmingham yesterday to have been racialist *in tone* and liable to exacerbate racial tensions. This is unacceptable from one of the leaders of the Conservative Party and incompatable with the responsibility of a member of the Shadow Cabinet.[24]

Heath, however, made it clear that he did not differ with the substance of Powell's remarks: 'I have repeatedly emphasized that the policy of the Conservative Party is that immigration must be more stringently limited and that immigrants wishing to return to their own countries should be helped financially to do so.'[25] The Labour Home Secretary indicated that the Government accepted this position too. On B.B.C. television on 29 April, James Callaghan stated that 'the Ministry of Social Security is willing to repatriate any immigrant family unable to pay for itself and wanting to return home'. He added that he was aware of unrest in the country regarding coloured immigration, declaring 'that is why I introduced the Commonwealth Immigrants Act in February[26] in order to limit the number of people coming into this country'.[27]

[23] Text of the speech in *Race* (Vol. X, July 1968), pp. 94-9.
[24] Ibid., p. 99. Italics added.
[25] Ibid.
[26] Mr. Callaghan, of course, was referring to the bill rushed through Parliament in February 1968 which introduced a voucher system for Kenyan Asians (1,500 per year) even though they held British passports. The bill was introduced after a brief but frenzied campaign, led by Powell and Duncan Sandys, that talked in the familiar terms of an uncontrollable flood of immigrants. It is noteworthy that Lord Butler has indicated that he would have voted against the bill had he been present at the vote in the House of Lords. Interview with Lord Butler, Cambridge (2 March 1968).
[27] *The Times* (30 April 1968), p. 1.

N

Powell repeated his proposals at Eastbourne in November, this time calling for a special Ministry of Repatriation and announcing a new doctrine of citizenship based on colour: 'The West Indian or Asian does not by being born in England become an Englishman. In law he becomes a United Kingdom citizen by birth; in fact he is a West Indian or Asian still.'[28] This time Heath condemned 'the character assassination of any racial group in this country' but called too for stricter controls based on the amalgamation of aliens and Commonwealth immigration legislation.[29] He repeated these proposals at Walsall in January 1969 (and moved to enact them in 1971). The Government responded by revoking the right of Commonwealth citizens to enter the United Kingdom to marry their fiancées regardless of whether the woman was born in the United Kingdom or not; this concessionary right was not revoked in the case of aliens.[30] Powell's substantive proposals, if not Powell himself, were on the legitimate agenda of political discourse and accommodation. The maintenance of the political consensus required continued systemic concessions, for the substance of the consensus was less important than the fact of consensus.[31]

III

Britain's Third World population could have been linked to the polity either by a legitimately colour-blind policy that would have permitted them to divide, like other Englishmen, as individuals based largely on class affiliation (individual integration) or by a recognition that the immigrants constituted, at least in the early decades of contact, a discrete political conflict collectivity, thus making possible bi-directional group linkages of boundary management and direct bargaining (collective integration).[32] The first alternative clearly would have been preferred by a majority of the West Indian immigrants who were moving away from colour-ascriptive societies; they wanted and expected to be accepted as Englishmen. Black (as opposed to coloured) West Indians have suffered most in their home islands from the white-bias legacy of colonial rule; in Thornton's telling phrase, they have only one world to belong to and are not at home in it.[33] Some reacted to this intolerable situation by affirming their blackness. Members of the Ras Tafari cult, for example, believe that Haile Sellassie (Ras Tafari) of Ethiopia is the living God, that the black

[28] *Sunday Times* (17 November 1968), p. 8.
[29] *The Times* (18 November 1968), p. 1.
[30] *The Times* (31 January 1969),p. 1.
[31] For a discussion of analogous 'cartel of elites' arrangements, see Arend Lipjhart, 'Consociational Democracy', *World Politics* (Vol. 21, January 1969), pp. 207ff.
[32] I am referring here, of course, to structural, not cultural, integration.
[33] A. P. Thornton, *For the File on Empire* (London, 1968), p. 320.

man must seek salvation by returning to Africa.[34] The West Indian blacks who came to Britain were afflicted by the same frustrations and feelings of inadequacy. Like the Ras Tafarians, they too seek to resolve those feelings through migration. But significantly, they have looked to and moved to England. Like the Ras Tafari movement, the migration to Britain was 'a lower-class thing; it was a black thing'.[35] But unlike their Ras Tafarian countrymen, the migrants to England moved toward 'whiteness', to the mother country.

To be sure, the West Indian migrants chose to come to Britain for economic reasons, for their frustrations at home have most often been defined in economic terms. The average migrant will state when asked that he has come to work, to better his economic position.[36] Yet, the migrants have come not simply for economic reasons, but for social and cultural ones as well. In moving to Britain, the West Indian migrant rejects implicitly the whole inhibiting colour-ascriptive network of his island's social structure. That system of relationships condemned him to inferior status, prevented him from achieving what the culture defined as good, and offered few compensations. He had little chance to achieve the positive cultural norms of 'whiteness' and 'respectability'. He could not assimilate; the middle-class solution was beyond his reach. As Philip Mason has put it:

There is a sense in which the Caribbean displays the essence of colonialism. It is true that in one respect this region is different from most of the colonial world; there are only fragmentary remains of a native population subjugated by invaders. But it is the essence of colonialism . . . that the few impose on the many a spiritual yoke which comes to govern their day to day actions, more constantly and pervasively, if less obtrusively, than the physical force which lies in the background. Nowhere did this happen more completely than in the Caribbean. Whole societies were persuaded to imitate a way of life that was quite unfamiliar to them, one they had little hope in attaining and not in itself particularly estimable; what was more serious, they came to despise themselves and their own way of life.[37]

[34] See M. G. Smith, Roy Augier, Rex Nettleford, 'The Ras Tafari Movement in Kingston, Jamaica', report for the Institute of Social and Economic Research, University College of the West Indies, 1960, and G. E. Simpson, 'The Ras Tafari Movement in Jamaica: A Study of Race and Class Conflict', *Social Forces* (Vol. 34, December 1955); 3,000 Jamaicans attended the movement's 1958 convention.

[35] V. S. Naipaul, *The Middle Passage* (London, 1962), p. 230.

[36] See Ceri Peach, *West Indian Migration to Britain: A Social Geography* (London, 1968) and R. B. Davison, *West Indian Immigrants* (London, 1962) for extended discussions.

[37] Philip Mason, *Patterns of Dominance* (London, 1970), p. 274. The dual theme of the rejection of European culture and colour values and the search for an African identity is the central issue in West Indian literature. According to G. R. Coulthard, there have been four principal variations on this theme: 'First, the feeling that the Caribbean Negro is somehow constricted in the moulds of European thought and behaviour patterns which are not fitted to his nature. Linked with this is the interest in African cultures, past and present, both in Africa and their remains in the West Indies.

The migration from the West Indies to Britain can be seen in part as an attempt to achieve social, cultural, as well as economic and political assimilation into the 'superior' society. The black migrant hoped to do one better than his coloured countryman—he would become English. To the West Indies, the Englishman had brought the prestige of his association with England. It was this esteem by association that the West Indian migrants wanted to share, and it was this ambition that caused most to reject agricultural and domestic work in England, though they had been farmers and domestics in the Caribbean.[38] It was this too that occasioned their surprise when they found that many white Englishmen did unskilled, even menial work. And it was this, ultimately, that contributed to the bitterness and frustrations of life in England, for there too they were and are defined by their colour. Seeking to escape the oppressions of colour, they found they were still black.[39]

Thus, the increasing political relevance and systemic expression of the folk prejudices of British society made impossible individual integration for most of the migrants. The realities of discrimination, the political conciliation of those who advocated colour-based immigration policies, and the development of a political consensus by white elites at the Third World immigrants' expense clashed too sharply with the hopes of individual acceptance. Yet the second possibility, that of collective integration, has been achieved only in the highly inadequate form of uni-directional buffering institutions.

The fluid period of the politics of race in Britain is over. The trend towards stricter immigration controls (and perhaps ultimately a programme of forced repatriation) aimed at reducing the number of black Englishmen appears irreversible. Two anti-discrimination laws have been passed, both with loopholes and weak enforcement provisions.[40] The buffer institutions created and sustained by the White Paper consensus

Second, the feeling that European civilisation has failed, by becoming excessively concerned with the production of happiness for the human individual. African, or Negro culture, is presented as being nearer to nature and nearer to man. Third, the rejection of Christianity as an agent or ally of colonialism; and finally, the attack on European civilisation for the brutality and cynicism with which it enslaved and exploited the Negro while still maintaining high-sounding principles of freedom and humanitarianism.' G. R. Coulthard, *Race and Culture in Caribbean Literature* (London, 1962), p. 52.

[38] See Robin Oakley, ed., *New Backgrounds* (London, 1968), p. 6.

[39] The most comprehensive survey of racial discrimination in Britain concluded, 'Of the three coloured groups, the experiences of the West Indians have been the worst. To a considerable extent this is due to their higher expectations on arrival and their greater desire to participate in a British pattern of life. This has caused them greater exposure to rejection and rebuff, and therefore to have a greater feeling that discrimination occurs.' Political and Economic Planning, *Racial Discrimination* (London, 1967), p. 8.

[40] See Anthony Dickey, 'The Race Relations Act, 1968', the Institute of Race Relations *Newsletter* (November/December 1968), pp. 338–41; and John Rex, 'The Race Relations Catastrophe', in T. Burgess, et. al., *Matters of Principle: Labour's Last Chance* (London, 1968), pp. 78–80.

have been put on a more permanent basis; section 25 of the 1968 Race Relations Act established the Community Relations Commission as the successor to N.C.C.I. Unlike N.C.C.I., the C.R.C. is a statutory body responsible to the Home Office.[41]

IV

In conclusion, I have argued that British race relations can only be understood as an amalgam of the colonial and voluntary migrant cases. The most significant feature of the politics of race in Britain has been its non-integration into an institutionalized class conflict framework. Thus, the Labour Government's White Paper of August 1965, 'Immigration from the Commonwealth', gave political expression to the immigrant–colonial amalgam in an effort by national and local party leaders to channel the issues of race to institutions outside of the usual political arenas. The issues of race, for British politicians, were incoherent and anomic. This central feature of domestic racial politics produced a political consensus that strictly controlled Third World immigration, and that—in the key structural decision of the period—linked the immigrants to the polity indirectly through quasi-colonial buffer institutions. These arrangements made impossible meaningful immigrant political participation, produced a group of broker leaders, formalized the institutional separation of the black population, and made it highly unlikely that Britain's Third World population would secure an equitable share of the scarce resource of political power.

This discussion is a corrective to the dominant research foci in the literature on immigrant assimilation, prejudice, and discrimination, and points the way to neglected research concerns. As such, it represents the beginning, not the end, of analysis. In part, then, this section should be read as an implicit research agenda. Much needed are additional studies (hopefully with some actional consequences) of the buffering institutions and their consequences for social and economic mobility, political participation rates, perceived satisfaction or deprivation, patterns of conflict and accommodation; in short, on the ways in which the political consensus buffer institutions define the limits of choice and racial justice.

A few speculative comments may be hazarded. The perceptual field of the Third World population, it is reasonable to assume, changes in

---

[41] For an extended discussion, see Community Relations Commission, *Report for 1969/70* (London, 1970). In a letter to the Bexley Community Relations Council on 28 May 1970 (at the onset of the election campaign), Edward Heath indicated strong support for the C.R.C., noting that it was not 'likely that we would favour a merger between the Community Relations Commission and the Race Relations Board'. Ioan Davies has recently commented, 'The retention of the Community Relations Commission is also an indication that—in one area at least—the Conservatives intend to try to keep the lid on.' Ioan Davies, 'Pretty Political Devices', *New Society* (18 March 1971), p. 439.

reaction to changes in the response of the white population, at the mass and elite levels, to them. It is to the institutionalized politics of race of the political consensus that the black population does and will respond. For many of the immigrants, the events of the last two and a half decades have been profoundly alienating. A recent study of the reaction of West Indian leaders to the national and local politics of race concluded that there was no doubt that most were convinced that there had been a rapid deterioration in race relations.[42] A Nottingham Jamaican put his reactions this way:

In 1944 I was a serviceman in the British air force fighting for freedom and democracy. In 1947 I became a settler in Nottingham. In the 1958 race riots I became a coloured man. In the 1962 Commonwealth Immigrants Act I became a coloured immigrant. And in 1968 I am an unwanted coloured immigrant. You tell me what's going to happen to me in 1970.[43]

The buffering institutions may have bought social peace in the short term. But, typically, when buffers lose their legitimacy, when one of the groups linked by the buffer breaks its connection with it, there is, to use Halpern's opaque terminology, a lapse into political incoherence.[44] Present evidence indicates the likelihood of this rejection of officially sanctioned buffers by most blacks; 'more and more, to put it succinctly, the immigrant sees himself less a West Indian or a Sikh in English society, and more as a black man in a white society.'[45] Writing in 1970, Gordon Lewis observed,

Not to collaborate is to lose financial aid, even more, is to abjure the English conviction that the way to get things done is to know the 'important people' at both the national and local government levels. To collaborate, on the other hand, is to run the risk of absorption, of being killed by official patronage, of seeming to betray the immigrant interests to a career of comfortable opportunism. It is not too much to say that most of the organizations in the field have decided by now in favour of complete independence, after a long experience of disillusionment.[46]

The short term peace bought by the buffers may soon yield to a continuing, and increasingly bitter, corrosive politics of racial confrontation and despair. This development, it might be argued, is not inevitable, but

---

[42] R. Manderson-Jones, in Abbott, ed., *The Prevention of Racial Discrimination in Britain*, based on unstructured interviews with twenty-one West Indians, most living in London.

[43] Quoted in John Heilpern and Dilip Hiro, 'The Town We Were Told Was Tolerant', the *Observer* (1 December 1968), p. 11.

[44] Manfred Halpern, 'Conflict, Violence, and the Dialectics of Modernization', unpublished paper (1968), p. 52.

[45] Gordon Lewis, 'Protest Among the Immigrants: The Dilemma of a Minority Culture', in Bernard Crick and William Robson, eds., *Protest and Discontent* (London, 1970), p. 89.

[46] Ibid., p. 91.

it surely is more likely than when the Third World immigrants first came in large numbers. In the 1950s, the problem was one of folk prejudices expressed in private acts of discrimination; by the late 1960s, the problem had become one of the political institutionalization of racism, a problem more resistant to change. In the United States, the change from black quiescent acceptance of the migration period linkages to non-violent protest to the Black Power Movement of the 1960s to violent ghetto rebellions to urban guerilla activity has taken place over a period of seven decades. In Britain, as a result of the unitary state (which provides fewer access points than the American Federal system), increased communications, awareness of the American experience, and the internationalization of Third World anti-colonial conflicts, the consequences of the unsatisfactory political linkages are liable to be felt much more rapidly as the process of disenchantment will be accelerated.

Institutions and linkages created by men can be reconstructed by men. This much is clear: existing political–structural race relations arrangements must not merely be tinkered with but transformed. The institutions created 'for immigrants' must be both representative of and made responsible to the constituency they claim to represent—black Englishmen themselves. At present, members of the C.R.C. are appointed by the Home Secretary, the majority of local committee representatives are white delegates of community organizations, and though the salaried local officers are hired by the local committees, the C.R.C. openly uses its control of funds to quash potentially embarrassing activism.[47] If the existing elaborate race relations structures are to be transformed, they must shed their ethos of benevolent paternalism; the dominant, controlling voice must be black.

Secondly, given the fact of pervasive racial discrimination in Britain, the C.R.C. and its committees (if they are to have any meaningful role at all) must, at the expense of their presently cherished pose of respectability,[48] become far more outspoken and active in seeking an equitable allocation of jobs, houses, and schooling for their Third World constituency. In short, if they are to be more than sham instruments of social control, these institutions need to become representative in all dimensions. At present, the C.R.C. and its affiliate local committees insulate politicians from the black community and permit them to handle the issues of race on politically manageable terms for them. Instead, I am suggesting that these organizations be transformed into vigorous advocates for the Third World population in a continuing process of boundary management and direct bargaining.

Given present political realities, of course, including the financial and

[47] Michael Dummett, 'Race and Colour in Great Britain', talk given to the Society for Philosophy and Public Affairs, Columbia University, 21 November 1970.
[48] See, John Reddaway, 'Whatever Happened to the CRC?', and William Taylor, 'Ariel's Revolt: Community Relations in the 1970's', *Race Today* (Vol. 2, 7 July 1970).

statutory position of these organizations, these proposals are hopelessly utopian. But this reality only indicates the scope of present and future tragedies, for only if just collective integration is made possible through transformed political relationships will future generations of black Englishmen not be strangers and afraid in a world they never made.

Part Four

Patterns of Political Linkage

Chapter Twelve

Potential Partisans, Parallel Institutions, and Social Control

THE place comparative studies occupies lies between what is true of all societies at all times and what is unique to one at a given time.[1] This comparative study, by examining the making and consequences of key structural decisions by white political elites during the fluid periods of migration in two 'immigrant–colonial' locales, has sought to contribute to the development of the embryonic field of comparative race relations; to suggest a particular research orientation and indicate its utility in probing the racial realities at hand; to explore critical themes in the history of American and British race politics in a manner that respects nationally unique developments; and, too, to indicate links between research, action, and social transformation.

Asking the same questions, utilizing the research guidelines discussed in Part I, the previous two sections have dealt with the genesis of racial linkages in the United States and Britain separately, on their own internally consistent terms. This chapter makes the implicit explicit by bringing the cases together.

I

Respecting the uniqueness of detail, the structural similarities of the cases, not the differences (of which more will be said later) are striking. The blacks who moved to the North and the West Indians who migrated to Britain left frustrating, colour-ascriptive, largely rural societies whose black–white relationships were essentially colonial to come to urban–industrial environments with tolerant, colour-blind, non-discriminatory official policies. In both of the adopted 'mother-country' societies liberal democratic forms, rhetoric, and processes accommodated themselves to the institutional expression of racism.

[1] For reviews of the scope of comparative politics see the two inaugural issues of *Comparative Politics* (Vol. 1, October 1968 and January 1969).

On arrival, in both cases, by virtue of their legal right to vote (as American and as Commonwealth citizens), the migrants were potential political participants. Hence this study of the politics of racial linkage, in Gamson's terms, is, most fundamentally, a study in developing relationships between *authorities* and *potential partisans*:

I shall argue that both the benign and threatening emphases among students of power concern a single relationship between *authorities and potential partisans*. One view takes the vantage point of potential partisans and emphasizes the process by which such groups attempt to influence the choice of authorities or the structure within which decisions occur. The second takes the vantage point of authorities and emphasizes the process by which they attempt to achieve collective goals and to maintain legitimacy and compliance with their decisions in a situation in which significant numbers of potential partisans are not being fully satisfied.[2]

Following Gamson's injunction that any satisfactory analysis must combine, in some way, both perspectives, the central point of orientation here has been to take the vantage point of authorities ('the social control perspective') to analyse their behaviour in making key structural decisions, and to assess the impact of those decisions from the vantage point of the potential partisans. Given that a modified interest-group pluralist model may describe accurately the political process for *included* represented groups and authorities, what Gamson aptly calls the *competitive establishment*,[3] our central concern has been with the precise terms of linkage between the migrant potential partisans and the polity, and with the consequential relative power of the relevant racial groups to make and carry out decisions and non-decisions.

This study's findings are consistent with Gamson's proposition that given the option of outcome modification or social control in dealing with potential partisans, those with power will prefer the latter since social control, if successful, maximizes the manœuvrability of the recipients of actual or potential pressure. Thus social control responses maximize both the security and choice possibilities open to authorities while, conversely, restricting the space of political choice open to potential partisans.[4]

The responses of national and local political elites to black migration in both the United States and the United Kingdom can be characterized in social control terms. In neither country, did the migrants fashion (or have fashioned for them) political linkages that, in terms of power, were bi-directional. In the United States, the attempt to secure patronage from the Republican party in exchange for mass support, the attempt to forge an electoral alliance with the Democrats and the attempt to secure protective

[2] William Gamson, *Power and Discontent* (Homewood, Illinois, 1968), p. 2.
[3] William Gamson, 'Stable Unrepresentation in American Society', *American Behavioral Scientist* (Vol. 12, November–December 1968), pp. 15ff.
[4] Ibid., pp. 18–19.

anti-lynching legislation from the Congress were all rebuffed, reflecting post-Reconstruction uni-directional national relationships. But more significant for the future were the uni-directional linkages fashioned in the cities of the North. By precluding black neighbourhood political control in New York City, the Tammany created institutional mechanism of the United Colored Democracy channelled potential black political power into non-threatening activity from the perspective of the party's white leadership. Charles Anderson's Republican machine achieved the same result. And in Chicago, where the possibilities for the political organization of the city's blacks were more promising than in any other Northern city, the Carey–Wright South Side machine compromised its independence and developed a stake in the racial *status quo*.

In the United Kingdom, in a period of only five years, the Labour and Conservative parties moved away from a principled rejection of colour-based immigration controls towards a bi-partisan consensus—whose existence was more significant for the politicians than its substance—that of institutionalized controls, and set up buffer institutions which provide for uni-directional participation.

Thus, in both cases, in the making of key structural decisions those who articulated cultural–folk prejudices were bargained with and conciliated at the expense of the powerless migrants. In the White House, in Congress, and in the political machines of the North, racist views became embodied in government policy. Similarly, at Westminster, Whitehall, and town halls, the content of the bi-partisan consensus differed substantively very little from the early proposals of the rigid control advocates on the Tory right.

Though Marcuse's well-known critique of the fundamental liberal tenet of tolerance has obvious prescriptive pitfalls, his analysis is relevant here, since it highlights the repressive potential of abstracted pure tolerance. Marcuse rightly points out that 'intolerance has delayed progress and has prolonged the slaughter and torture of innocents for hundreds of years'. Yet, if we ask with him, in light of the discussion of the previous chapters, 'Are there historical conditions in which such toleration impedes liberation and multiplies the victims who are sacrificed to the *status quo*? Can the indiscriminate guarantee of political rights and liberties be repressive?' at a minimum our reply surely cannot be a glibly uttered, 'ridiculous'.[5]

Nationally and locally, as the policy products of liberal, tolerant, political systems, in both the United States and the United Kingdom, political elites acted to link potentially partisan black and Third World migrants to the polity *indirectly* through institutions over which the elites could exercise significant control—institutions which precluded direct group inclusion in the relevant competitive establishments. Thus, if democracy is viewed not simply in formalist terms, but in terms of socially

[5] Herbert Marcuse, 'Repressive Tolerance', in Robert Paul Wolff, Barrington Moore, Jr., and Herbert Marcuse, *A Critique of Pure Tolerance* (Boston, 1965), p. 91.

descriptive, substantive, and actual representation as well, formalist democracy produced anti-democratic, non-representative linkages.[6]

In his work on democracy, Rustow has urged that we recognize critical differences between socio-economic and communal issues:

There is a fundamental difference in the nature of the issues. On matters of economic policy and social expenditures you can always split the difference. In an expanding economy, you can have it both ways: the contest for higher wages, profits, consumer savings, and social welfare payments can be turned into a positive-sum game. But there is no middle position between Flemish and French as official languages, or between Calvinism, Catholicism, and secularism as principles of education. The best you can get here is an 'inclusive compromise'—a log-rolling deal whereby some government officials speak French and some Flemish, or some children are taught according to Acquinas, some, Calvin, and some, Voltaire. Such a solution may partly depoliticize the question. Yet it also entrenches the differences instead of removing them, and accordingly it may convert political conflict into a form of trench warfare.[7]

This formulation of the differences between the politics of class and the politics of race and ethnicity is convincing in only the most limited, short-term way. It assumes an expanding economy, over-stresses the extent to which class conflicts are objectively positive-sum games, and, most importantly, misses the point that racial groups are not simply cultural or status conflict groups, but material and political conflict groups as well. In Fanon's terms, 'the economic substructure is also superstructure. The cause is the consequence; you are rich because you are white, you are white because you are rich.'[8]

Hence the relationship between race and the three stratification dimensions of class, status, and power is a complex one. 'The race relations situation is not just stratification plus racialist ideology and ascription, but the very dynamics of the stratification system become profoundly influenced by its racial elements.'[9] It is for this reason that race and ethnic relations can only be understood fully in terms of the precise linkages between racial and ethnic groups and the society's economic, normative, and political structures.

In this respect the broad orientation of the 'plural society' approach which challenges the dominant comparative politics consensual conventional wisdom, provides an analytical anchor. Pluralism, in this sense (as opposed to other usages common among social scientists), 'is not a theory ... but an analytical concept to help us deal with heterogeneous societies'. Thus van den Berghe defines plural societies as 'those that are segmented

---

[6] See Chapter 2 for an extended discussion.

[7] Dankwart Rustow, 'Transitions to Democracy: Toward a Dynamic Model', *Comparative Politics* (April 1970), pp. 359–60.

[8] Frantz Fanon, *The Wretched of the Earth* (London, 1969), p. 31.

[9] Sami Zubaida, 'Introduction', in Sami Zubaida, ed., *Race and Racialism* (London, 1970), p. 7.

into two or more groups that have distinct and duplicatory sets of institutions, except in the political and economic spheres where the institutions are shared'.[10]

But *how* the institutions are shared is the crucial issue to which this study has been addressed. Pure class stratification occurs within a single total shared institutional framework; but in a racially heterogeneous society the groups are linked to what Despres has called the maximal institutions of the market and polity. Thus the terms of linkage between racial groups in these arenas is so important. Accordingly, Rothchild has recently urged a focus on inter-ethnic bargaining in these 'brokerage arenas'. I would concur, but urge that such a focus utilize the structural-behavioural dichotomy to stress the nature of representation and relative distributions of power which racial bargaining groups bring to the inter-racial bargaining process.[11]

Seen in this light, the central political issue cannot simply be defined in terms of participation alone, but rather must focus on the terms of participation. And the issue is not simply one of crying racism, but of identifying the structures in which racist values inhere. As Cruse has put it:

> To say that America is a racist society is not enough—there is more to it than that. If American racism created the institutions, it is now the institutions themselves which legitimize the racist behavior of those who are the products of the institutions. The problem, then, is how to deal *structurally* with these institutions—how to alter them, eradicate them, or build new and better ones.[12]

II

With this perspective, let us review comparatively the key structural features of New York's United Colored Democracy and Nottingham's Commonwealth Citizens Consultative Committee, each being new linkage mechanisms established in the critical periods of migration.

The United Colored Democracy was founded at the initiative of the leader of Tammany Hall in 1898 as an electoral organization to secure black votes while permitting the neighbourhood clubhouses to remain segregated. The Consultative Committee, by contrast, created in 1954, was set up by the city's leading voluntary welfare and religious organizations, but after 1958 when it was funded by the local authority, had more direct political involvement. The U.C.D. was officially a partisan organization, the Nottingham Consultative Committee (N.C.C.) officially non-partisan. With respect to authorship, though, the most salient feature is

[10] Pierre van den Berghe, *Race and Ethnicity* (New York, 1970), pp. 16, 14.
[11] Donald Rothchild, 'Ethnicity and Conflict Resolution', *World Politics* (Vol. 22, July 1970), pp. 597ff.
[12] 'The Fire This Time?' *The New York Review of Books* (Vol. XII, 8 May, 1969), p. 18.

shared: namely, that neither organization was created by the migrants for the migrants. Both, rather, were created *by* authorities *for* potential partisans.

The U.C.D. was an all-black organization. Its members need not have had other institutional identifications. The N.C.C., on the other hand, was from the beginning multiracial, indeed predominantly white, whose black members were selected as representatives of the 'responsible' West Indian, Indian, and Pakistani visible, predominantly social, organizations. In both cases, however, the mass of migrants did not have available to them formal mechanisms of selecting the leadership that white elites recognized as legitimate. And in neither organization were the black leaders' social characteristics (measured in terms of class, status, and length of residence in the North or Britain) congruent with black mass social characteristics. Both in New York and Nottingham blacks ultimately served with the approval of the relevant whites. Tammany appointed the first leader of the U.C.D. directly, cut off patronage from one of his successors who challenged the racial *status quo*, and later restored the flow of rewards to his more compliant successor. The whites on the N.C.C., in parallel fashion, were instrumental in removing from the organization the one set of blacks who raised fundamental objections to its assumptions, arrangements, and actions.

Both the U.C.D. and N.C.C. blacks were given material and symbolic rewards by white elites, but the 'mix' differed in each case. In the former, the rewards were largely material in the form of patronage for the appointed black leaders and mass. N.C.C. black leaders were given some direct patronage, but the bulk of rewards received were symbolic. The main currency of mass rewards was assistance in dealing with welfare state bureaucracies.

The most significant shared feature of the American and British racial linkage organizations was their nature as parallel political institutions, as uni-directional buffers interposed between the migrants and mainstream political arenas. Black political participation was channelled away from the clubhouses in New York and party politics in Nottingham, into organizations whose essential direction was controlled by white elites. From a 'system' perspective, these organizations were functional in the short run by providing well-defined patterns of access and defusing social conflict; but from the migrants' perspective they were not formally, socially, or substantively representative, nor were they efficient even in achieving their limited aims. It is in this sense that the new linkage arrangements are analogous to classic patterns of colonial governance.

Gamson has argued that there are four general types of social control mechanisms available for elite use: insulation, sanctions, persuasion, and co-optation. The first controls the differential access 'of potential partisans to resources and their ability to bring these resources to bear on decision makers'. Sanctions 'affect the situation of potential partisans by making rewards or punishments contingent on attempts at influence'. Persuasion refers to attempts to alter the normative orientation of potential partisans; and co-optation, as Selznick has classically defined it, 'is the process of absorbing new elements into the leadership or policy-determining structure of an organization as a means of averting threats to its stability or existence'.[13]

In dealing with the potentially partisan migrants, both American and British political elites utilized a similar combination of these mechanisms of social control. The buffering institutions created—the U.C.D. in New York, the Carey-Wright machine in Chicago, N.C.C.I. and its constituent committees in the United Kingdom—were co-optive mechanisms in that they publicly absorbed new elements into the political arena. Potentially threatening partisans were brought *inside* 'legitimate' political organizations, but not directly. Thus the buffers were insulating organizations that provided the black populations with differentially lower access to political resources than other groups. Paradoxically, the buffer institutions both incorporated blacks into the relevant respective political arenas while, at the same time, insulating those arenas from unwanted pressures and demands. It was hoped that this indirect, relatively powerless (unidirectional) mode of participation would be sufficient to convince potentially troublesome migrants that they were being dealt with equitably. And, finally, sanctions in the form of rewards and punishment kept a compliant leadership in line. In short, to borrow a phrase from Gamson once again, this similar combination of social control mechanisms, from an elite vantage point, was aimed at institutionalizing a situation of *stable unrepresentation* (in the sense of not being included in the competitive establishment) for the black and Third World populations.

In both countries in the critical period of migration the institutional linkages established were promoted by their creators as being progressive innovations in the migrants' interest. Thus the black political organizations in New York and Chicago, and the local structures in Nottingham were cited repeatedly by local politicians as evidence of significant racial progress. But what is striking about them, of course, is that these organizational linkages structured participation, created persistent, well-defined patterns of access, and established orderly procedures for reaching the migrant populations *on elite terms*, leaving the distribution of political power largely intact.

It is in this sense that these structural arrangements can be appropriately labelled repressive reforms. Gorz has distinguished between 'reformist' and 'non-reformist' reforms:

A reformist reform is one which subordinates its objectives to the criteria of rationality and practicality of a given system and policy. Reformism rejects

---

[13] Gamson, op. cit., Chapter 6; Philip Selznick, *TVA and the Grass Roots* (New York, 1966), p. 13.

o

those objectives and demands—however deep the need for them—which are incompatible with the preservation of the system.

On the other hand, a not necessarily reformist reform is one which is conceived not in terms of what is possible within the framework of a given system and administration, but in view of what should be made possible in terms of human needs and demands.[14]

He distinguishes, then, between reforms that widen the space of choice within a given structure, that is behavioural changes, and reforms that alter the structure itself to transform behavioural choice possibilities. But the 'reforms' of the U.C.D., N.C.C.I., etc., did neither; they constricted rather than widened choice possibilities. Hence they are examples of repressive reforms, i.e., reforms that appear to restructure relationships to widen choice but actually are extensions of and/or the creations of new mechanisms of social control; they are boundary-maintaining mechanisms that utilize the rhetoric of responsiveness and participation. It is probably precisely because these structured relationships have been cast in reformist, emancipatory imagery that they have been so ill-understood. Confusing, too, is their nature as pre-emptive or anticipatory rather than restorative (and thus overtly counter-revolutionary) control mechanisms.

III

The political responses to black migration in the two leading liberal democracies teach us some harsh truths about the limits in practice of the liberal self-conception. Dahrendorf, an advocate of a liberal democratic future for his native Germany, has succinctly summed up the core elements of liberal relations:

Liberal democracy can become effective only in a society in which, (1) equal citizenship rights have been generalized; (2) conflicts are recognised and regulated rationally in all institutional orders; (3) elites reflect the color and diversity of social interests; and (4) public virtues are the predominant value orientation of the people.[15]

Utilizing these conditions as checkpoints, the capabilities of the liberal democracies of the United States and Great Britain to incorporate the politics of race can be assessed.

Regarding his first condition, Dahrendorf notes that 'the relation between political constitution and social structure is determined by the ways in which individuals participate in the life of their society.'[16] For black and Third World migrants, their participation as individuals was dependent on the nature of their inclusion as a group. The individual's life chances—his behavioural choice possibilities—are shaped and

[14] André Gorz, *Strategy for Labor: A Radical Proposal* (Boston, 1968), p. 7.
[15] Ralf Dahrendorf, *Society and Democracy in Germany* (London, 1968), p. 31.
[16] Ibid., p. 29.

limited by the structural position of the group in the class, status, and political power stratification hierarchies. For newcomers in both locales, viewed as a collectivity, equality of citizenship existed in form only. The most striking feature of the terms of the political linkages fashioned, as we have seen, was their one-directional character in terms of power (hence choice).

Once structural arrangements are established that are uni-directional in character, the liberal process of bargaining can continue, thus preserving the liberal face of the system, even though bargaining outcomes are really not in doubt. Given the continued appearance of black participation in the political process as citizens with equal rights, their plight can be blamed on them; the victimized are seen as guilty, the victimizers free of responsibility.

Liberal mechanisms of social control, though less obvious than totalitarian coercion, can be equally devastating for the target group. Rogin, for example, has chillingly described the ways in which American Indians were driven off their lands. The Creek in Mississippi were placed under state law which stripped them of all legal rights and protection against marauding traders, thus making life intolerable. The Government's treaty with the Creek divided the communal lands into individual plots owned by the Indians who were then free to sell and cross the Mississippi river to the West, or stay and remain vulnerable under Mississippi state law. 'Since the government had left each Indian free to make his own decision, it was not implicated in the extraordinary fraud, thievery, and violence which followed.'

As this process of Indian removal proceeded, the Government in Washington disclaimed any responsibility, for the Indians had chosen freely: 'Liberal contractural relations defused guilt; no one could be held responsible for the condition of anyone else. . . . The principle was to structure the environment so that the dice were loaded strongly in favor of a single alternative, and then give the target of planning the onus of the choice.'[17]

Given the onus of choice, the powerless internalize their impossible situation and internalize their guilt. Thus, Elkins has argued, the complete powerlessness of the slave (and of the inmates of German concentration camps) 'produced noticeable effects on the slave's very personality'. The slave often identified with his master, and accepted society's estimate of himself as being without worth.[18] The less complete, but nonetheless pervasive powerlessness of blacks in America's northern ghettoes, in large part the product of the uni-directional linkages established in the period of migration, has had similar effects. The Group for the Advancement of Psychiatry found that:

[17] Michael Paul Rogin, 'Liberal Society and the Indian Question', *Politics and Society* Vol. I (May 1971), pp. 305–12.
[18] Stanley Elkins, *Slavery* (New York, 1963), pp. 82, 130.

The damaging effects of powerlessness and inferior social status are reflected in unrealistic inferiority feelings, a sense of humiliation and constriction of potentialities for self-development. This often results in a pattern of self-hatred and rejection of one's own group expressed by anti-social action toward one's own group.[19]

The low self-esteem of the powerless may be especially acute in liberal democratic societies with an ethos of equality of opportunity, for then the individual, 'free' to choose, may blame himself and/or his group for his predicament. In extreme cases, write Parker and Kleiner, low self-evaluation can lead to mental illness.[20] What is striking of course, and this point is missed by many urban ethnographers, is that these self-evaluative and behavioural patterns are the product of objective structural conditions; this remains true even if the victims do not perceive their condition in these terms.

The behavioural consequences of relationships that institutionalized black powerlessness made possible the detachment of a token, symbolic leadership group from the masses. One is struck, in fact, by the similarity in response of black 'leaders' in Britain and the United States who sought individual solutions to a collective problem. White-sanctioned leadership positions as patronage referees and powerless machine politicians in the United States, and as participants in buffer institutions in Britain were positions which permitted a form of escape for the individual.[21] In both countries, a black leadership group, rewarded by white conferred prestige and limited patronage, tangible and intangible, and considered reliable, moderate, and responsible by their patrons, accepted positions on the periphery of power. Charles Anderson in New York and Eric Irons in Nottingham shared more in common than one would have thought possible given the differences in time and place.

Dahrendorf's third condition (I shall return to his second shortly) for the success of liberal democracy, a representative elite, has thus not been fulfilled in either locale, both in numerical terms (fewer blacks than members of other groups achieved elite positions, however loosely defined), and in terms of effectiveness in that the blacks placed in visible leaderships positions, like the group they were said to represent, were essentially without power. In neither country, in short, have blacks had access on an equal basis with whites to local and national decision-making positions.

Dahrendorf's final condition, it will be recalled, asserted that 'the constitution of liberty works to the extent to which a society is dominated

[19] The Group for the Advancement of Psychiatry, Committee on Social Issues, 'Psychiatric Aspects of School Desegregation', report no. 37 (May 1957).

[20] Seymour Parker and Robert Kleiner, *Mental Illness in the Urban Negro Community* (New York, 1966), pp. 168ff.

[21] There is an illuminating discussion of this issue in Ralph Bunche, 'A Brief and Tentative Analysis of Negro Leadership', MS. in the Schomburg Collection, New York Public Library, 1940.

by public virtues'.[22] Cultural folk prejudices, which can scarcely be regarded as public virtues, achieved systemic political expression in anti-democratic uni-directional linkages which, in turn, have sustained prevailing racial stereotypes. For without continuing bi-directional relationships, the prevailing racial myths are not only left unchallenged, but concretized.[23]

With Baldwin we can say that 'power *is* real, and many things, including very often love, cannot be achieved without it'.[24] This view has been confirmed by most social psychologists interested in questions of prejudice. Gordon Allport, in his classic review of the relevant research, concluded that 'prejudice (unless deeply rooted in the character structure of the individual) may be reduced by equal status contact between majority and minority groups in pursuit of common goals'. This especially holds if the contact 'is of a sort that leads to the perception of common interests and common humanity between members of the two groups'.[25] Similarly, Muzafer Sherif has argued that prejudice is best reduced by bringing groups into contact in situations where they agree on goals which 'are urgent and compelling for all groups involved'.[26] Co-operation in political parties, pressure groups, or coalitions between groups with roughly equal power capabilities to achieve common ends suggest themselves as possibilities; but these forms of common interracial political action are foreclosed by uni-directional linkages and parallel institutions.

Since the bargaining process made possible by the migration periods' political arrangements was so skewed, the rational regulation of conflict, in the sense of persistent, continuing mutual dialogue and adjustments (Dahrendorf's second condition), was not possible. In this respect too the 'reform' institutional linkages in both countries, though justified by liberal rhetoric, were fundamentally antithetical to the liberal self-conception.

IV

Ironically, the American experience since 1930 and recent events in Britain indicate that the racial stability sought by the white elites who shaped the terms of linkage in fact was undermined by precisely those structural relationships they made possible. In this respect the study of the failure to fashion successful linkages (in terms of the criteria of Chapter 2) in the early and fluid periods of interracial contact is in part the study of a significant source of contemporary conflict in the United States and of actual and potential conflict in the United Kingdom.

[22] Dahrendorf, op. cit., p. 30.

[23] For the classic discussion of the self-fulfilling prophecy, see Robert Merton, *Social Theory and Social Structure* (New York, 1967), pp. 421–4, 434.

[24] James Baldwin, *The Fire Next Time* (London, 1963), p. 81. Emphasis in original.

[25] Gordon Allport, *The Nature of Prejudice* (New York, 1954), p. 281.

[26] Muzafer Sherif, *Intergroup Relations and Leadership* (New York, 1962), p. 19.

In his *Political Order in Changing Societies*, Huntington explores the relationship between political participation and political institutionalization, the relationship which, in his view, determines the stability of a political system: 'The primary thesis of this book is that [violence and instability are] in large part the product of rapid social change and the rapid mobilization of new groups into politics coupled with the slow development of political institutions.'[27] Sharp rises in instability accompany sharp rises in participation when a low level of political institutionalization (defined in terms of the adaptibility, complexity, coherence, and autonomy of political institutions) 'makes it difficult, if not impossible for the demands upon the government to be expressed through legitimate channels and to be moderated and aggregated within the political system.' Thus, for Huntington, if political stability is to be maintained, 'as political participation increases, the complexity, autonomy, adaptability, and coherence of the society's political institutions must also increase.'[28]

Though I would sharply question Huntington's elite-maintaining, stability-oriented, contentless perspective,[29] and although the book loosely utilizes 'developed' societies, including the United States and Britain, as models of political stability, his work does point usefully to connections between institutions (a structural dimension) and participation (a behavioural dimension). From his normative perspective—as well as from mine, stressing democratic representation, equality of choice possibilities, and racial justice—the institutions created in the migration periods were failures, in that in all but the very short term they were inadequate to provide either stability or meaningful participation.

Yet his work, paradoxically, would not point to this conclusion. In a situation of fundamental racial inequalities in material and status resources, and in a locale where cultural folk prejudices are widely shared, the stability of the system in the long run, when faced with demands of potential partisans, depends not only on the strength and scope of the institutions created to channel their participation, but also on the terms of participation they make possible. But to achieve bi-directional linkages, in both the United States and Britain, during the periods of migration many existing myths, assumptions, and practices would have

---

[27] Samuel P. Huntington, *Political Order in Changing Societies* (New Haven, 1968), p. 4.

[28] Ibid., p. 79.

[29] Here I would echo Kesselman who has questioned 'the high priority assigned to political stability. . . . When Huntington suggests that, "A government with a low level of institutionalization is not just a weak government; it is also a bad government. The function of government is to govern," he comes perilously close to affirming the converse: that a government which *does* govern (i.e., a strong government) is incapable of governing *badly*. And the identification of strong presidents with good presidents is no longer self evident.' Mark Kesselman, 'Overinstitutionalization and Political Constraint: The Case of France', *Comparative Politics* (Vol. 3, October 1970), p. 22. Emphasis in original.

had to be challenged. The situation in these years was fluid in that these temporarily destabilizing decisions *could* have been made.

If one sees the migration periods as periods of developing institutional relationships between authorities and potential partisans, then Huntington's work, though sensitive to these issues, provides almost no help in understanding the shortcomings of organizations like the U.C.D. and the N.C.C., even on his own normative terms, since his conditions for stability were met: new institutions to aggregate and moderate the demands of the new participants *were* created; they were autonomous, increased the complexity of the polity, and made the politics of race coherent. The problem, then, was not the low level of institutionalization as compared to participatory demands, but, rather, had to do with the new institutions themselves.[30]

Building on Huntington's work, Kesselman has taken a large, helpful step forward by developing the notion of *over*-institutionalization— which occurs frequently, his view, in developed polities—where:

The institutionalization process outstrips mobilization . . . participation is stifled by institutional development. . . . A major problem of developed systems is overinstitutionalization—a plethora, not a paucity of institutions. If in transitional societies it is easier to destroy old institutions than to build new ones, the problem is reversed in developed polities, where established institutions may be outmoded but still able to withstand challenge.[31]

For us, this formulation is only partially helpful. Moving beyond Huntington, Kesselman incisively sees that institutional development of a particular kind or kinds stifles participation; he convincingly cites France as a case in point. But the kind of institutional barrier to participation (producing the outcome he calls political constraint) he has in mind deals with a clogged political landscape 'with institutions that have outlived their original purposes but refuse to die', the product of organizational success and the development of organizational loyalties where they come to be valued for their own sake, irrespective of the benefits they deliver.[32] But the problem with the linkages fashioned in the Northern cities of the United States and in Britain was not that they had outlived their purpose; on the contrary, they were created with well-defined social control purposes in mind. Rather, the institutions themselves were flawed, providing ultimately neither for meaningful participation nor stability. Though the level of institutionalization was in Huntington's terms appropriate to the demand for participation, the ultimate outcome was unsatisfactory from the vantage points of both authorities and potential partisans (for different reasons, of course).

[30] See Immanuel Wallerstein's review of *Political Order in Changing Societies* in the *American Journal of Sociology* (Vol. 76, November 1969), pp. 440-1.

[31] Kesselman, 'Overinstitutionalization . . .', op. cit., pp. 24, 44.

[32] Ibid., pp. 24-5.

We have already spent considerable time detailing why this was so in terms of substantive democratic norms. But by was it so in terms of stability? Why in short are Huntington's indicators, predictively applied, misleading? The answer, I think, as should now be clear, must be found by examining the precise nature of the participation made possible by the linkage institutions; that is, the analysis of structural limitations on behaviour must precede the analysis of behaviour including protest movements, violent insurrection, and the like. Since objective group situations cannot simply be inferred from the group's own perceptions of its interests and by its actions, we must inquire first if the structured relationships that obtain objectively affect a group adversely (thus being necessary, but not sufficient conditions for destabilizing behaviour); and secondly, given these objective conditions, what transforms the group, in the classic Marxist sense, from a collectivity 'in itself' to a collectivity 'for itself'.[33]

An extended fully satisfactory discussion of these issues is not possible here, but the following considerations seem compelling. As a result of the uni-directional linkages established in the United States after the turn of the century and in Britain since 1948, blacks were denied bi-directional political access. If, broadly, politics is about 'who gets what how', political bargains reached by competing collectivities in all likelihood are made at the expense of the relatively powerless. We defined power, with Champlin, as an actor's generalized capacity to get others to do what he wants without having to make unacceptable sacrifices.[34] This formulation is consistent with Blau's, who writes that 'power is a generalized means for the achievement of various ends. The higher a powerful group's expectations of what it wants to accomplish, the greater its needs for power.'[35] Thus groups relatively without power lack the means to achieve their collective aims.

Thus Coser notes that: 'to make oneself understood and to get others to listen is contingent upon the possession of power to give force to one's argument. A group that is not able to assert its interests will not gain consideration of its claims.'[36] Denied this consideration—that is, not that there is an absence of institutions to moderate and aggregate a group's demands, but rather those institutions which do exist fundamentally compromise the interests of the group—relatively powerless groups are likely to transcend 'legitimate' modes of political activity. There is a two-directional relationship between the extent to which a group trusts the political system and the tactics employed by the group to achieve its ends. Both Etzioni and Gamson have noted a congruence between trust in the

[33] For an illuminating discussion, see Isaac Balbus, 'The Concept of Interest in Pluralist and Marxian Analysis', *Politics and Society* (Vol. I, February 1971), pp. 151ff.

[34] See below, Chapter 2, pp. 37ff.

[35] Peter M. Blau, *Exchange and Power in Social Life* (New York, 1964), pp. 228-9.

[36] Lewis Coser, *Continuities in the Study of Social Conflict* (New York, 1967), p. 106.

system and the means employed to influence outcomes.[37] Thus Gamson hypothesizes that while 'a confident solidary group will tend to rely on persuasion as a means of influence, . . . an alienated solidary group will tend to rely on constraints as a means of influence'.[38] Where authorities are perceived as sharing the group's orientation, their commitments are mobilized through friendly contacts, the presentation of information, and the like. At the other end of the continuum, where groups perceive authorities as being fundamentally hostile to their interests, they seek to alter outcomes by imposing sanctions on the authorities (in the broad middle of the continuum, the use of inducements is the most likely influence technique). Lipsky thus views non-violent protest as a political resource, as an attempt by the relatively powerless to induce authorities to act by activating 'third parties to enter the implicit or explicit bargaining arena in ways favorable to the protesters'.[39] Protest activity of this sort—the rent strike movement in New York city in the early 1960s being a leading case in point[40]—is aimed at mobilizing the support of those with bi-directional political relationships.

The Civil Rights Movement of the 1950s and early 1960s in the United States can be comprehended in these terms, as an effort to garner the support of morally anguished white Americans who would grant black demands once heard because the condition of America's blacks belied the country's corporate belief system. This kind of activity proved only partially successful at best in achieving its goals because it misread the commitment of its potential white allies, but more importantly because attempts to bargain through third parties are likely to be inadequate substitutes for direct bargaining based on boundary management. In curious fashion, the buffer institutions created by the national and local political communities in Britain share the Civil Rights Movement's assumption that indirect bargaining through intermediaries can be effective.

'The assertion of interest', Coser has written, 'can ordinarily proceed on a non-violent basis in those social systems in which channels for such assertions have been legitimized. But where this is not the case, the chances are high that violence will be one of the ways in which interest is being asserted.'[41] The absence of viable political linkages makes violence a high possibility outcome. Indeed, in his comprehensive overview of collective violence in European perspective, Tilly suggests that the most persuasive interpretation of collective violence is a *political* one:

Far from being mere side effects of urbanization, industrialization, and other large structural changes, violent protests seem to grow most directly from the

[37] Amitai Etzioni, *A Comparative Analysis of Complex Organizations* (New York, 1961); Gamson, op. cit.

[38] Ibid., pp. 164, 169.

[39] Michael Lipsky, 'Protest as a Political Resource', *The American Political Science Review* (Vol. LXII, December 1968), p. 1145.

[40] See Michael Lipsky, *Protest in City Politics* (Chicago, 1970).

[41] Coser, op. cit., p. 106.

P

struggle for established places in the structure of power. . . . Over the long run, the processes most regularly producing collective violence are those by which groups acquire or lose membership in the political community.[42]

Lupsha writes too in his survey of theories of urban violence that 'one area that has been neglected . . . is the political side of urban violence. Politics, political values and the political system are intimately linked in the recent riots.' Urban blacks in the United States, he notes, have developed a riot ideology which views violence as a legitimate means of influencing a distant authority structure that only permits them token and powerless participation.[43] Put another way, if we take it 'to be axiomatic that human beings—other than those systematically trained to use legitimate or illegitimate violence—will resort to violent action only under extremely frustrating, ego-damaging, and anxiety-producing conditions',[44] we can view collective racial violence as the behavioural choice that is the product of structural arrangements that limit choice possibilities to this alternative; for the violent actor there is little or nothing to lose.

Thus the linkage arrangements of the migration periods promoted the transformation of the black and Third World migrants from collectivities 'in' to collectivities 'for' themselves. The parallel institutions created for the newcomers contributed directly to the groups' institutional enclosure, and the terms of these institutions insured a high degree of control by white authorities over the groups' access to scarce class, status, and power resources.[45]

As Despres reminds us, 'it can't be assumed that maximal cultural sections are incompatible and conflict producing in terms of the transactions that occur between their respective members . . . cultural sections are not in themselves politically functional. They become so only when individuals and groups make them so.'[46] But, we should add, when institutional enclosure is superimposed on structural inequalities, the prospects are that individuals and groups will 'make them so', for, paraphrasing Michels, the issue can't possibly be decided by the passage of individual molecules from one side to the other. The life chances of the individual black in both countries have been and are bound up directly with the position of his group as a whole.[47]

At the wrong end of uni-directional colonial-type relationships, the colonized, as Memmi has brilliantly shown, in internal as well as external

[42] Charles Tilly, 'Collective Violence in European Perspective', Ted Gurr and Hugh Graham, *Violence in America: Historical and Comparative Perspectives* (New York, 1969), p. 10.

[43] Peter Lupsha, 'On Theories of Urban Violence', unpublished paper, 1968.

[44] Coser, op. cit., p. 83.

[45] See R. A. Schermerhorn, *Comparative Ethnic Relations* (New York, 1970), pp. 255-7.

[46] Leo A. Despres, *Cultural Pluralism and Nationalist Politics in British Guiana* (Chicago, 1967), p. 276.

[47] Robert Michels, *Political Parties* (New York, 1962), p. 237.

colonies, have only two options: individual or collective solutions. Individual solutions, however, are ultimately untenable; the price is too high, it cannot be paid: 'He soon discovers that, even if he agrees to everything, he would not be saved. In order to be assimilated, it is not enough to leave one's group, but one must enter another; now he meets with the colonizer's rejection.'[48] It is clear, he continues,

. . . on the other hand, that a collective drama will never be settled through individual solutions. The individual disappears in his lineage and the group drama goes on. In order for assimilation of the colonized to have both purpose and meaning, it would have to affect an entire people; i.e., that the whole colonial condition be changed. However, the colonial condition cannot be changed except by doing away with the colonial relationship.[49]

Since the colonized cannot collectively (or, hence, individually) benefit from uni-directional linkages, a classic Marxian 'two-class' stratification dynamic emerges whereby subordinates and superordinates come into structural conflict with fundamentally contradictory interests, 'an interest in the preservation of existing power relationships or destruction of existing power relationships'.[50] And it is precisely the institutional enclosure of the subordinate that facilitates their organization and the growth of an anti-system movement since that enclosure makes easier group communication and mobilization.[51]

V

There is a need for more research in the periods covered by this study. In particular, it would be useful to explore the politics of race in other American and British cities during the early stage of interracial contact to explore more fully the varieties of linkages that were fashioned by the newcomers, and the extent to which they resemble or diverge from those analysed here. A large number of case studies would permit the development of a richer, more sophisticated comparative work, both within and between countries.

But I am not simply calling for more research, more ways to squander money to find our way to a brothel. To have an impact on the possibilities for social transformation, as I suggested earlier, we must transcend dominant 'value-free' 'objective' technically-oriented, largely behavioural research orientations, what Rioux has aptly labelled 'asceptic' social science, to a critical posture that, by examining structured linkages, can

[48] Albert Memmi, *The Colonizer and the Colonized* (Boston, 1965), p. 124.
[49] Ibid., p. 126.
[50] Isaac Balbus, 'Ruling Elite Theory vs. Marxist Class Analysis', *Monthly Review* (Vol. 23, May 1971), p. 38.
[51] For a discussion, see Maurice Pinard, 'Mass Society and Political Movements: A New Formulation', in Hans Peter Dreitzel, *Recent Sociology, no. 1* (New York, 1969), pp. 99ff.

help clarify and widen the space of political choice. This stance recognizes the public nature of social science, and is committed to the values of substantive political, social, and economic democracy, to the quest for liberation.

In taking this position, as Stephen Warner reminds us:

. . . we must recognize the odds against us. A critical social science of the variety I and most of the people I know and respect would favor would operate against the interests of the most powerful segments of our society and in favor of those of unorganized or powerless masses. Conflicts of interest or values are a part of our world, whether they may be transcended, as Marx suggests, or not, as is Weber's insistence. Thus it is not enough to call for value relevance and value-commitment; *whose values* and *what kind* of values will remain at issue. To fail to recognize this is to risk abandoning a critical for a technical role for social science.[52]

In this view, reality is not simply what prevails now, or has prevailed in the past; *true* reality, in Ernst Bloch's terms, 'is contained not in the "how", but in the "not yet"—that is, in the future and in all that *can* come into being, but has not yet done so because of the restraining forces of the present'.[53] Identification and analysis of those constraints is the first step in undermining them and in providing the means to define and attain the new. It is in this sense that race relations research which pinpoints the institutional constraints on racial justice can contribute to concrete social change and transformation. For social scientists in the last third of the twentieth century, there are few equally compelling tasks.

[52] R. Stephen Warner, 'Critical or Technical Sociology? A Comment on Somers', *Berkeley Journal of Sociology* (Vol. 15, 1970), p. 70.

[53] David Gross, review of Ernst Bloch, *A Philosophy of the Future*, in *Radical America* (May–June 1971), p. 96.

Index

New York—*cont.*

age, declining share of, 83, distribution of types of patronage appointment, 82, in street-cleaning department, 79, black patronage related to population, 82, and Tammany, 66–7, 70–1, 79; political features in settlement era, 66 *et seq.*; political linkages and white elite strategy, 84; population, increase in, 62; Republicans, disenchanted, 68; Tammany, black leader, 118, pattern of relations with blacks, 67–8; uneven formal representation, 110; United Coloured Democracy, 69 *et seq.*, Democratic patronage appointments, 79, compared with Nottingham Commonwealth Citizens Consultative Committee, 195–68, 203, Osofsky's view of, 72–3, politicians compared with those in Chicago, 91, structural buffer, 84, and white party organizations, 110, 161, 193; ward politics, exclusion from, 88

Nottingham, black leadership, character of, 170–1; black patronage, 174; black police, recruitment of rebuffed, 167; the Camden resolution, 167; black communities, function of the Consultative Committee organizer, 161–2; black leaders, role of, 155; black people, difficulty of contacting, 158; black population, 154; black reaction to White Paper, 163; Coloured People's Housing Association, 158; Commonwealth Citizens' Consultative Committee, 164–9, Budget 31 March 1967, 170, and English classes for immigrants, 167, ineffectuality of, 169, as a political safety valve, 170; Consultative Committee for the Welfare of Coloured People, 157–61, 164; council nomination versus co-option of blacks, 172–3; course in basic English, 1957, 158; economic characteristics and patterns of immigrant settlement, 152; ethnic records in housing office, 168; housing of blacks, 167–8; immigrants offered 'token, powerless participation', 173; immigration controls, 165; and Indian Workers' Association, 156; integration, mechanisms wanting, 174, new programme for, 166, February 1968 questionnaire on, 154–5; Eric Irons and needs of immigrants, 163–4; a Jamaican comment on racial situation, 186; labour shortage, 153; 'liaison',

164–5; managerial and highly paid work, 153; and National Committee for Commonwealth Immigrants, 152; compared with New York, 195–7; Pakistanis 'not politically-minded', 156; political community's attitudes, and those of rest of Britain, 155; politics of, 154; politicization of blacks not encouraged, 169; race, inter-party uniformities on, 154, 161, politics of, 152 *et seq.*; race relations before 1958, 157 *et seq.*, after 1958, 160 *et seq.*, as a political problem, 161; race riots 1958, 129, 157, 160, 165; reputation accounted for, 174; voluntary committees to assist newcomers, 130; West Indians and political consciousness, 156

Notting Hill Gate, 1958 race riots, 129, 157

Osborne, Cyril, M.P., bill on immigration, 148; *Economist* calls the 'voice of his party', 148; immigration controls, 126, 129, 131, 132, 147; as 'spokesman for the white man', 127

Oxford, consultative committee, 167

Pacey, Harry, Nottingham's welfare officer, 166

Paddington, voluntary committees to assist immigrant newcomers, 130

Pakistani immigrants to Britain, 34; in Nottingham, 156, 163, 167

Pakistani Friends League, Nottingham, 156, 164

Pakistani Welfare Association, Nottingham, 163

Pannell, Norman, M.P., 126–7, 131–2

Peabody, Philip, and NAACP anti-lynching campaign, 55

Phalanx Forum, 97

Pitt, David, on West Indian political consciousness, 156

Plateau Tonga of Northern Rhodesia, 177

Pluralism, 194–5

Political science, Cobban's observation on, 13; 'divorce from history', 23; 'grand theory', 14; and political choice, 17; and race, 14, 21; uniqueness of national historical circumstance, 16

Political stability, 202

Populist Movement, 106–7

Powe, George, and 'colonial stooges', 165; and Commonwealth Citizens' Consultative Committee, 165, 170, resigns